Christopher Hales Wilkie

The Parish Registers of S. Giles, Kingston

Baptisms, 1558-1812 - Marriages, 1558-1837 - Burials, 1558-1812...

Christopher Hales Wilkie

The Parish Registers of S. Giles, Kingston
Baptisms, 1558-1812 - Marriages, 1558-1837 - Burials, 1558-1812...

ISBN/EAN: 9783337260279

Printed in Europe, USA, Canada, Australia, Japan

Cover: Foto ©ninafisch / pixelio.de

More available books at **www.hansebooks.com**

The Parish Registers

OF

S. GILES, KINGSTON.

Baptisms - - 1558-1812.
Marriages - - 1558-1837.
Burials - - 1558-1812.

PREFACED BY

A List of the Rectors of the Parish,

SUPPLEMENTED BY

The Monumental Inscriptions in the Church and Churchyard.

BY THE

REV. CHRISTOPHER HALES WILKIE,

M.A., EXETER COLLEGE, OXFORD,

RECTOR OF KINGSTON, KENT.

Fifty Copies only Printed, of which this is No. 41.

SIGNED *C. Hales Wilkie*

BRIGHTON :
PRINTED BY J. G. BISHOP, "HERALD" OFFICE.
1893.

CONTENTS.

PREFATORY NOTES - - - - - - v.—vi.

LIST OF RECTORS - - - - - - vii.—xvi.

REGISTERS OF BAPTISMS - - - - - 1—85

" MARRIAGES - - - - 86—108

" BANNS - - - - - 108—111

" BURIALS - - - - - 112—155

NOTES OF CHURCH REPAIR

(2nd REGISTER BOOK) - - - - 156—158

APPENDIX—MONUMENTAL INSCRIPTIONS - - 159—170

INDEX OF BAPTISMS - - - - - 171—178

" MARRIAGES - - - - - 179—183

" BANNS - - - - - 183—184

" BURIALS - - - - - 185—189

PREFATORY NOTES.

This Volume somewhat exceeds the size originally intended. After transcribing the Registers of the Parish, it seemed to me that the Registers of Burial might with advantage be supplemented by the Monumental Inscriptions in the Church and Churchyard. Meanwhile, having drawn out a list of the Rectors of Kingston, I thought that this also would find an appropriate place in a collection of such Parish records.

The Registers of the two earliest books here printed have been copied *verbatim*. The first book, 1558-1745, consists of 50 leaves of parchment, about 15in. by 6in. The second book, 1745-1812 (Marriages, 1745-53), similar in size, though but half filled, is bound in leather and stamped on the cover with the lettering—"The Register Book of Kingstone, 1744. Peter Innes, Rector; Ralph Dilnot, Churchwarden."

By the kind courtesy of the Deputy Diocesan Registrar, Mr. ALLEN FIELDING, I have been able to compare the Registers with the Transcripts in the Diocesan Registry. (See foot-note on page 4).

The List of Rectors has been compiled chiefly from the Institutions in the Registers of the Archbishops at Lambeth, by means of Ducarel's Index. Such biographical notices have been added as I have been able to collect from various sources. In this portion of the work I must express my thanks to Mr. KERSHAW, the Librarian of Lambeth Library, for kind assistance, also to Dr. SHEPPARD, of Canterbury, in my reference to the MSS. in the Chapter Library.

In the Appendix my special thanks are due to Mr. R. HOVENDEN, who at my request has most kindly been entirely responsible for the Notes at the foot of the Inscriptions, giving the heraldic description of the Arms, &c., where such occur on the Monuments.

It only remains for me just to refer to the etymology of " Kingston." From the form in which it appears in the majority of the earlier Institutions, I have been led to the conclusion that its derivation is King's *ton*, not King's *stone*, and that the final *e* with which it is now commonly spelt is a corruption of later times. In a manuscript in the Bodleian Library (Steel Collection, Gough MS. 26, f. 5), among some similar notes professing to give the etymologies of Kentish names, is the following, "Kyngham-ford [1] now called Kingston, near Berhamdown, that belonged to the King, and all about it to the Archbishop and Church,"— referring probably to the adjoining parish of Bishopsbourne. The Manor of Kingston was held in chief of the King from the time of William the Conqueror downwards.[2]

C. H. W.

Kingston Rectory, Canterbury,
September, 1893.

---

[1] The name of the Hundred in which Kingston is situated, which was originally called the "Hundred of Berham." From this it seems that the Hundred of Kynghamford takes its name from this parish.

[2] See *Hasted* (III. 748) in his account of this Parish. He gives the name without the final *e*.

RECTORS OF KINGSTON.

1279. **Maurice de Dalbanergh.**[1]

> 5 Non. Julii. A.D. 1279 apud Lyminge, dns. Mauricius de Dalbanergh, Presb. institutus fuit in Eccl. de Kyngeston juxta Cant. ad præsent. dni. Alexaudri de Balioll, &c. *Peckham, f. 10 a, 48 a.*

1291. **John de Wattone.**

> 15 Kal. April. A.D. 1291, institutus fuit Johes. Wattone clericus ad Eccl. de Kyngeston, &c. *Peckham f. 41 a.*

> John de Wattone was ordained subdeacon with title to the Church of Kingston, in South Mallyng Chapel, the 1st Sunday in Lent 1290-1 and priest the following year by the Bp. of Hereford in Wye Church. (Abp. Peckham's Register, *Rolls Series*.)

1313. **William Seward.**[2]

> 23d. Nov. A.D. 1313 admisit doms. Will. Seward Cleric. ad Eccl. de Kyngestone vacant. ad præsentat. dni. Bartholomei de Badelsmere militis spectati, &c. *Winchelsey f. 57 a.*

1316. **Robert de Staunford.**

> 4 Id. Nov. A.D. 1316, institutus fuit Rob. de Staunford, Subdiac. in personâ dmni. Nic. perpetui Vicarii de Chileham, in Eccl. de Kyngeston vacant, ad præsent. dni. B. de Badlesmere, &c. *Reynolds, f. 18 a.*

1321. **Bonoditus.**

> 13 Kal. Aug. A.D. 1321, admissus fuit Bonoditus quondam Reymund. de Conterone ad Eccl. de Kyngestone vacant. ad præsent. dmni. Bartholomei de Badlesmere Militis, veri patroui [3] &c. *Reynolds f. 23 b.*

-1364. **Hugh de Nottingham.**[4]

> See following entry.

1364. **Edmund de Godwyneston.**

> 5 Kalend. Junii A.D. 1364, apud Chevnyng admissus fuit Mag. Edm. de Godwyneston, Presb. ad. Eccl. Paroch. de Kyngeston Cant. diœc. per resignat. dni. Hug. de Nottyngham ult. Rect. ejusdem vacant. ad præseut. dni. Rob. Typetot, Militis &c. *Islip f. 304 a.*

---

(1) This rector was instituted by Abp. Peckham, on the occasion of his first visit to Lyminge ("History of Lyminge Church," *Canon Jenkins*).

(2) W. Seward, subdeacon, R. of Kingston obtained (1313), a license of non-residence for 2 years, for the purpose of study. (Chapter Library, Canterbury, MS. Reg. Q. f. 102.)

(3) The entry in the Register, which continues to some length, states that Bonoditus, who was an acolyte and of the age of 27 years, was instituted by proxy, his proctor, Pannucius de Conteroni, Physician (Rector of Chevenyng, *Hasted I.* 367) undertaking to present him to the Archbishop within the year. Bonoditus was Rector here in 1328, obtaining in that year a similar license for nou-residence as W. Seward. See preceding note. (Chapter Library MS., Reg. Q. f. 129.)

(4) Hugo de Notingham was presented by the widow of Barthol. de Badlesmere to the Rectory of Stambridge Parva, Essex, in 1328, resigning it in 1333 (*Newcourt's Repertorium*). Probably the same with this rector.

-1400.   William Haddow.

Died A.D. 1400.   See following entry.

1400-1414.   Robert Wilcock. [1]

24 die Martii A.D. 1400, apud Cant. dmns. Rob. Wilcok Capellanus admissus fuit ad Eccl. paroch. de Kingeston juxta Dover, Caut. 1 loec. per mortem dni. Will. Haddow ultimi Rectoris ibidem vacant. ad presentat. Phil. de Despenser Militis, &c. *Arundel f.* 275 *b.*

Robert Wilcock exchanged in 1414 with Thomas Boteler, Vicar of Elham. He exchanged from Elham in 1424 with John Neel, Rector of Dunton, in the Diocese of London, but held that benefice for one year only.

(Chichele. 136 a. & Newcourt's Repertorium.)

1414.   Thomas Boteler.

4 die mensis Jan. A.D. 1414, apud Cant. dns. auctorizavit Permutationem inter duos. Robert. Wilkok rectorem Eccles. paroch. de Kyngeston ad presentationem dni. Philip. Le Despencer veri &c.—Et Thomam Boteler Vicarium perpetuum Eccles. paroch. de Elham, Cant. Dioec ad praesentationem Custodis et Scholarum Collegii sive Aulae de Merton, Universitatis Oxoniensis, &c. *Chichele f.* 62.63.

Thomas Boteler, who was previously Vicar of St. Mary Haddelee, in the Diocese of Rochester (Bp. Beaufort's Register of Institutions, Lincoln), exchanged from there May 2, 1403, with Geoffrey Gleg, Rector of Stryxton, in the Diocese of Lincoln. From Stryxton he exchanged in the following August with John Appulton, Vicar of Elham (Arch. Cant. x 55). In 1414 he exchanged to Kingston, where he probably died. [2]

1422.   John Blackborn.

17 die mensis Novemb. A.D. 1422 apud Lambeth admisit dom. Johan. Blakborn Capellanum ad Eccl. paroch. de Kyngston Cant. dioec. vacantem ad praesentationem Philipp. le Despenser Militis veri. &c. *Chichele f.* 136 *b.*

1450.   George Hawys.

20 die Jan. A.D. 1450 apud Lambeth admissus fuit dnus. Georgius Hawys, capellanus ad Eccl. Paroch. de Kyngeston Cant. dioc. vacant. ad praesentationem Rogeri Wentworth armigeri & Margeriae Consortis suae, &c. *Stafford f.* 107 *b.*

-1472.   William Denby.

Died in 1472.   See following entry.

1473-1479.   William Newman.

29 die mensis Martii A.D. 1473 apud Knole dnus. admisit ad Eccl. Paroch. de Kyngeston, Cant. dioec., per mortem Will. Denby ult. rectoria ibid. vacant. ad praesentat. dmnae Margeriae de Roos verae, &c., dnm Will. Newman, &c. *Bourchier f.* 109 *b.*

---

(1) John Dygge, of Barham, in the 4th year of Henry IV., granted to Robert Wylkok, Parson of Kyngston, his Manor of Swanton (in Lidden). *Hasted* III. 354.

(2) *Parsons* (" Monuments, &c., of Churches in Kent," 1794) in his account of this Church gives the following:—On a fragment of brass now lying in the parish chest,

Hic jacet Thomas Botiller C——
Obiit XII° die Octobr. Anno Dni. Mill——

1479. Thomas Barnby.

22 Octob. A.D. 1479 admissus fuit dns. Thos. Barnby ad Eccl. Paroch. de Kyngeston. Cant. diœc. per mortem Will. Newman ult. rectoris ibid. vacantem ad pɩæsent. Henrici Wentworth Militis veri, &c. *Bourchier* f. 122 b.

1498-1538. William Chevenyng.

21 die Aug. A.D. 1498 dns. admisit Will. Chevenyng ad Eccl. de Kyngston, Cant. diœc. vac. ad presentat, dni. Henrici Wentworth Militis, ᴧc. *Dean* f. 165 b.

Died in 1538.[1] See following entry.

1538. William Allright.

(Louis More) [2]

19 die mᴇnsis Aug. A.D. 1538, apud Lambehith dns. admisit dnm. Will. Allright Capellanum ad Eccl. Paroch. de Kingst ɩn juxta Bourne, Cant. diœc., per mortem ult. Incumb. vacantem, ad quam per Thomam Polnynges Militem ratione Advocationis ejusdem sibi per Nobilem virum dnm. Thomam Wᴇntworth dɩɩm. Wentwoɩth concess., ac el iɩ ᴇx parte facto ipsius Eccl. patrou. duo. præsentat. extitit, &c. *Crᴧnmer* f. 365 b.

17 die mensis Septemb. A.D. 1538 apud Lamhehith, dnus. admisit dnm. Lodovicum More clericum ad Ecc'. Pᴧroch. de Kiɩɩg-ton Cant. diœc, per mortem dmnl Wi l. Chevenyng ult. Incumb ibid vacɩɩnt. ad quam per Rogerum Wentworth Militem ratioue donationis et concessiouis advocationiɩ dictœ Ecclesiœ per Richaɩd Wentworth armig-rum sibi concess. ipsius Eccles. patrouo dɩɩ. presentat. extitit, &c. *Crᴧnmer* f. 365 b.

Subsequent entries in the Register show that the dispute as to the patronage of the living was compromised by the resignation of Louis More (after a second Institution) in favour of W. Allright, the latter and his successors undertaking, out of the fruits of the living, to pay an annual pension of £5 to Louis More during his lifetime. W. Allright was Rector here in 1550 (See *Visitations* for that year, Chapter Library MS.)

-1554. Richard Barkiston.[3]

Died 1554. See following entry.

1554-1560. Robert Russell.

The Presentation of Robert Russell clerk, of Sherborne, Dorset, by Anthony Aucher, Kt. dated 11 Dec., 1554, is preserved in the Chapter Library at Canterbury. The living is declared vacant by the death of Richard Barkiston. The petition is addressed, 'sede vacante,' to Dean Nicholas Wotton. Robert Russell died 1560. See following entry.

1560-1569. John Butler, LL.B.

21 die mᴇnsis Septemb. A.D. 1560 apud Lambeth dns. admisit Joh. Butler clericum ad Eccl. paroch. de Kingstoɩe juxɩa Bourne Cant. diœc. per mortem Rob. Russell Clerici ult. Rectoris ibid. vacantem ad præsent.

---

(1) In his will (proved 1st Oct., 1538) he directs—" My body to be buryed within the Chauncel of the Chuɩch of St. Gyles, Kingstoue, where my stoue doth lay." The tomb cannot be now identified.

(2) Lod More, cap. Rector of All Hallows the Wall, 21st Oct., 1515, resig. 1532. (*Newcourt's Repertorium*, vol. 1, 257.)

(3) Ric. Barkiston was instituted to the Rectory of Sutton Vallance in 1519. " First Fruits Compos. Bk "—Record Office.

Gilberti Hyde generosi ipsius Eccl. ratione ejusdem advocationis juris patronatus ejusdem eidem Gilberto in hac parte facti per dominam Auger &c. *Parker f.* 346 *a.*

John Butler held the Vicarage of Minster, Thanet, with this living till his death in 1569. He was Canon of Canterbury where he resided.[1] In his Will he directs his body to be buried in the Chapter House 'besyde Mr. Newton.' From the same source we learn that in addition to his other benefices he was Rector of Brandon-ferry in Suffolk and was Prebend of a Cathedral in Wales.

1569-1573. William King.[2]

Ultimo die mensis feb. A.D. 1569 dns. admisit Will. King clericum ad Eccl. paroch. de Kington juxta Bourne, Cant. diœc. per mortem Mag. Joh. Butler clerici ult. Incumb. Ibid. vacantem ad præsentat. Will. Auger generosi, veri &c. *Parker f.* 398 *b.*

William King resigned in 1573. See following entry.

1573-1600. John Hastlyn.

30 die Jan. A.D. 1573 dns. admisit Joh. Hastlyn ad Eccl. paroch. de Kingston Cant. diœc. per resign. Will. King ult. Rectoris ibidem vacant. ad præsentat. Will. Auger armigeri, veri &c. *Parker f.* 97 *b.*

John Hastlyn died Aug. 24, 1600, and is buried in the Chancel (*Append. XV.*). The burial of his first wife Alice,[3] and the baptisms of his four children by Margaret, his second wife, are entered in the Registers. His Will is in the Probate Registry at Canterbury.

1600-1632. Daniel Nicols.[4] M.A.

8 die mensis Sept. A.D. 1600, Institutio Mag. Daniells Nicols ad Eccl. paroch de Kingston Cant. diœc. per mortem Joh. Haselinge ult. Rectoris ibid vacant. ad præsentationem Afræ Patricke viduæ &c. *Whitgift. f.* 260.

Daniel Nicols was married, Dec 12 1603, at Eastry to Martha Hickes of Worth. 8 children, by this marriage, were baptised at Kingston. He died in 1632 and both himself and his wife are buried here, but no Stone remains to his memory. His Will and the Will of his brother, Rev. Matthew Nichols, who is also buried at Kingston, are in the Canterbury Probate Registry.

---

(1) It appears from a ' Return of the Condition &c. of Parishes in the Diocese,' made by order of Abp. Parker in 1569, that Mr. Hunt was then resident curate at Kingston. According to the same Return, there were 26 houses in the parish and 102 Communicants.

(2) Possibly the same with William King vicar of Appledore 1569-73, & Canon of Canterbury—who became afterwards Archd. of Northumberland, Canon of Windsor, &c.

(3) *Parsons* ("Monuments of Churches in Kent") in his account of this Church gives—Round a pew is the following inscription cut in the wood,

' Here lyeth Alis Haslyn '
' Buried in this place
' Who made a virtuous end '
' And only by Gods Grace '
' the 21st April 1557

(4) The condition of the Church furniture during this incumbency must have been deplorable. The following answer is given to Articles of enquiry at the Archdeacon's Visitation in 1608. "We have an old rotten communion table with a carpit of Buckeram; we have noe pulpit clothe, neither cushion of silke."

1632-1639. Walter Balcanqual, D.D.

27 die mensis Novemb. A.D. 1632, Institutio Walteri Balcanquall, S. T. D. ad Rectoriam Eccl. Paroch. de Kingeston, Cant. diœc, per mortem Danielis Nicolles, cler. ultimi Incumbentis ibidem vacantem ad præsent. Anthonii Aucher de Bishopsborne in com. Cant. Militis, &c. *Abbott f. 55.*

A notice of the Life of this Rector is given in the *Dictionary of National Biography.* The son of a Presbyterian Divine of the same name, he was educated at the University of Edinburgh, where he graduated in 1609. He took his degree of B.D. at Cambridge in 1611 as a Fellow of Pembroke Hall, and was incorporated at Oxford, July 16, 1617, in which year he was appointed Master of the Savoy by King James, who made him one of his Chaplains and sent him to represent the Church of Scotland at the Synod of Dort. His other subsequent preferments bear date as follows:—Rector of Adisham Kent, 1618. Dean of Rochester and Vicar of Goudhurst in 1624. Dean of Durham 1638, deprived 1642. He died at Chirke Castle, Denbighshire, Dec 25, 1645 (*Append. LIII.*). He was married Sept 21, 1624 at Bishopsbourne Church to Elizabeth widow of Sir William Hammond Kt. of St. Albans, and daughter of Anthony Aucher Esqr. of Bishopsbourne by his wife Margaret, daughter of Edwin Sandys, Archbishop of York.[1] All that is known of Dr. Balcanqual as an author is that he drew up ' The Declaration of King Charles I. concerning the late tumults in Scotland' (1639), and was the writer of Letters on the Synod of Dort, preserved in *John Hales' Golden Remains;* he also published some sermons.

1639-164x Thomas Blechynden, D.D.

Instituted 5 March, 1639.[2] (Bk. of Institutions, Record Office.) It may be assumed that this is the Dr. Blechynden who was Vicar of Eastry and Prebendary of Canterbury. He was ejected from his Canonry in 1642, when he probably vacated this living.[3] The Prebendary was the eldest son of Humphry Blechynden of Aldington. Succeeding to the family estate in 1639 he resided there till his death in 1663 (*Hasted III.* 456). By his wife Margaret he left a family of 2 sons and 4 daughters.

164x-1671. Nicholas Dingley.

This Rector was appointed in the time of the Commonwealth. His name first occurs in the Register Books in the entry of the Baptism of one of his children,[4] Dec. 10th, 1648. On page 36 will be found his Nomination by the parishioners as " Register " —according to the Act passed in the Long Parliament. At the Restoration an attempt was made to eject him (See the

(1) *Wood* in his Athenœ Oxon. (Vol II. Fasti 87) mentions a daughter of Dr. Balcanqual the wife of Sir Thos. Thynne of Longleat.

(2) The Institution is not quoted in Ducarel's Index at Lambeth.

(3) From the Return of the Churchwardens at a Visitation in 1640 the condition of the Church appears to be no better than it was thirty years before. (See note 4, p. x.) " Dr. Blechindius Chancel wants Tyling, and it doth rain in upon the Communion Table."

(4) The different members of his family are mentioned in his will (Probate Registry, Canterbury.) He then gives his instruction " my body to be buried at the upper end of the little chancel of Aldington Ch. at my most deare deceased ffather's foote there to sleep with my ancestors in a bed of dust with hopes to awake unto everlasting life at the glorious appearing of my blessed Lord and Saviour Jesus Christ."

(4) 3 children were baptised here; others are also named in his Will (Probate Registry, Canterbury).

appended note, also *Kennett's* Register and Chronicle p. 231).
Mr Dingley however continued in possession of this benefice
till his death. He was buried at Kingston Feb. 1st 1671.

The Institution of Miles Barnes to the Rectory of Kingston Aug·
2nd 1660 on the presentation of Sir A. Aucher is entered in the
"Bishop's Certificates" and "Liber Institut." at the Record
Office, though he failed to displace Mr Dingley. He was
probably resident in Kingston[1] at the time. He was Rector of
Lyminge 1634-1641, also of Brooke 1640-1661, and his name
appears as Vicar of Tenterden in 1649. He was subsequently
appointed Vicar of Folkestone in 1667, but only held the living
for 2 years. He died Sept 1, 1670 and was buried at Barham.
(*Append. LIV.*)

1672-1681. Robert Aucher, M.A.

26 die mensis Jun. A.D. 1672 institutio Rob. Aucher ad Rector. de Kingston'
Cant. diœc., per mort. Nic. Dingley vac. ad præsentat. Frederici Primrose.
Sheldon f. 352.

Robert 3rd son of Sir A. Aucher, Kt. was born Jan 21st 1643 and
baptised at Bishopsbourne. Matriculated at Queen's College,
Oxford, June 10th, 1664; B.A. 1668; M.A. 1670. Shortly after
his Institution to this Living the Archbishop granted him "a
licence to absent himself for 3 years from his Rectory and to
reside in Oxford, in order to the gaining of some more knowledge in the study of Divinity."[2] In 1676 he obtained a
dispensation to receive and hold the Vicarage of Eastchurch
with the Rectory of Kingston. He was, however, never instituted to Eastchurch, though he held the right of presentation.[3] The date of his death and his place of burial have not
been ascertained.

1681-1692. John Maximilian De L'Angle, D.D.

18 Jun. 1681, Instit. Maximilian De L'Angle ad Rect. de Kingeston, Cant.
Diœc. per mortem Rob. Aucher vacant. ad præsentat. Johnis. Stonyng,
&c. &c. *Sancroft f.* 397.

The son of Jean Maximilian De L'Angle a French Protestant
Divine for 25 years Minister of the Reformed Church at Rouen.
After his appointment to this living he obtained in 1684 a dis-
pensation to hold with it the Vicarage of Sibertswold-with-
Coldred, which however he exchanged two years afterwards for
the Rectory of St. George's-with-St. Margaret's Canterbury.
He vacated both benefices in 1692 and in 1695 was appointed to
the Rectory of Chartham, where he remained till his death,

---

(1) In the Marriage Licence of his daughter Ann to Bernard Gibbard dated June
23 1662 he is described "of Kingston, clerk." From his Will in the Probate Registry
we learn that he died possessed of a house and lands in Kingston. He also left 20s. to
the poor of each of the Parishes of Kingston, Barham, and Folkestone. A pedigree of
the Barnes family given in *Drake's* new edition of Hasted's Kent (*Hundred of Blackheath*,
p. 160), shows the connection of Miles Barnes with the Wilsfords of Heden in this parish,
through his mother a daughter of Abp. Sandys and his wife Cicely Wilsford. Another
daughter of the Archbishop had married Anthony Aucher Esq., of Bishopsbourne. The
pedigree erroneously states that Miles Barnes was Rector of that parish.

(2) Act Books of the Archbishops, Vol. III., Lambeth. His father made an un-
successful application in 1678 for a renewal of the licence for another 3 years—"the
parish being well satisfyed with the Life and Doctrine of the Curate." *Towner MS.* 41,
f. 83, Bodleian Library.

(3) Mr. Hatton Aucher as administrator of the goods of Rev. R. Aucher in July
1682 presented Rev. Anthony Woolrich to the Vicarage of Eastchurch vacant by the
death of the last incumbent—Rev. Thos. White. Mr. White was instituted to Eastchurch Feb. 16 1666. Arch. Cant. XIV. 381.

Nov. 24, 1724. *(Append. LV.)* Dr. De L'Angle was made a prebendary of Canterbury in 1671. His elder brother Samuel was prebendary of Westminster.[1]

1692-1718. Gilbert Burroughs.

16 Dec. 1692 Instit. Gilberti Burrough ad Rect. de Kingston Cant. Diœc. per cess. Joh. Maximilian de L'Angle vacant. ad præsentat. Edward Crayford &c. *Tillotson f.* 150 *b.*

Gilbert Burroughs was appointed Second Master of the King's School Canterbury in 1689. In the following year he became curate of this parish, succeeding to the living on the resignation of Dr. De L'Angle in 1692. His first wife Mary, daughter of Rev. T. Seyliard rector of Deal, and three of her children are buried in the North Aisle of the Cathedral.[2] He married secondly, in 1712 Jane daughter of Tristram Stevens and shortly after resigned his mastership in the King's School, residing on his benefice the last few years of his life. *(Append. XIV.)*

1718-1769. Peter Innes, M.A.

24 Dec. 1718. Instit. Petri Innes ad Rect. de Kingston, Cant. Diœc. per mortem Gilb. Burroughs vacant. ad præsentat. Elizabethæ Peters viduæ. *Wake f.* 3040.

The son of the Rev. Gilbert Innes [3] and Susanna his wife daughter of John de la Pierre (or Peters) M.D., of the Black-friars Canterbury. Baptised at St. John's Margate 24 June, 1692. B.A. University College Oxford 1713, M.A. 1716. Mr Innes was chaplain to the Rt. Hon. Heneage, Earl of Aylesford. In 1740 he was appointed to the Vicarage of Burham near Rochester [4] which he held by dispensation with Kingston till his death. He married Mary daughter of Stephen and Catherine Nethersole who died in 1748 and was buried at Kingston. *(Append. XVIII.)* Soon after this time Mr Innes seems to have fallen into ill health, requiring the assistance of a curate and to have been for a time non-resident.[5] He returned however to Kingston where he is buried—presumably by the side of of his wife, but no inscription remains to his memory.

1769-1806. John Nairn, M.A.

Mr. Nairn graduated at Peterhouse, Cambridge, B.A. 1750, M.A. 1764. Ordained Deacon 1750, Priest 1754, by the Bishop of Norwich. After holding the curacy of Great Mongeham he was appointed Perpetual Curate of Wingham in 1756. Five years later he was presented by the Bishop of Rochester to the Rectory of Stourmouth, and in 1769 he obtained a dispensation to hold with it the Rectory of Kingston on the presentation of the Rev. W. Dejovas Byrche and Elizabeth his wife. He resigned the incumbency of Wingham in 1771, but held his other two benefices till his death. Mr. Nairn was Chaplain to the Rt. Hon. George Lord Viscount Torrington. He married first, in 1760 Elizabeth * daughter of Dr. Hall, Physician of

---

(1) See the De L'Angle Pedigree by Mr Henry Wagner, F.S.A., Arch. Cant. XV., 31-33.

(2) *Dart's* Canterbury, and *Hovenden's* Cathedral Registers.

(3) Successively Vicar of Chislet, St. John's Margate, and Maidstone. *Haslewood's* Chislet, p. 92.

(4) Act Books of the Archbishops, Vol. VIII., Lambeth.

(5) "Parochial account of the Diocese by Archd. Head", MS. 1138 Lambeth.

* Buried at Kingston. *Append. XII.*

Greenwich Hospital, and Elizabeth * his wife; secondly in 1792 Ann * daughter of Rev. R. Jenkin, Rector of Westbere and his wife Catherine daughter of Rev. Ralph Blomer, D.D. Prebendary of Canterbury. He is buried in the Chancel of this Church. *Append. XII.*

1806-1816. Cooper Willyams, M.A. †

The son of John Willyams of Plaistow House, Essex, Commander R.N. [1] He graduated at Cambridge, Emm. Coll., B.A. 1784, M.A. 1789. While Vicar of Exning Suffolk he was appointed Chaplain of the "Boyne" under Lord St. Vincent in his campaign in the W. Indies in 1794, and subsequently Chaplain of the "Swiftsure," Capt. Ben. Hallowell, in the Mediterranean, being present at the Battle of the Nile. He published narratives of both expeditions illustrated by his own drawings. [2] Lord St. Vincent, to whom he was private Chaplain, presented him afterwards to a living in Kent, which he exchanged for Stourmouth. At the same time his old friend and schoolfellow Sir Egerton Brydges appointed him to the Rectory of Kingston. [3] Having obtained, like his predecessor, a dispensation to hold these two livings together, he was instituted to them both in June 1806. Mr Willyams married Elizabeth daughter of Peter Snell, Esqre of Whitley Court, Gloucester; two sons, by this marriage, were baptised at Kingston. Mr Willyams died July 17, 1816, and is buried in Fulham Churchyard in the same vault with his sister. *Append. III. & LVI.*

1816-1852. Thomas Bartlett, M.A.†

The Son of Thomas Bartlett Esqre of Henley. [4] St Edm. Hall Oxford B.A. 1813, M.A. 1816. He was appointed in 1814 assistant minister of St John's Bedford Row London, under Rev. Dr. Wilson afterwards Bp. of Calcutta. In the following year he accepted a curacy at Beckenham, and on Aug 1st. 1812 was instituted to this Rectory on the presentation of Mrs Catherine Susannah Cowper and Miss Sarah Butler of Wantage. [5] While Rector of this parish he also held from 1828 to 1839 the Rectory of St. Mildred, Canterbury, though without any emolument. He was appointed in 1832 one of the Six Preachers of the Cathedral and was Domestic Chaplain to the Marquis of Cholmondeley 1828-1850. After an incumbency of 36 years at Kingston Abp. Sumner conferred on him the Rectory of Chevening. Here however he remained only two years, removing in 1854 to the living of Luton, Beds. 3 years later he was presented by the Rev. D. Barclay Bevan to the rectory of

* Buried at Kingston: *Append. XII.*

† For notes of Church Repair &c. during this incumbency see pp. 156-157.

[1] His mother was a granddaughter of Sir Edward Goodere Bart. of Burghope. In the preface to one of his books quoted in the following note, Mr Cooper Willyams claims descent from Edwin Sandys, Abp. of York.

[2] "An Account of the Campaign in the West Indies in 1794." London 1796, 4to. "A Voyage up the Mediterranean in H.M.S. Swiftsure with description of the Battle of the Nile Aug 1st 1798." London 1802, 4to.

[3] Sir Egerton Brydges in his Autobiography Vol. I. p. 44, refers to the presentation and gives a personal account of this rector.

[4] A family of Norman origin, the same with Barthelot or Bartelott.

[5] Great nieces of Bp. Butler. Miss S. Butler buried at Kingston April 1st 1843, æt. 82.

Burton Latimer, Northants., which he resigned a few years before his death. Mr Bartlett was twice married. His first wife Catherine Sarah, daughter of Dr. Gilbert Cowper, was granddaughter of the Rev. Joseph Butler, Prebendary of St. Paul's London and Rector of St. Paul's Shadwell, a nephew of Bishop Butler. By this marriage he had several children, one of his sons Philip George succeeding him at Kingston. He married secondly Dec 8th, 1864 Lucinda Grace daughter of Rev. Henry Hoare, Vicar of Framfield, Sussex, who survived him. He died May 28th. 1872 and is buried in Burton Latimer Churchyard by the side of his first wife. See *Append. LVII.* Mr Bartlett was the author of a "Memoir of the Life, Character & Writings of Bishop Butler" also of an Index to the Analogy, and published various pamphlets and sermons. A notice of this Rector appears in the Dict. of National Biography.

1852-1861. Philip George Bartlett.

Son of the preceding Rector, baptised at Kingston Jan 18, 1820. He passed the Divinity Course at the Theo: Coll: Toronto in 1842, and was appointed Rector of St. George's Carryingplace, Ontario in 1845. Returning to England he was appointed Curate in Charge of Rudstone, Yorks, in 1850, and succeeded to the Rectory of Kingston in March 1852.[1] He exchanged in 1861 with the Rev. James Percy Croft, then Rector of Kirton, Suffolk. Mr Bartlett married Margaret Lucy daughter of Rev. Daniel Ferguson Rector of Walkington, Yorks. He continued Rector of Kirton till his death, though non-resident for some years previously through ill health. He died at Walkington Park, Beverley, March 19. 1876, and was buried at Carleton Forehoe, Norfolk, by the side of his wife who had died there in the previous year, while on a visit to their son the Rev. John E. P. Bartlett, who was at the time Rector of that parish. *Append. LVII.*

1861-1884. Percy James Croft, M.A. †

The second son of the Ven. James Croft [2] (Archdeacon of Canterbury and Rector of Saltwood) and Charlotte his wife, daughter of Charles Manners Sutton, Archbishop of Canterbury. Educated at Eton and Trinity, Cambridge; B.A. 1842, M.A. 1862. Ordained to the curacy of Saltwood 1843; curate of Tachbrooke, Worc. 1847. Vicar of Exning, Suffolk 1848, whence he removed in 1854 to the Rectory of Kirton in the same county. After holding that living for seven years he exchanged with the preceding Rector to Kingston [3] where he remained till his death in 1884. *(Append. XX.)* Mr Croft was domestic Chaplain to the Duke of Northumberland. He married, first, Annabella Mary daughter of Rev. H. Torre of Syndale, Yorks, who died Jan 28th 1851. By his second wife Mary Ellen (dec. Sept. 13th 1869, *Append. XX.*), daughter of Rev. C. Greenall Davies, Vicar of Tewkesbury, he had a numerous family. Mr Croft married, thirdly, Amelia Anna, daughter of Rev. H. Todd, Rector of Occold, Suffolk, who is also buried at Kingston *(Append. XXI.)*, surviving her husband barely two years.

---

† For notes of Church repair &c. during this incumbency see pp. 157, 158.

(1) On the presentation of Queen Victoria, "by reason of the Lunacy of the true Patron." *Bk. of Inductions,* Diocesan Registry.

(2) Eldest son of Rev. Nic. Croft, Canon of York. See pedigree of Croft of Aldborough Hall & Stillington Hall, Yorks. *Burke's* "Landed Gentry."

(3) On the presentation of Josiah Iles Wathen of Mickleham Surrey, patron for this turn. *Bk. of Inductions,* Diocesan Registry. Inducted Sept. 7th, 1861,

1884.   Christopher Hales Wilkie, M.A. †

> 3rd son of E. C. Hales Wilkie Esqre of Ellington, St. Laurence, Thanet, and Mary his wife, daughter of Thomas Wood Esqre of Chislet Court. (1) Exeter Coll. Oxford, B.A. 1862, M.A. 1866. Wells Theo. Coll. 1863. Curate of Glemham, Suffolk, 1864-66; St. Margaret's Rochester 1866-67; Cranbrook, Kent, 1867-70; Sunning-hill 1870-71; St. Peter's Thanet 1871-74; in charge of Edburton Sussex 1874-77. Presented by Archbishop Tait to the Rectory of Edburton 1877. Instituted(2) to the Rectory of Kingston Sept. 23d 1884. Married 1875 Melian Augusta daughter of F. Pembroke Jones Esqre and Emma his wife, daughter of William Delmar Esqr J.P. & D.L. for Kent, of the Elms Canterbury.

CURATES.

1498.   Richard Bole. (3)

1567.   John Wylcock. (4)

1569.   — Hunt. (5)

1633-36.   James Shipton, M.A. (6)

1636-42.   Michael Huffam.

1679-82.   Robert Garrett, M.A. (7)

1687-89.   Simon D'Evereux, M.A. (8)

1690-92.   Gilbert Burroughs. (9)

1750-56.   Bryan Faussett, M.A. (10)

1756-63.   William Barrett.

1764-65.   Hopkins Fox, B.D. (11)

1765-67.   William Taswell, M.A. (12)

† For notes of Church repair during this incumbency, see p. 158.

(1) For pedigrees of Wood and Wilkie see *Haslewood's* Chislet, p. 172. Pedigree of Hales—*Burke's* " Extinct Baronetcies," (Hales of Coventry); also " Miscell. Geneal. & Herald." New Series Vol. 1 pp. 69-71 (1874).

(2) On the presentation of Mrs Mary Wilkie of Ellington.

(3) *Archd. Visit.* Chapter Library.

(4) Signs the transcripts this year. Married at Kingston (p. 86).

(5) See the first footnote on page x.

(6) Curate of Adisham, 1636. Married Jeane d. of Rev. W. Master, D.D. Preb. of Canterbury. Vicar of Patrixbourne 1659, St. Peter's Thanet 1662 till his death in 1665.

(7) Rector of Wootton 1680. Died there 1712, æt. 70.

(8) Minor Canon of Canterbury. Rector of Harbledown and Perpetual Curate of Nackington for more than 40 years. Vicar of Brookland 1731 and died there 1733.

(9) Rector of Kingston 1692.

(10) Chichele Fellow of All Souls Oxford. Vicar of Alberbury Salop 1748-50. Rector of Monks Horton 1765, Perpetual Curate of Nackington 1767. The Journal of his excavations on Kingston Downs &c. published by Roach Smith under the title of ' Inventorium Sepulchrale.' Died at Nackington 1776. See Dict. National Biography.

(11) Son of Hopkins Fox of Nackington. King's School Canterbury, and Trinity Cambridge (Fellow). Vicar of Linstead 1767, Ruckinge 1780.

(12) Minor Canon of Canterbury, Vicar of Brookland   Rainham 1772, Aylsham, Norfolk, 1777.

THE BOOK OF

BAPTIZINGES MARYAGES AND BURYALLS

OF THE

PARISHE OF KINGESTONE IN KENT 1558.

ANNO PRIMO REGNI REGINE ELIZABETHE.

BAPTIZINGES 1558.

Julye.

1558. 9 daye was baptized Richard Browninge sonne
of Jeames Browninge   Anno supra.

28 daye was baptized Richard Argill sonne
of George Argill   Anno supra.

Septembr.

1 daye was baptized Egidius Wealls sonne
of Roger Wealls   anno supra.

6 daye was baptized Katherine Packers   *anno* supra.

October.

1 daye was baptized Katherine Stonedaers daughter
of Robert Stonedares   anno supra.

Januarye.

4 daye were baptized Agnis and Mercie gryme
daughters of Thomas Gryme   anno supra.

29 daye was baptized Thomas Trewe sonne of
William Trewe   Anno Supra.

30 daye of January was baptized Katherine Turner
daughter of Richard Turner · anno supra.

August 1559.

1559. 4 daye was baptized Peeter Horton sonne
of Sampson Horton   Anno supra.

ffebruary.

2 daye was baptized Katherine Cole daughter
of Nicholas Cole   Anno Supra.

19 daye was baptized Mathew Boulton sonne
of John Boulton   Anno supra.

June 1560.

1560. 29 daye was baptized Mary Davie Daughter
of Richard Davie   Anno Supra.

July.

24 daye was baptized Vincent Younge sonne
of Thomas Younge   Anno Supra.

ffebruary.

20 daye was baptized . . . . wallys daughter
of Roger Wallys.   Anno Supra.

October 1561.

1561. 26 daye was baptized John Moyse sonne of
Richard Moyse   Anno Supra.

ffebruary.

1 daye was baptized Elizabeth Turner
daughter of Richard Turner   *anno* supra.

ROBBE. BASSOCKE * } Churchwardens.
JOHN HOPKYN   }

Marche 1561.

1561. 21 daye was baptized Alice Baker daughter
of Michaell Baker   Anno Supra.

Aprell 1562.

1562. 5 daye was baptized Simon Grime sonne
of Thomas Gryme   Anno Supra.

Septembr.

6 daye was baptised Mary Rugley   *anno* sup.

21 daye was baptised William Sturdye   *anno* sup.

---

* The signatures of the Churchwardens for the year 1598, when
all existing Registers were ordered to be transcribed from paper to
parchment books.   These names appear at the foot of each page of
the Register Book up to that date, certifying the correctness of the copy.

November.

5 daye was baptized Alice Affeild   *anno* supra.

October 1563.

1563.   6 day was baptized Elizabethe Gould daughter
of Thomas Gould   Anno Supra.

December.

25 daye was baptized John Horton sonne
of Sampson Horton   Anno Supra.

Itm was baptized Joane Argor daughter
of George Argor   Anno Supra.

Idem die was baptized Margery Argor
daughter of George Argor   *anno* supra.

Marche.

18 daye was baptized Anthonye Packer *anno* supra.

Aprell 1564.

1564.   15 daye was baptized Vincent Silke *anno* supra.

Maye.

23 daye was baptized Annes Younge *anno* sup*ra*.

June.

21 daye was baptized Alice Gansine *anno* sup*ra*.

Marche.

4 daye was baptized Richard Rugley *anno* sup*ra*.

Aprell 1565.

1565.   2 daye was baptized Thomas Johnson *anno* supra.
7 daye was baptized John Groome *anno* sup*ra*.

June.

3 daye was baptized Luke Boultane *anno* sup*ra*.

December.

16 daye was baptized Anna Arger daughter
of George Arger   Anno Supra.

January.

19 daye was baptized william Nethersole   *anno* supra.

Marche.

3 daye was baptized Marye Peckar daughter
of Roger Peckar   Anno supra.

Septembr. 1566.

1566.* 15[1] daye was baptized Mathew Browninge sonne
of John Browninge   Anno Supra.

Januarye.

5[2] daye was baptized William Groome sonne
of William Groome   *anno* supra.

ROBE. BASSOCKE ⎫
JOHN HOPKINS   ⎬ Churchwardens.

January. 1566.

1566. 17[3] daye was baptized Edward Bradshawe sonne
of Grygorye Bradshaw   *anno* supra

eod. die[4] was baptized Robert Rugley a*nno* supra
the sonne of John Rugleye.

(· · · · ·) [5]

Maye 1567.

1567. 18 daye was baptized William Younge sonne
to Thomas Younge   Anno Supra.

October.

18 daye was baptized Christofer Packer sonne
of Roger Packer   Anno Supra.

---

* The foot notes within inverted commas that follow are extracts
from the Transcripts in the Diocesan Registry, showing where any
variation occurs or where they furnish additional particulars, and, occa-
sionally, entries which are not found in the Register Book itself. These
Transcripts (Archdeacon's) commence in 1566, and are continuous with
the exception of a hiatus of 20 years, 1640—1661, at the time of the
Commonwealth. From 1603 down to the beginning of the present
century the Transcripts are in duplicate, a yearly return being required
by the Archbishop also from that date. The two series are referred to
as *(a)* and *(b)* respectively in the foot notes.

[1] "23 Aug." *(a)*   [2] "7 Jan." *(a)*.   [3] "17 Sept." *(a)*.
[4] "eodem die." (17th Sept). *(a)*.
[5] "17 March Joannis Bolt*un* filius qui *de* Joannis Boult*on*." *(a)*
Not in the Register.

June 1568.

1568. 29 daye was baptized Peter Hollowaye sonne
of John Hollowaye   Anno supra.

August.

22 daye was baptized Nicholas Browninge sonne
of John Browninge   Anno Supra.

September.

12 daye was baptized William Sayer sonne
of Jeames Sayer   Anno Supra.

26 daye was baptized Thomas Blackewood sonne
of William Blackewood   Anno Supra.

ffebruary.

2 daye was baptized Henry Bradshawe sonne
of Grigory Bradshawe   Anno Supra.

August 1569.

1569. 7 daye was baptized Thomas Sherman sonne
of Robert Sherman   anno Supra.

Septembr.

13 daye was baptized Elinor Harffeild daughter
of Thomas Haffeild   anno supra.

Novembr.

13 daye was baptized John Bownes ye sonne
of John Bownes   anno supra.

20 daye was baptized Annis Rugly daughter
of John Rugley   anno Supra.

Decembr.

9 daye was baptized Marye Gookin daughter
of John Gookine   anno Supra.

18 daye was baptized John Robins sonne
of John Robins   anno Supra.

23 daye was baptized Thomas Perye sonne
of John Perrye   anno Supra.

August 1570.

1570. 28 daye was baptized Christyan Browninge
daughter of John Browninge   *anno* supra.

Novembr.

26 daye was baptized William Bradshawe sonne
of Grigorie Bradshawe   anno supra.

Decembr.

24 daye was baptized Christofer Sayer sonne
of James Sayer   anno supra.

ROBBE. BASSOCKE ⎫
JOHN HOPKYNS ⎬ Churchwardens.

Marche 1570.

1570.   7 daye was baptized John Vittell sonne
of William Vittell   Anno Supra.

November 1571.

1571.   4 daye was baptized Affra Robins daughter
of John Robins   anno Supra.

December.

21 daye was baptized Isacke Rugley sonne
of John Rugley   anno Supra.

Marche.

5 daye was baptized James Sherman sonne
of Roberte Sherman   anno Supra.

July 1572.

1572.   13 daye was baptized Isabell Haddinge daughter
of Jefferye Haddinge   anno Supra

December.

10 daye was baptized Thomas Hopkin sonne
of John Hopkin   anno Supra.

January.

1 daye was baptized Martha Bradshaw daughter
of Grigory Bradshaw   anno Supra.
26 daye was baptized Joane Boykines daughter
of Elyas Boykines   Anno Supra.

ffebruary.

4 daye was baptized Alice Haule daughter
of Thomas Haule   Anno Supra.

Marche.

17 daye was baptized Silvester Vittell sonne
of Richard Vittell   anno Supra.

Maye 1573.

1573. 1 daye was baptized Richard Sayer sonne
of James Sayer   Anno Supra.

August.

16 daye was baptized Jane Browninge daughter
of [1] (· · · ·) Browninge   Anno Supra.

September.

6 daye was baptized Jane Denne daughter
of Vincent Denne   anno Supra.

October.

4 daye was baptized Thomas Robins sonne
of John Robins   Anno Supra.

11 daye was baptized Margarett Dorne daughter
of John Dorne   Anno Supra.

November.

8 daye was baptized Jone Bunce daughter
of John Bunce   Anno Supra.

December.

20 daye[2] was baptized Jone Pery daughter
of John Pery   Anno Supra.

ffebruary.

14 daye was baptized Jane Bradshaw daughter
of Grigory Bradshawe   anno supra.

ROBT. BASSOCKE ⎱ Churchwardens.
JOHN HOPKYN   ⎰

---

[1] " John." (a).   [2] " 20 Sept." (a).

September 1574.

1574. 26 daye was baptized Thomas Denne sonne
of Vincent Denne.   Anno Supra.

Aprell 1575.

1575. 24 daye was baptized Elizabethe Austen
daughter of Edmond Austen   Anno Supra.

Maye.

8 daye was baptized Jone Boughton daughter
of John Boughton   Anno Supra.

24 daye was baptized Thomas Gould sonne[1]
of William Gould   Anno Supra.

October.

16 daye was baptized william Dorne sonne
of John Dorne   Anno Supra.

ffebruary.

15 daye was baptized Alice Cosbye daughter
of Roger Cosbye   Anno Supra.

19 daye was baptized Vincent Bunce sonne
of John Bunce   anno Supra.

Marche.

11 daye was baptized John Vittell sonne
of William Vittell   Anno Supra.

18 daye was baptized John Matson sonne
of James Matson   Anno Supra.

The same daye was baptized Charles Bradshaw
sonne of Grygorye Bradshaw   anno Supra.

1576. 25 daye was baptized Marye Sayer daughter
of James Sayer   anno Supra.

Julye 1576.

22 daye was baptized Jone Nethersole daughter
of John Nethersole   anno Supra.

---

[1] " Thomas, the daughter of," &c, *(a)*.

ffebruary.

8 daye was baptized Elizabethe Pantry daughter
of William Pantrye *anno* supra.

17 daye was baptized Jeramye Rugleye sonne
of John Rugley   anno supra.

Maye 1577.

1577. 16 daye was baptized John Craye sonne
of John Craye   anno supra.

July.

14 daye was baptized Thomas Haddin sonne of
Jefferaye Haddin   anno Supra.

September.

1 daye was baptized Thomas Denne sonne
of Robert Denne ˙ anno supra.

22 daye was baptized Mary Denne daughter
of Vincent Denne   anno supra.

The same day also was baptized Elizabethe
Lawrence daughter of John Lawrence[1]   *anno* supra.

Also Robert Gould sonne of William Gould   *anno supra.*

November.

24 daye was baptized John Browninge sonne
of John Browninge   *anno* supra.

December.

ROBBE. BASSOCKE ⎱ Churchwardens.
JOHN HOPKYN ⎰

December 1577.

1577. 1 daye was baptized Anna Austen daughter
of Edmond Austen   anno supra.

29 daye was baptized Thomasine Collens
daughter of Thomas Collens   *anno* supra.

Januarye.

5 daye was baptized Martha Cosbye daughter
of Roger Cosbye   Anno Supra.

---

[1] " John Larrence, gent." *(a).*

ffebruary.

2 daye was baptized Marye Nethersole daughter
of John Nethersole   anno Supra.

23 daye was baptized Mary Bunce daughter
of John Bunce   anno Supra.

Marche.

2 daye was baptized Robert Matson sonne
of James Matson   anno supra.

Aprell 1578.

1578. 6 daye of Aprell was baptized John Cooly
sonne of Michaell Cooly   anno supra.

25 daye was baptized Edward Sayer sonne
of James Sayer   anno Supra.

September.

29 daye was baptized Richard Smithe sonne
of James Smithe   anno Supra.

ffebruary.

8 daye was baptized Simon Rugley sonne
of John Rugley   anno Supra.

24 daye was baptized Mary Rugley daughter
of Robert Rugleye   anno Supra.

Maye 1579.

1579. 3 daye was baptized Henry Denne sonne
of Vincent Denne   anno Supra.

31 daye was baptized Nicholas Trome* anno supra.

July.

19 daye was baptized Elyzabethe Boykett
daughter of Elyas Boykett   anno supra.

26 daye was baptized Jone Peerson daughter
of vincent Boykett[1] anno supra.

---

* Crome (?)

[1] "John Peerson ye daughter of Vincent." (a).   "Boykett"
evidently copied in error from preceding entry.

November.

15 daye was baptized Susan Haddin daughter
of Jefferay Haddin   anno supra.

30 daye was baptized Vincent Denne sonne
of Robert Denne   anno supra.

January.

24[1] daye was baptized Jone Hopkine daughter
of John Hopkins   anno supra.

27[2] daye was baptized Dennis Hopkine daughter
of Thomas Hopkine   anno supra.

ffebruary.

7 daye was baptized Anne Nethersole daughter
of John Nethersole   anno supra.

March 1580.

1580   25 daye was baptized Henry Pearse sonne
of Richard Pearce   anno Supra.

ROBBE BASSOCKE }
JOHN HOPKIN   } Churchwardens.

Maye 1580.

1580.   1 daye was baptized Phillip Gould sonne
of William Gould   Anno Supra.

July.

17 daye was baptized Alice Matson daughter
of James Matson   anno Supra.

August.

14 daye was baptized Jone Pearsy daughter
of Vincent Pearse   Anno Supra.

19 daye was baptized Elizabethe Craye daughter
of John Craye   Anno Supra.

Septembr.

25 daye was baptized Paule Browninge sonne
of John Browninge   Anno Supra.

---

[1] " 27 Jan." (a).   [2] " 24 Jan." (a).

October.

2 daye was baptized Margarett Bunce
   daughter of John Bunce   Anno Supra.

December.

22 daye was baptized John Rugley sonne
   of Robert Rugley   anno supra.

24 daye was baptized Josias Nethersole
   sonne of John Nethersole   Anno Supra.

ffebruary.

5 daye was baptized Elizabethe Sayer
   daughter of James Sayer   anno Supra.

12 daye was baptized Abraham Rugley
   sonne of John Rugley   Anno Supra.

19 daye was baptized Gylion Culline
   daughter of Henry Culline   anno supra.

26 daye was baptized Arthur Boykett
   sonne of Elyas Boykett   anno supra.

Marche 1581.

19 daye was baptized Mercye Chandler
   daughter of Richard Chandler   anno supra.

1581. 28 daye was baptized Edward Browninge
   sonne of Thomas Browninge   anno supra.

Aprell.

23 daye was baptized Vincent Denne
   sonne of Vincent Denne   anno supra.

Maye.

7 daye was baptized Thomas Simons
   sonne of John Simons   anno supra.

June.

4 daye was baptized Marye Stokes
   daughter of Christofer Stokes   anno supra.

December.

17 daye was baptized Danyell Rugley
   sonne of Robert Rugley   anno supra.

13

January.

9 daye was baptized Nicholas Denne sonne
of Thomas Denne of Adsham   anno supra.

28 daye was baptized Jone Vittell
daughter of William Vittell   anno supra.

ROBBE BASSOCKE
JOHN HOPKIN   Churchwardens.

Maye 1582.

1582. 6 daye was baptized Silvester Denne daughter
of Robert Denne   Anno Supra.

August.

5 daye was baptized Jone Mason daughter
of Anthonye Mason   anno supra.

September.

21 daye was baptized Vincent & Mathew Pearson
sonnes of Vincent Pearson   anno supra.

23 daye was baptized Susan Bunce ·
daughter of John Bunce   anno supra.

30 daye was baptized Thomas Richard
sonne of John Richard   anno supra.

October.

7 daye was baptized Marye Coulson daughter
of Esdras Coulson   Anno Supra.

November.

11 daye was baptized Dennis Haddyne
daughter of Jefferye Haddine   anno supra.

Decembr.

9 daye was baptized Elizabethe Balducke
daughter of William Balducke   anno supra.

16[1] daye was baptized James Rugley
sonne of John Rugleye   anno Supra.

23 daye was baptized Mildred Hopkin
daughter of John Hopkine   anno supra.

[1] "6th Dec." (a).

28 daye was baptized Susan Hopkine
daughter of Thomas Hopkine   anno supra.

January.
13 daye was baptized Elnor Gould
daughter of William Gould.   anno supra.
27 daye was baptized Jane Sayer
daughter of James Sayer   anno supra.

Marche.
6 daye was baptized John Boykett & Margarett
children of Elyas Boykett   anno supra.

Aprell 1583.
1583. 21 daye was baptized John Palmer
sonne of John Palmer   anno supra.

July.
21 daye was baptized John Browninge
'sonne of Thomas Browninge   *anno* sup*ra*.

September.
15 daye was baptized Margaret Rickewood
daughter of Rickewood[1]   anno supra.

January.
19 daye was baptized John Nethersole
sonne of John Nethersole[2]   anno supra.

The same daye also was baptized Jane Craye
daughter of John Craye[3]   anno supra.

May 1584.
1584. 17 daye was baptized Jane Bunce
daughter of John Bunce   anno supra.

June.
29 daye was baptized Anne Denne
daughter of Mr. Vincent Denne[4]   *anno* supra.

---

[1] " Margaret Rycarde, daughtr of John Rycarde." *(a)*.
[2] " Mr. John Nethersole." *(a)*.
[3] " John Craye, y° sonne of John Craye." *(a)*.
[4] " Mr. Vincent Denn, Doctor." *(a)*.

September.

13 daye was baptized Jane Rugley
daughter of Robert Rugley   anno supra.

ROBBE BASSOCKE } churchwardens.
JOHN HOPKIN }

October 1584.

1584. 4 daye was baptized Mary Peerson
daughter of Vincent Peerson   anno supra.

Decembr.

6 daye was baptized John Denne
sonne of Robert Denne   anno supra.

ffebruarye.

28 daye was baptized Mathewe Baldocke
sonne of William Baldocke   anno supra.

Aprell 1585.

1585. 18 daye was baptized John Gould
sonne of William Gould   anno supra.

June.

6 daye of June was baptized Thomasine Laborne
daughter of Richard Laborne   anno Supra.

August.

29 daye was baptized Robert Boykett sonne
of Elyas Boykett   anno Supra.

September.

19 daye was baptized John Sayer
sonne of James Sayer   anno supra.

October.

28 daye was baptized Jeffery Haddine
sonne of Jefferye Haddyne *anno* supra.

Decembr.

27 daye was baptized John Richard[1]
sonne of John Richard[1]   anno supra.

---

[1] " Rycard." (*a*).

The same daye was baptized Thomasine Hopkine
daughter of Thomas Hopkine *anno* supra.

January.
16 daye was baptized Wilsford Nethersole
sonne of John Nethersole[1] anno supra.

ffebruary.
13 daye was baptized Alice Rayner
daughter of Mathew Rayner[2] a*nno* supra.

Aprell 1586.
1586. 25 daye was baptized Alice Bunce
daughter of John Bunce anno supra.
also Elizabethe Mason daughter of
Anthonye Mason anno supra.

December.
11 daye was baptized John Nethersole
sonne of John Nethersole anno supra.

ffebruarye.
12 daye was baptized Jone Rugleye
daughter of Robert Rugley anno supra.
26 daye was baptized ffrancis Nethersole
sonne of Mr. John Nethersole & John Newstreet
sonne of Thomas Newstreete. anno supra.

Julye 1587.
1587. 30 daye was baptized Marye Denne
daughter of Robert Denne a*nno* supra.

Septembr.
17 daye was baptized Marye Craye
daughter of John Craye a*nno* supra.

ROBBE BASSOCKE } Churchwardens.
JOHN HOPKIN }

---

[1] " Mr. John Nethersole." *(a)*.
[2] " Alice Rayner, daughter of Wydow Rayner, her father Matthew." *(a)*.

Decembr 1587.

1587. 10 daye was baptized Thomas Culline[1]
daughter of William Culline *anno* supra.

ffebbruarye.

4 daye was baptized Catherine Denne
daughter of Mr. Vincent Denne[2] *anno* supra.

Aprell 1588.

1588. 8 daye was baptized Nicholas Boyket
sonne of Elyas Boykett anno supra.

June.

23 daye was baptized John Laban
sonne of Richard Laban anno supra.

October.

6 daye was baptized Annis Rugly
daughter of Richard Rugleye anno supra.

Novembr.

17 daye was baptized Marye Hastlyn
daughter of John Hastlyne *anno* supra.

Januarye.

1 daye was baptized Mary Browninge
daughter of Thomas Browninge *anno* sup*r*a.

Aprell 1589.

1589 20 daye was baptized Katherine Mershe
daughter of William Mershe & William Odley
sonne of Jobe Odleye anno supra.

Maye.

18 daye was baptized Elizabethe Wayte
daughter of George Wayte anno supra.

June.

21 daye was baptized John Gould
sonne of William Gould *anno* supra.

---

[1] " Tamsen Cullyn." (*a*)
[2] " Mr Vincent Denne, Doctor." (*a*)

C

July.

6 daye was baptized John Coorte
  sonne of John Coorte   anno supra.
20 daye was baptized Mary Churchman
  daughter of John Churcheman   anno supra.

September.

14 daye was baptized Annis Younge
  daughter of Vincent Younge   *anno* supra.
28 daye was baptized James Rugley
  sonne of Robert Rugley   anno supra.
The same daye also was baptized William
  Nethersole sonne of Mr. John Nethersole.

Decembr.

7 daye was baptized Edward Denne sonne
  of Robert Denne & John Haddine
  sonne of Jefferye Haddine   anno supra.

ffebruarye.

1 daye was baptized Vincent Craye
  sonne of John Craye   anno supra.
8 daye was baptized Mary Chambers
  daughter of Edward Chambers   anno supra.

ROBBE BASSOCKE }
JOHN HOPKIN   } Churchwardens.

Julye 1590.

1590 26 daye was baptized John Boykett
  sonne of Elyas Boykett   anno supra.

August.

9 daye was baptized Marye Allen
  daughter of John Allene[1]   anno supra.

Novembr.

1 daye was baptized Margarett Rugley
  daughter of Richard Rugley   anno supra.

---

[1] " Mr. John Allyn." (*a*)

January.
6 daye was baptized John Hastlyne
sonne of John Hastlyne   anno supra.

Maye 1591.
1591 6 daye was baptized Henry Maple
sonne of Henry Maple   anno supra.

September.
26 daye was baptized Thomas Butler
sonne of Mr. Robert Butler   anno supra.

November.
21 daye was baptized John Odleye sonne
of Jobe Odleye   anno Supra.

December.
19 daye was baptized Margarett Gould
daughter of William Gould   anno supra.

ffebruarye.
6 daye was baptized William Younge
sonne of William Younge   anno supra.

Marche.
19 daye was baptized Anne Nethersole
daughter of Mr. John Nethersole & Robert
Denne sonne of Robert Denne   anno supra.

September 1592.
1592   3 daye was baptized George Richard
sonne of John Rickard   anno supra.

ffebruarye.
11 daye was baptized Grace Scriben
daughter of Thomas Scriben   anno supra.

Aprell 1593.
1593. 8 daye was baptized Sara Vsmor
daughter of Ralfe Vsmor   anno supra.
& Jane Boykett daughter of Elyas Boykett
29 daye was baptized William Rugley
sonne of Richard Rugley   anno supra.

June.

10 daye was baptized Margaret Browninge
daughter of Thomas Browninge   *anno* sup*ra.*

August.

19 daye was baptized Joane Hastlyne
daughter of John Hastlyne   anno supra.

ROBB. BASSOCKE } Churchwardens.
JOHN HOPKIN }

Aprell 1594.

1594. 16 daye was baptized Vincent Younge
sonne of Vincent Younge[1]   anno supra.

June.

23 daye was baptized William Brigg
sonne of Richard Brigge   anno supra.

Septembr.

30 daye was baptized Jone Browninge
daughter of Mathew Browninge   *anno* sup*ra.*

Novembr.

3 daye was baptized Jone Courte
daughter of John Courte   anno supra.

Decembr.

26 daye was baptized Margarett Goodwine
daughter of Danyell Goodwine   *anno* supra.

Maye 1595.

1595.   4 daye was baptized Thomas Chambers
sonne of Edwarde Chambers   anno supra.

June.

11 daye was baptized Jone Rugleye
daughter of Richard Rugley   anno supra.

22 daye was baptized Willyam Rickard
sonne of John Ryckard   anno supra.

30 daye was baptized Katherine Browninge
daughter of Thomas Browninge   *anno* supra.

---

[1] " Sonne of Vincent desseased." (*a*)

July.

1 daye was baptized Jone Maple
daughter of Henry Maple   anno supra.

Marche.

7 daye was baptized James Morley
sonne of James Morley   anno supra.

Aprell 1596.

1596. 25 daye was baptized Sara Nethersole
daughter of Mr. John Nethersole   anno supra.

June.

6 daye was baptized John Browninge
sonne of Mathew Browninge   anno supra.

13 daye was baptized George Bassocke
sonne of Robert Bassocke   anno supra.

August.

29 daye was baptized John Mughole
sonne of Samuell Mughole   anno supra.

ffebruarye.

20 daye was baptized Stephen ffoorde
sonne of Edward ffoorde   anno supra.

Marche.

4 daye was baptized Sibell Dale
daughter of Edward Dale   anno supra.

Julye 1597.

1597. 31 daye daye was baptized John Denne
sonne of William Denne   anno supra.

ROBBE BASSOCK }
JOHN HOPKIN } Church Wardens.

August 1597.

1597.   7 daye was baptized Jane Baker
daughter of Edward Baker   anno supra.

28 daye was baptized Elizabeth Chambers
daughter of Edward Chambers   anno supra.

September.
11 daye was baptized Affra Hastlyne
    daughter of John Hastlyne   anno supra.

January.
10 daye was baptized Elizabeth Goodwine
    daughter of Danyell Goodwine   anno supra.
11 daye was baptized Elizabethe Davis
    daughter of Richard Davis   anno supra.

Marche.
5 daye was baptized Marye *T*oppin*
    daughter of John *T*oppin   anno supra.
12 daye was baptized Marye Bassocke
    daughter of Robert Bassocke   anno supra.

September 1598.
1598. 10 daye was baptized Rebecka Nethersole
    daughter of Mr. John Nethersole   anno supra.

† By me JOHN HASTLYN p*a*rson.
    ROBERT BASSOCK Churchwarden.
    JOHN HOPKINS | his m*a*rke.

1598. The. 25. of Decebr was Baptised Daniell Rycard y⁶ sonn
    of John.
1599. The. 26. August was Baptised Jayne Ruglye the daughter
    of Rycharde.
The. 3. of ffebruary was baptised Ann Robinson the daughter of
    Edward.
The. 10. Was baptized Dennis Mughole the Daughter of Samuell.
1600. The 11 of Maye was baptised Rycharde Chambers the
    Sonne of Edwarde.
Aprill 7. Anna the daughter of William Denn was baptised.
Novebr. 16. Jane the daughter of John Dale was baptised.
Novemb. 21. Jane y⁶ daughter of Robert Bassocke baptised.

---

* Coppin (?)
† Thus far in the Register the entries have been transcribed from
an earlier book. (See foot note on page 2) The Rector here signs
with the Churchwardens, at the end of the copy, to attest the whole.

Novebr. 30.   Margaret the daughter of Henric Rigden baptised.

An. dom. 1601.

An. 1601.   Aprill 19.   Was baptised Robert Browninge the sonne of Matthewe Browninge.

Novebr. 15.   Was baptised Marget the daughter of George Baldocke.

An. 1602.   April 5.   Was baptised Lucy the daughter of William Denn.

January 2.   Was baptised Edwarde Dale the sonne of John Dale an*no* supra.

Marche 13.   Was baptised Richarde Gloover the sonne of Richarde Gloover.

An. 1603.   Marche 25.   Was baptised Mary the daughter of Edwarde Robinso*n*.

Marche 27.   Was bap. Richarde the sonne of Richard Rugley.

May 1.   Was baptised James Browninge the sonne of Matthewe Browninge.

May 29.   Was baptised Vincent Denn the sonne of Mr. John Denn.

An. 1604.   July 15.   Was baptised Robert Smithson the sonne of Gregorie Smithson.

Octob. 7.   Was baptised John the sonne of Richarde Rugley.

Octob. 11.   Was baptised Roberte the sonne of Samuel Mughall.

March 17.   Was baptised John Nicols ye sonne of Daniel Nicolls pa*r*son.

Decemb. 16.   Was baptised Martha the daughter of Edwarde Chambers.

1605.   June 16.   Was bap. Ann the daughter of John Loude.

August 4.   Was baptised Amie the daughter of John Huse.

Marche 16.   Was bap. Mathie y^r base sonne of Elsabethe Boyket.

1606.   Sep. 14   Was bap : Jone the daughter of Gregory Smithson.

Decemb. 7. was bap. Daniel the sonn of John Lowde.

Decebr. 14.   was bap. Thomasine the daughter of Edwarde Robinson

1607   Marche 29.   was bap. George the base borne sonne of Elsabeth Johnson.

May 5 was bap : Daniel the sonne of John Heringe.

May 10 was bap. Ann the daughter of Thomas Luckas.

May 31 was bap. John the sone of Auerey Sabin.

Novebr. 8. was bap. Richarde Nicols ye sonne of Daniel Nicols. parson.

1608. April 3. was baptised John the sonne of John Loude.

April 24. was bap. Jane the daughter of Thomas Pierse.

Octob: 25. was baptised James Wilforde the sonne of Sr. Thomas Wilforde Knight.

Novemb: 1. was bap: Thomas Ingester the sonne of Timothy Iniester.

The same day was bap: Elsabethe the base born daughter of Ann Johnson.

Deceb: 4. was bap: Clemente the sonne of Thomas Hogbin.

February 26: was bap: Anthony Woodd the sonne of John Woodd.

The same day was bap: Mary Woodd the daughter of John Woodd.

March: 12 was bap: Elene the daughter of Thomas Gregorie.

1609. April 9 was bap: Gregory Smithson the sonne of Gregory Smithson.

Octob: 1. was babtised Katerine Wilforde the daughter of Sr. Thomas Wilforde Knight.

The same day was bap: Martha George the daughter of Thomas George.

Visitat. Octobr. 10.

Decebr: 24 was bap: Jane the daughter of Daniel Nicols parson.

February 18 was bap: Roberte the son of John Cullen.

1610. Aprill 15. was bap: Richarde ye sonne of Richard Preble.

Visitat. April 24.

July 15 was bap: Joane the daughter of John Wood.

August 19. was bap: James ye sonne of James Sayer.

Visitat: Sep. 25.

Octob: 7. was bap. Marget the daughter of Robert Eaton.

1611. April 7. was bap. Jane ye daughter of John Simons.

April 28 was bap: Joane ye daughter of Edwarde Browninge.

July 22 was bap: Roberte the sonne of Daniel Rugley.

Sep: 1 was bap: Judithe ye daughter of Gregory Smithson.

Octob: 27. was bap: dionys the daughter of Richarde Hopkin.

The same day were bap: John and Roberte the sonns of John Rickwoode.

Noveb : 21 was bap : Daniel the sonne of Daniel Nicols parson.

Anno 1612. March 29. was bap. william yᵉ sonn of Roberte Eaton.

    Visitat. 28 of April.

Septemb. 13 was bap. Marget the daughter of Thomas Norington.

Octob. 25 was bap : Vincent yᵉ sonne of William Denn.

    Visitat. 21 of April. Anno 1613.

May 30 was bap. Sara the daughter of Edwarde Browninge.

July 11 was bap : Elsabeth yᵉ daughter of John Wood.

August 8 was bap. John yᵉ sonne of John Simons.

    Visitat. 28 of September.

Octob : 17 was bap : Edwarde the sonne of Sr. Thomas Wilforde
    Knight.

January 23 was bap. Catharine yᵉ daugh : of William Denn.

The same day was bap : william yᵉ sonne of Robert golde.

February 27. was bap. Edwarde yᵉ sonne of John Hatcher.

March 13 was bap. Elsabethe yᵉ daughter of Robert Eaton.

An : 1614.

March 25 was bap. Elisabethe yᵉ daugh : of Daniel Nicols parson.

    Visitat. Aprill 30.

May 1 was bap : Elias yᵉ sonne of John Boykett.

May 29 was bap : Ann the daughter of Ingram Hogbone.

Septemb : 4 was bap : Mary yᵉ daughter of John Rickwood.

    Visitat. Sep : 28.

Octob. 9 was bap John yᵉ sonne of Mr.* Thomas Marshe.

Octob. 23 was bap: Richard yᵉ sonne of Paule Browninge.

Noveb. ii. was bap: Jane Smithson yᵉ daughter of Gregory
    Smithson.

Deceb. 26 was bap. Stephen the sonne of Thomas Norington.

An: 1615.

March 26 was bap: Elizabethe the daughter of Sr. Thomas
    Wilforde Knight.

April 30 was bap: Ann the daughter of Edwarde Browninge.

May 21. was bap: Mary yᵉ daughter of Roberte Golde.

---

* " Mr " inserted by a later hand.

May 28 was bap: Ann the daughter of Nicolas Rayner.

June 11. was bap: Joane the daughter of Henry Grigg.

July 9 was bap: William ye sonne of William Bridge.

Febru: 11. was bap: William ye sonne of Edmunde. Vden.

    Visitat. April 10, 1616.

May 12 was bap: Ann the daughter of Mr. John Nethersole the younger.

June 2. was bap: Ann the daughter of Robert Younge.

August 25. was bap: Matthewe ye sonne of Daniel Nicols parson.

    Visitat. Octob. 1 An: 1616.

Octob: 13 was bap: Mary ye daughter of Thomas Hopkin.

Decemb. 8. was bap: Edwarde the sonne of Mr. William Denn.

January: 12. was bap: Marget the daughter of Edwarde Browninge.

March 16 was bap: Mary ye daughter of Paule Browninge.

    Visitat. April 30. Anno 1617.

May 11. was bap: Mary ye daughter of John Giles.

May 25 was bap: John the sonne of Roberte Golde.

    Visitat. Octob: 3.

Octob: 5. was bap: John the sonn of William Bridges.

Octob: 19 was bap: Luke ye sonn of Thomas Smithet.

Deceb: 7. was bap: Roberte ye sonn of Robert Eaton.

Decemb. 28. was bap: Catherine Rickwood the daughter of John Rickwood.

Febr: 15. was baptised Marget the daughter of John Boyket.

March 1 was bap: William ye sonn of Thomas Hopkin.

April 12 was bap: William ye sonn of Daniel Nicols parson.

    Visitat. April 14. An. 1618. (28. Ap:

Septemb. 6. was bap: Elsabethe ye daughter of Roberte Younge.

    Visitation ye. 1. of Octobr. an. sup.

Novemb: 8 were bap: Jane & Thomasine ye daughters of John Loude.

January 17. was bap: Paul ye sonne of Paul Browninge.

January 31. was bap : Margery ye daughter of Henry Taylor.

ffebruary 14. was bap : Mary ye daugh : of John Waginer.

An : 1619.

May 2. was bap : Sara ye daughter of Thomas Hopkin.

May 30 was bap : Ann : yᵉ daugh : of John Ventiman.

July 11. was bap : Edwarde the sonne of Edwarde Browning.

Septeb : 19 was bap : Marget yᵉ daughter of William Allen.

Visitat. yᵉ 27. of Septembr.

Octob : 24 was bap : John yᵉ sonne of John Giles.

An : 1620.

April 23 was bap : Marget yᵉ daughter of William Bridges.

April 30 was bap : Edwarde yᵉ sonne of Thomas Hastefer.[1]

August, 20 was bap : Matthewe yᵉ base borne sonne of Amie Smithe.

Septembr. 10 was bap : Roger yᵉ sonne of Roberte Golde.

Oct. 29 was bap : Mary yᵉ daughter of John Boyket.

The same day was bap : Marget yᵉ base borne daughter of Marget Mughole.

Noveb : 26 was bap : Roberte the sonne of John Everden.

Decemb : 10 was bap : Edmonde yᵉ sonne of Thomas Hopkin.

The same day was bap : Margery yᵉ daughter of John Giles.

Deceb : 24 was bap : Thomas yᵉ sonne of Daniel Nicols parson.

March 4 were bap : Vincent & Thomas the sonns of John Rickwood.

April 8 was bap : Ann yᵉ daughter of Paule Browning.

Visitat. yᵉ 10 of April.

Visitat. Sept. 28. Ann : 1621.

Octob. 14 was bap : John yᵉ sonne William Sally.

Noveb : 25 was bap : Mary yᵉ daugh : of Thomas Kingsmel.

March 3. was bap : Thomas yᵉ sonne of Vincent Cray.

An : 1622.

April 7 was baptised Joane yᵉ daughter of William Allen.

April 14 was bap : Mary yᵉ daughter of John Everden.

July 5 was bap : Ann the daughter of Sr. Thomas Wilford Knight.

Octob : 13 was bap : Mary yᵉ daughter of William Bridges.

Noveb : 17 was bap : Martha yᵉ daughter of James Wrathe.

January 1. were bap : Stephan & George yᵉ sonnes of Robert Golde.

---

[1] " Hasley " (a).

ffebruary 2. was bap : Mary ye daughter of Edward Browninge.

An : 1623. Marche 30 was bap : Martha ye daughter of Thomas Hopkin.

August 10. Was bap : George ye sonne of Thomas Tallies.

Septeb : 14 was bap : Marget the daughter of John Rickwood.

Septemb. 21. was bap : Marget ye daughter of Robert Younge.

Visitat ye 23 of Septemb.

Novemb. 30 was christened Elisabethe Marshe ye daughter of Mr.* Thomas Marshe.

Deceb. 26 was bap : John ye sonne of Matthew Shoveler.

ffebruary 1. was bap : William ye sonne of William Sally.

An : 1624.

May ye 2 was bap : Thomas ye sonne of Thomas Hastifer.

July 4 were bap : Catherine & Jane ye daughters of Thomas Hopkin.

Sep. 26. was bap : Elsabeth ye daughter of Paule Browninge.

Visitat. Sep. 30.

Octob. 3. was bap : Jane ye daughter of Mr. Edwine Auger.

March 13 was bap : Thomas ye sonne of Thomas Branslet.

March 20 was bap : Thomas ye sonne of Matthew Shoveler.

1625.

April 17. was bap : Jhon ye sonne of William Allen.

Visitat. April 26.

May 1. was bap : Thomas ye sonne of Thomas Kingsmeele.

Sep. 18 was bap : John ye sonne of John Giles.

The same day was bap : Mary ye daughter of Vincent Cray.

Octob : 9 was bap : Joane ye daughter of Austen Godfray.

Decemb. 11. was bap : John ye sonne of John Boyket.

Decemb. 18. was bap : Thomas ye sonne of Robert Younge.

An : 1626.

May 11 was bap : Mary ye daughte. of Thomas Mershe.

July 16 was bap : Robert ye sonne of Robert Gold.

July 23 was bap : Water ye sonne of Sr. Thomas Wilforde Knight.

---

* " Mr " inserted by a later hand.

August 27. was bap : Edwin yᵉ sonne of Thomas Dewell.

Octob. 1. was baptised William yᵉ sonne of Thomas Tallies.

The same day was bap : Elsabethe yᵉ daughter of William Sally.

Octob. 22.[1] was bap : Mergery yᵉ daughtr of Thom : Kingsmeel.

1627.

April 15 was bap : Vincent yᵉ sonne of Thomas Branslet.

May 27. was bap. Joane yᵉ base borne daughter of Joane Ladd.

June 24th was bap : Homfray yᵉ sonne of Paule Browninge.

July 8 was bap : Alise yᵉ daughter of William Silke.

October 18 was baptised Lucke Richard yᵉ sonne of John Richard.

Decemb. 9 was bap : ffrances yᵉ daughter of William Sabin.

January 29.[2] was bap : Jeremy yᵉ sonne of William Sally.

1628.

April 27 was bap : Daniel yᵉ sonne of Robert Younge.

August 17 was bap : Mildred yᵉ daughte of William Allen.

Octob. 12 were bap: Nicholas & Richard yᵉ sonns of James Wrathe.

Noveb. 2. was bap : John yᵉ sonne of Richard Winter.

Deceb. 4. was bap : Ann yᵉ daught. of John Boyket.

1629.

May 3. was bap. Susan yᵉ daughter of William Sauin.

May 17 was bap : Jane yᵉ daught. of John Rickwood.

Septemb : 17 was bapt. Benet yᵉ daught. of Thomas Branslit.

Noueb. 1 was bap. Thomas yᵉ sonne of Richard Tallies.

Deceb. 6. was bap. ssusan yᵉ daught. of Richard Wood.

Deceb. 20 was bap. Augustine yᵉ sonne of Samuel Branslet.

January 10 was bap: James yᵉ sonne of Nicholas Smithe.

ffebruary 7. was bap: Nicholas yᵉ sonne of John Barber.

1630.

June 22 was baptised ffrancis the daught. of Sʳ Thomas Baker Knight.

July 25 was bap: Joane yᵉ daughter of John Rickwood th'elder.

---

[1] " Oct. 27 " (a).   [2] ' Jan 27 " (a).

August 29 was bap: Mary the daughter of William Allen.

October 17 was bap: Alexander yᵉ sonne of William Silke.

January 2 was bap: John yᵉ sonn of Thomas ffriend.

1631.

July 10 was bap: Mary yᵉ daughter of Thomas Claringbold.

November 4 were bap: Paule & Jonas yᵉ sonns of William Sally.

January 22 was bap: William yᵉ sone of William Cullen.

The same day was bap: Sara yᵉ daughter of Thomas Bransley.

Marche 18 was bap: Samuel yᵉ sonne of Samuel Bransley.

1632.

April 30 was bap: Hezechias the sonne of Whittingam ffogg gentl.

June the 24th was baptized Thomas the sonne of John Mughall.

ffebruary the 17th was baptized Thomas the sonne of Thomas Claringbolle.

March yᵉ 3rd was Baptized Elizabeth the daughter of William Alleine.

1633.

1633. Thomas the sonne of Sʳ Thomas Baker Knight was baptized the 9th of May.

Elizabeth the daughter of Whittingam Fogg gent. was baptized the same day.

Vincent & Richard the sonnes of Nicholas Bonham were baptized yᵉ 13th day of August.

Isaac Winter the sonne of Richard was baptized the 13th of October.

Barbara the daughter of Thomas *bee*re bapti the 20 of Novemb.

Thomas the Sonn of Thomas Freind was baptized the 8th of December.

Richard Solly the Sonne of William was baptized the last of January.

Stephen Hogben the Sonne of Jonas was baptized the 2nd of February.

1634.

1634. Annah Tallice the daughter of Richard & Mary was baptized the 13th of Aprill.

Thomas the Sonne of Whittingam Fogge gent. & Katherine was baptized y 24th of Aprill.

Margaret the daughter of Sʳ Thomas Baker Knight & Frances Lady baptized the 5th of September.

John White the Sonne of Thomas & Margaret was baptized the 5th of October.

Joane Branslet the daughter of Thomas & Katherine baptized the 18th of January.

James Pittocke the Sonne of John & Sarah baptized the 8th of February.

1635. Elizabeth the daughter of James Shipton Clerke & Joane baptized the 29th of May.

Anne Kingsmel the daughter of John & Joane baptized the 9th of June.

1635. Thomas Hopkin yᵉ son of John yᵉ yonger & Anne was bapt: yᵉ 19. of July.

William Fogg yᵉ Sonn of Whittingham. Gent: & Katharyne was bapt: yᵉ same day.

Elizabeth Jones yᵉ daughter of David & Elizabeth was bap: yᵉ 26 of July.

James yᵉ sonn of Sʳ Thomas Baker Knight & ffrancis his lady was bapt: yᵉ 26 Septemb.

Mary Winter yᵉ daughter of Richard & Elizabeth bapt: yᵉ 1st of November.

Anne Browne yᵉ daughter of John & Elizabeth bapt: the same day.

Mary Beake yᵉ daughter of Henry & Joane bapt. yᵉ 15th of Novemb.

Robert Turner yᵉ Son of Richard & Susan bapt: yᵉ 14th of February.

Ann Myhell yᵉ daughter of Richard and Mildred bap: yᵉ 28 February.

1636 John Branchly yᵉ sonne of Samuell & Parnell baptiz: yᵉ 27th of March.

James Pittock yᵉ sonn of John & Sarah bapt: the 3rd of Apryll.

William Beer yᵉ Sonne of Thomas & Anne bapt: yᵉ 15 of May.

Anne Rickwood yᵉ daughter of John and Mary bapt: yᵉ 26 of June.

Elizabeth Hobdy yᵉ daughter of ffrancis, & ffrancis his wife bapt : yᵉ 1st of January.

John Sterling yᵉ Sonn of John & Mary bapt : the 15th day of January.

Richard yᵉ Sonn of Ambrose Snapes and Allyce his wife was bapt. yᵉ 19th of February.

1637. Elizabeth yᵉ daughter of Richard & Ann Thraps was baptiz : yᵉ 25 of June.

William yᵉ son of Richard and Mildred Myhel was baptiz : yᵉ 9th of July.

Mary yᵉ daughter of John & Margery Godwyn was bapt : yᵉ 16th of July.

Myhill yᵉ Sonn of David & Elizabeth Jones was baptiz : yᵉ 30th of July.

Thomas the Sonn of Henry & Joan Beak bapt : yᵉ 3rd of Septemb.

Ann yᵉ daughter of William & Judeth Gould, bapt : yᵉ 4th of March.

1638. Dorathy yᵉ daughter of John & Joane Kyngsmell was baptiz : Apryll yᵉ 10th.

Danyell the Son of Nathanyell & Mary Nash was baptiz : Apryll yᵉ 29th.

Sarah yᵉ daughter of John & Sarah Pittock was baptiz : June yᵉ 17th.

Danyell Rickwood yᵉ Son of John and Mary Rickwood bapt : July yᵉ 22.

Ruthe yᵉ daughter of John and Ann Barber Baptiz : September yᵉ 2nd.

Richard the Sonn of Sʳ Thomas Baker Knight bapt : yᵉ 7th Septemb.

Leah yᵉ daughter of Thomas and Ann Beer was baptized Septemb. yᵉ 23d.

Elizabeth yᵉ daughter of John & Elizabeth Browne[1] was baptised Octob. yᵉ 28th.

John yᵉ Sonn of Richard and Myldred Myhell bapt : yᵉ 23d Decemb.

1639. Richard the Son of Richard Tallis[2] was baptiz : March yᵉ 31.

Abraham yᵉ son of Abraham Wood was baptiz : Apryll yᵉ 7th.

Steven the Sonne of Michaell Huffam Cleark and Leah his wife was baptiz : July the 28th.

Mary yᵉ daughter of Samuelle & Parnell Branchley was bapt. Octob : yᵉ 6th.

---

[1] " John & Ann Brown." (a)
[2] " Richard & Mary Tallis." (a)

Mary ye daughter of Richard & Ann Marsh was baptiz: Decemb. y^n 29th.

John ye Son of John & Margret Hedgcock bapt: January ye 19th.

Richard Hobdy ye son of ffrancis was baptized ye 23d of February.

Susan ye daughter of Richard & Susan Turner baptized March ye 1st.

1640. Thomas the son of Richard and Sarah Wood was bapt. August ye 27th.

Elizabeth ye daughter of Richard & Ann Traps was bapt: August ye 30th.

ffrancis the daughter of Mr. James Wilsford gent. was baptized Decemb: the 20th:

William the sonne of Henry Beake was baptized Januarye ye 24th.

John the Son of John Hedgcock bapt: ffebruary ye 2nd.

Michaell ye Sonne of Michael Huffam Clerke and Leah his wife was baptized March the 2nd.

1641. Henry ye Sone of Sr Thomas Baker Knt. bapt: March ye 28th.

The same day was bapt: Elizabeth ye daughter of Sr Thomas Baker.

Gregory the sonn of Antony Cullen and Jane his wife was baptis: March the 16th.

Griffin the son of William Allen was baptis: Septemb. ye 10th.

Thomas ye sone of John Browne and Elizabeth his wife was baptized the 3rd of October.

Margaret Woodle daughter of William & Elizabeth Woodle Baptized June ye 27th 1641.

1642. Apryll the 12th was baptised Elizabeth the daughter of Richard and Myldred Myhell.

Apryll the 24th was baptised William the sone of John and Mary Rickwood.

Steven the sonn of Thomas and Mary Phylpott was baptised.

Richard the sonn of Richard and Martha Burton baptised August the 7th.

William the sonn of Samuell and Parnell Branchly baptis: Septemb: ye 11th.

Thomas the sonn of Michael Huffam Clerk and Leah his wife was bapt : Septemb yᵉ 25th.

Richard the sonn of Abraham Wood was bapt : the 2d of October.

Thomas the sonne of Richard Dixon & Marie his wife was baptised October the twentie third.

December the 8th was babtised Charles, the sonn of Sʳ Thomas Baker Knight.

Januarie the 3rd was baptized Margaret the daughter of Henry Beeke and Joane his wife.

Thomas Hopkin the sonn of William and Margaret Hopkin baptized feb : 5th.

Margaret Godwin the daughter of Griffith Godwin baptised feb : 5th.

Richard Wood the sonne of Richard & Sarah Wood was baptised March the 19th.

1643. Thomas Sawyer the sonne of James & Joane Sawyer baptised Aprill the 4th.

Henrie Hidgecocke the sonne of John & Margarett Hidgecocke was baptised June the 28th.

Marie Gould the daughter of William & Judith Gould was baptised Julie the 16th.

Thomas yᵉ sonn of William Oldfeild and Ann his wife baptized Aprill yᵉ 10.

Francis Mihil daughter of Richard & Mildred Mihil baptized October 15th 1643.

Elizabeth Kingsmell daughter of John & Joane Kingsmell baptized October 22 1643.

Thomas Question yᵉ son of Charles & Anne Question baptized November 19 1643.

James Wood yᵉ son of James & Mary Wood baptized November 19th 1643.

John Hobday yᵉ son of Francis & Francis Hobday baptized December 17th 1643.

Tomasin Court yᵉ daughter of Robert & Ellen Court baptized March 17th 1643.

1644.

Griffin yᵉ son of Griffin and Elizabeth Godden bapt. March 12th.

1645. baptized John Godden ye sonn of Griffin Godden.

Christian Bushell daughter of Thomas Bushell and Anne his wife was baptized the 28th of October 1644.

William Oldfeild sonne of William Oldfeild and Ann his wife babtised June ye 24 1645.

1647. Septembr. 28. was babtized Elizabeth daughter of Richard & Sarah wood.

1648. June the 18 was baptized Sarah the daughter of Griffin Godden.

June the 25 was baptized Sarah the daughter of Goodman Budds.

Decemb. ye 10 in the same yeare, was babtized Paull the sonn of Nicolas Dingley, (minister of Kingston) and Christian his wife.

the same year June ye 15th was baptized John ye sonn of Vincent & Mary Rickwood.

Feb. 18 in the same yeare was babtized the · · · · of James Sayer.

Jan. 13 was baptized Nicolas the sonn of Nicolas Dingley (parson of Kingston) and christian his wife.

1649. Jan. 27. was baptized John ye sonn of Robert White and Alice his wife.

1649. febru ye 27 was baptized Henry ye son of Steven Mapple & Elizabeth his wife.

John the sonn of Thom^s Grey and Margaret his wife was baptized the 26 day of November.

was baptised Rich Myhill ye sonn of Richard Myhill & Myldred his wife ye 24 of June 1650.

William the sonne of Richard Gibbon gent and Mary his wife was babtized the 2d of ffebru. 1649.

Elizabeth the daughter of Richard Gibbon gent and Mary his wife was baptized the 12th of Aprill 1650.

Dameris Gibbon borne ye 4th of Octob, 1655.

Anne the Daughter of Thomas Kingsmell Junior and his Marye his wife was baptized the 2 : of August 1652.

Octob. 20 1650 was baptized Elizabeth fowell daughter of Thomas and Ann Fowell.

1653. March ye 15th was baptized Ann : ye daughter of Steven Mapple & Elizabeth his wife.

1653. March yᵉ 2

> * We the parishioners of Kingston
> doe nominate you Nicolas Dingley our
> minister to be keeper of yᵉ Register
> booke of yᵉ said parish of Kingston
> and doe desire the justices of
> yᵉ peace to approve yereof according
> yᵉ late Act of Parliament
> in wittnes wherof we subscribe
> our names

> ROBERT YOUNG Church warden of yᵉ said parish
> THO. KINGSMELL RICH. WOOD WILL. ADDAMS
> RICH : PETTIT *RICHD. TRAPPS.*

1653. March yᵉ 12 were baptized Samuell and Will*man* Brenchley sonn and daughter of Austen Brenchley and Joane his wife.

March yᵉ 19 was baptized Thomas fowell sonn of Thom: fowell.

1654. Aprill yᵉ 2. was baptized Nicolas Cox Sonn of Andrew Cox.

Aprill yᵉ 9 was baptized Mary daughter of Goodm. Frierson & his wife.

Aprill yᵉ 24 was baptized William Sonn of Stephen & *Fillis* Fittell.

Novemb. yᵉ 30 was baptized Elizabeth Maple yᵉ daughter of Stephen Maple.

Decemb. yᵉ 31 was baptized Hellen Salley daughter of William Salley.

1655. November yᵉ 10 was baptized Elizabeth yᵉ daughter of Steven Mapple & Elizabeth his wife.

1655. Octob. yᵉ 2 was baptized Mary yᵉ daughter of Austen and Joane Brenchly.

1652. Sara the daughter of Thomas Grey and Margare*t* his wife, was baptized the 2 of Decemb. 1652.

1656. Thomas the Sonne of Thomas Grey and Margaret his wife was baptized the Eleventh of May 1656.

---

* By an Act of Parliament passed 24 Aug. 1653, it was ordered that every parish should forthwith proceed to the election of a 'Parish Register' (*sic*) who was to be the keeper of the Register Books, and to enter all marriages, births, and burials. This Act only continued in force till the Restoration.

1662.* ffebrey the first was baptised susane the dafter of William Brise and Jone his wife.

1656. Janry. yᵉ 17 was babtized Thomas sonn of Robert Boys & Mary his wife.

1661. was baptised Robert the sun of Robert Jull and an his wife.

1656. december yᵉ 27 of the same yeare was borne Bennet Browne the daughter of John Browne & Mary his wife, & January yᵉ 10 of yᵉ same yeare was yᵉ said Bennet Browne baptized.

March yᵉ 12 of yᵉ same yeare was baptized Augustine the sonn of August : & Joane Brenchly.

1658. Aprill yᵉ sixth was baptised Mary Read daughter of John Read of Kingston which Mary Read was borne march yᵉ last the same day on which her father John Read was buried.

1669. March the 6 was baptised John the sun of William Brice and Jonne his wife.

febr : the 10 at 3 of the clock in the morning was borne Christian second daughter of Nicolas Dingley and Christian his wife which Christian was baptized in the parish church of Kingston feb. yᵉ 13 1658.

1659. May the twelfth of the same yeare was baptized Richard sonn of Richard and Jane Strowd of yᵉ parish of Barham.

Novmb yᵉ 14 1658 was baptized Anna the daughter of Edward Ewell gent. & Katherine his wife.

1658. August yᵉ 22 was baptised Robart yᵉ sonne of Robart Boyes & Mary his wife.

March yᵉ 8 was borne Thomas Wilsford sonn of James Wilsford Esq. & Elizabeth his wife. yᵉ said Thom. Wilsford was baptized March yᵉ 20 of yᵉ same yeare.

1659. Nuember the 12 was baptized eles the dafter of Robert Jule and ane his wife.

1659. march yᵉ 11 was baptized Ann the daughter of Andrew wanstall & Elizabeth his wife.

Septemb. yᵉ 10 of yᵉ yeare was baptized Elizabeth Attwood. daughter of Thomas Attwood & Ann his wife.

---

* The Baptisms in this part of the Register are not in order of date. It appears that some were not registered at the time, but were subsequently entered, being inserted where space could be found on the page.

1660. Aprill y⁰ 5 was baptized George the sonn of John cocklinn & Martha his wife.

1660. April y⁰ 15 was baptizised Damoris y⁰ daughter of Steven Mapple & Damoris his wife.

1660. June y⁰ 24 was baptized John the Sonn of John Hedgcock and Mary his wife.

March y⁰ 11 was baptised Mary y⁰ daughter of Robart Boyse & Mary his wife.

1659. Feb. 24 was baptised Thomas Sonn of Augustin & Joan Brenchléy.

July the 7 of the same yeare was baptized Clement the sonn of Thomas and Elizabeth Court.

1660. Octob. y⁰ 29 was baptized Sam: y⁰ sonn of Augustin Brenchley & Joane his wife.

1661. Jan: y⁰ 18 was baptised Elizibeth y⁰ daughter of Robart Boyse & Mary his wife.

1661. March y⁰ 27 was baptized Ann the daughter of Thomas & Elizabeth Court.

(. . . . .) [1]

1662. June y⁰ 24 was baptised Anne y⁰ daughter of Arthur Hayward & Elizibeth his wife.

1662. febru y⁰ 6 was baptised Steven y⁰ sonn of Steven Mapple & Damoris his wife.

1662. November y⁰ 23 was baptized Martha Cocklinn daughter of John & Martha his wife.

1661. May y⁰ 9 [2] was baptised Edward son of Augsten & Joan Branchle.

1662. febuary 22 [3] was baptised Elizabeth dafter of Robert Jull and An his wife.

1663. Aprill y⁰ 5 was baptised Steven y⁰ sone of Thomas Woodland & Elizibeth his wife.

Ye same day. was baptised Henry y⁰ sone of Richard ffoord & Elizibeth his wife.

1663. Aprell the 1 [4] was baptised Thomas the sun of John Hallaidy and Mary his wife.

---

[1] "1661. September 30 was baptized Samewel the sun of Asten Brenchly and Jone his wife." (a) (Not in the Register.)
[2] "May 14th." (a) [3] "March 8th." (b) [4] "Feb. 21" (b)

1662. January ye 17[1] was baptised Ann daughter of Thomas and Ann Attwood.

NIC. DINGLEY Rector.
RICHARD WOOD Churchwarden.

March ye 16.[2] 1662 was baptized Robt. sonn of Robert Sanchey & Elizabeth his wife.

(. . . . .) [3]

July ye 12 1663. The same day & yeare was baptized James Ford sonn of Henry Ford and Dorothea his wife.

December the 6 in the same yeare was baptized Samuel Brenchley sonn of Augustine and Joane Brenchley.

Janry 17 of the same yeare was baptised Jane the daughter of Robert Boys and Mary his wife.

March ye 13 of ye same yeare was baptized Edward Sonn of Robt. & Elizabeth Sanchey.

1664. July ye 10 of ye same yeare was baptized Richard Hedgcock sonn of John and Mary Hedgcock.

Septembr. yu 18 of ye same yeare was baptized Mary daughter of Stephen Maple & Damaris his wife.

November the 13 of the same yeare was baptized John Hopkin sonn of Edward Hopkin & . . . . his wife. ·

NIC. DINGLEY Rector EDWARD STURGES Churchwarden.

January 22 1664 was baptized Jane Ford daughter of Richard Ford and Elizabeth his wife.

1665. Aprill ye 30 1665 was baptized William Sonn of John Holliday and Mary his wife.

May 28 of the same yeare was baptized Mary Draper the base borne daughter of Vincent Draper & Ann his wife.

June the 4 of ye same yeare was baptd. Katherine daughter of Elias Gammon & Katherine his wife.

---

[1] " March 16th." (b)   [2] " May 16th." (b)

[3] " Jan 6. was baptised Mary daughter of Edward and Mary Hopkin " (b)

" March 8 baptised Susanna Adams daughter of Ralph & Margaret Addams." (b) (These not in the Register.)

[4] " 1663. April 21 was baptised Margaret Grey daughter of Thomas Grey & Margaret his wife." (b) (Not in the Register.)

June ye 11th of the same yeare was baptizd Affery daughter of *Augustine and Joane Brenchley.

June ye 18 was baptized Sarah daughter of Henry & Dorothea Ford.

July the 30 of the same yeare was baptised Elizabeth the daughter of John & Martha Cocklin.

Nouember the 5 of the same yeare was baptised John the sun of James donn and ann his wife.

Nouember the 26 the same yeare was baptised Catherine the daughter William Brice and his wife.

1666. Aprill the 1 the same yeare was baptiseed Catherine the daughter of Ralf Addams Margret his wife.

NIC DINGLEY Rector.
. . . . STROOD Churchwarden.

1666. Aprill ye 6 in ye same yeare was baptized Abraham sonn of Thomas & Ann Attwood.

Aprill ye 22 was baptised John the Son of Robart & Mary Boyce.

June ye 24[1] of ye same yeare was baptized Mildred daughter of Rich and Ann White.

July ye 29 of ye same yeare was baptized Ann ye daughter of Edward & . . . .

Septemb 21 of ye yeare was baptised Elizabeth daughter of Elias Gammon & Katherine his wife.

Novemb 4 of ye same yeare was baptized Margaret daughter of Thomas & . . . . Grey.[2]

Novemb. 18 of ye same yeare was baptized Thomas sonn of Stephen & Damaris Maple.

1667. May ye 12 of the same yeare was baptized Mary daughter of Richard & Elizabeth Ford.

Novembris ye 24 of ye same yeare was baptized Ann daughter of Thomas And Avis mihill.

february 9th of ye same yeare was baptised Thomas sonn of Thomas & Ann Bushell.

NIC DINGLEY. HENRY FORD ch. warden.

---

[1] "June 10." (a)   [2] "Mary Grey." (a)

1667*

ffebruary 16. Tho. yᵉ sonne of Tho : and Mary Grey was baptized.

1668. October 4. James the sonne of James and Anne Donne was baptized.

January 24. Anne daughter of Robert and Mary Boyes was baptized.

1669 October 7. Mary yᵉ daughter of Sʳ Robert ffaunce and Elizabeth his Lady was baptized.

November 28. Henretta yᵉ daughter of Augustin and Joane Brensly. was baptized.

December 5. Elizabeth yᵉ daughtr. of Thomas and Aves Mihill was baptized.

January 16. Anne yᵉ daughter of Richard and Marjery Tallis was baptized.

January 18. Daniell the sonne of John and Mary Holyday was baptized.

1670. April 16. Abigall yᵉ daughter of Thomas and Anne Atwood was baptized.

May 21. Judeth the daughter of Thomas and Mary Grey was baptized.

June 21. William the sonne of Vincent and Anne Draper was baptized.

September 18. Anne yᵉ daughter of John and Susan Soale was baptized.

November 5. Mary the daughter of Robert and Mary Browning was baptized.

November 6. John the sonne of John and Mary Muggole was baptized.

1671. November 19. William the sonne of Robert and Mary Boyes was baptized.

December 21. Elizabeth daughter of Sʳ Robert ffaunce and Elizabeth his Lady was baptized.

---

* From this point to the end of 1680 the Baptisms have been copied into the Register, probably by Robert Garrett, the Curate. A leaf of the original (containing the entries from the above date down to March, 1675) is bound up at the end of the Register Book.

E

(. . . .)⁽¹⁾

January 27. Jane the daughter of Henry and Dorothy fford was baptized.

1672. March 31. Richard the sonne of Richard and Elizabeth fford was baptized.

Aprill 30. Richard the sonne of Richard and Margery Tallis was baptized.

June 2ᵈ Dorothy daughter of Nicholas and Parnell Soale was baptized.

June 9. Thomas the sonne of John⁽²⁾ and Mary Holyday was baptized.

October 13. Elizabeth daughter of John and Elizabeth Saxton was baptized.

December 27. John the sonne of Thomas and Aves Mihili was baptized.

December 29. Sarah the daughter of John & Susan Soale was baptized.

1673. May 25. Anne the daughter of Vincent and Anne Draper was baptized.

October 31. Margarett daughter of Sʳ Robert and his Lady Elizabeth ffaunce was baptized.

January 11. Edmund the sonne of Edmund and Jane Grant was baptized.

1674. Aprill 19, Richard the sonne of Richard and Anne White was baptized.

August 13, Edward the sonne of Robert and Mary Boys was baptized.

November 22. John the sonne of John and Margaret Kingsmell was baptized.

December 20. Edward the sonne of John⁽³⁾ and Mary Holyday was baptized.

January 31. Elizabeth daughter of Thomas and Mildred Maxtead was baptized.

⁽¹⁾ " 1671. Thomas Kingsmill sonne of John Kingsmill & Margaret his wife. bapt. 16 Jan." (*b*). (Not in the Register.)

⁽²⁾ " Thomas " (*a*) & (*b*).   ⁽³⁾ " Thomas " (*b*)

1675. March 28. John the sonne of John and Susanna Soale was baptized.

Aprill 22. Robert sonne of Sr Robert and his Lady Elizabeth ffaunce was baptized.

May 23. Elizabeth the daughter of Thomas and Mildred Sayer was baptized.

July 18. Anne the daughter of Abraham and Anne Atwood was baptized.

August 29. William the sonne of Henry and Dorothy fford was baptized.

September 5. Thomas the sonne of Gregory and Elizabeth Smithsun was baptized.

October 17. Mary the daughter of Richard and Margery Tallis was baptized.

October 24. Peter the sonne of Edmund and Jane Grant was baptized.

November 28. Elizabeth the daughter of John and Anne Morris was baptized.

January 2. Thomas the Sonne of Thomas and Aves Mihill was baptized.

1676. Aprill 2. Jane the daughter of Vincent and Anne Draper was baptized.

May 16. Nicholas the sonne of Nicholas and Parnell Soale was baptized.

ffebruary 4. Thomas the sonne of Richard and Anne White was baptized.

ffebruary 27. Elizabeth the daughter of Richard and Elizabeth Shrubsole.

March 4. David the sonne of John [1] and Mary Holiday was baptized.

1677. May 27. Jane the daughter of Edward and Jane Brice was baptized.

July 29. Alice the daughter of Vincent and Anne Draper was baptized.

September 9. Henry the sonne of Edmund and Jane Grant was baptized.

---

[1] " Thomas " (b)

44

September 30. John the sonne of Thomas and Mildred Sawyer baptized.

October 18. Elizabeth the daughter of Edward and Elizabeth Hogben was baptized.

November 15. Mary the daughter of Richard and Mary Robars was baptized.

December 11. Elizabeth the daughter of William and Elizabeth Hopkin was baptized.

December 16. Thomas the sonne of Stephen and Mary Wry was baptized.

ffebruary 17. Thomas the sonne of Nicholas and ffrances Saddleton was baptized.

1678. March 26. Sarah ye daughter of Gregory & Elizabeth Smithsun was baptized.

Aprill 14. John ye sonne of Robert & Mary Browning was baptized.

May 19. John ye sonne of Henry & Mary Stringer was baptized.

June 30. Isaacke ye sonne of Michael & Everell Steed was baptized.

July 22. Edward ye sonne of Edward & Margarett Soale was baptized.

September 12. Anne ye daughter of Thomas & Aves Mihill was baptized.

December 13. Susanna daughter of John Cason Gent. and Mary his wife was baptized.

December 30. Mary ye daughter of John Morrice and Anne his wife was baptized.

1679. Aprill 27. John the Sonne of John & Mary Inkepitt was baptized.

May 11. Elizabeth the daughter of Henry & Mary Stringer was baptized.

June 8. Richard the Sonne of Thomas & Mildred Maxtead was baptized.

August 17. Elizabeth ye daughter of Richard & Elizabeth Shrubsole was baptized.

September 28. Anne ye daughter of Richard & Mary Mihill was baptized.

November 20. Anne ye daughter Nicholas & Parnell Soale was baptized.

1680. Aprill 16. Thomas ye sonne of William & Elizabeth Hopkin was baptised.

June 13. Edward ye sonne of John & Susanna Soale was baptized.

July 18. Elizabeth ye daughter of Edmund & Jane Grant was baptized.

September 19. Thomas ye sonne of Thomas & Mildred Sawyer was baptised.

November 16. Thomas ye sonne of William & Elizabeth Jure [1] was baptized.

December 27. Elizabeth ye daughter of Stephen & Mary Wry was baptized.

March 13. Thomas ye sonne of John & Mary Inkepitt was baptized.

June 30, 1680. Henry ye son of Mr* Henry Marsh & Leah his wife was baptized.

ROBERT GARRETT, Curate.

1681. April 25. Mary ye daughter of Richard & Elizabeth Shrubsole was baptized.

May 22. Elizabeth ye daughter of John & Margarett Kingsmell was baptized.

June 9. Nicholas ye son of Nicholas & ffrances Saddleton was baptized.

July 3. William ye son of William & Sarah Knott was baptized.

September 25. Anne ye daughter of Richard & Mary Mihill[2] was baptized.

September 25. Mary ye daughter of Roger & Mary Golder was baptized.

ffebruary 12. William the son of William & Elizabeth Hopkin was baptized.

1682. Octob. 29. James ye son of William and Anna Hambrook was baptized.

---

[1] " Juce " *(a)* & *(b)*.

* " Mr " inserted by a later hand. The same has been done in previous entries of this name.

[2] " Brenchley " *(a)* — " Brenchley " has been erased in the Register and " Mihill " written over.

Nov: 5. Anne daughter of Robert and Elizabeth Rye was baptized.

Dec: 3d. John y^e son of Steeven and Mary Rye was baptized.

Dec. 10th. John son of Edward and Jane Grant was baptised.

168$\frac{3}{4}$. Jan: 20. Francess Cason Daughter of Esq. John Cason and Mary Cason his wife was Baptized.

Aprill 1. Mary y^e Daughter of John Atwood and Jane his wife was Baptized.

June 10th. Elizabeth Daughter of Tho : Golder and Christian his wife was baptized.

1684. Apr. 13th. Rich. son to Rich. Mihill and Mary his wife was baptized.

May 23. Hewly Bayns son to Tho : Bayns Gentleman and Elysabeth his wife was baptized.

June. 8. John son to Gregory Smithson and Elizabeth his wife was Baptized.

June 15th. Annah daughter to Nicholas Sadleton and Francess his wife was Baptized.

Aug : 7th. Henry Son to John Cason Esq : and Mary Cason his wife was baptised.

Nov : 2. Thomas son to Mary Sharp was baptized.

Nov 16. Aime daughter to Stephen Rye and Mary his wife was Baptized.

Nov. ye 23. Margrit ye Dauther to Edward ford and An his wife was baptised 1684.

March 30th 1685. Susannah Daughter to Richard Shrubsole and Eling his wife was baptized.

Apr: 19 1685. Jane Daughter of Edw : Grant and Jane his wife was baptized.

1685. Sept 20. Richard y^e son of William and Annah Hambrook was Baptized.

1686. July 11. Alice the Daughter of Sarah Prickett[1] base born & baptized the 11 : of July 1686.

Dec: 26 168$\frac{6}{7}$. Stephen y^e son of Stephen & Mary Rye was baptized.

---

[1] " 1686 June 11. Sarah Prickett baptised." *(a)*

Jan 9 168⁶⁄₇. John yᵉ son Edward Brice & Jane his wife was baptized.

Jan 16 168⁶⁄₇. Nicholas yᵉ son of Nicholas Pilcher & Hannah his wife was baptized.

March 6 168⁶⁄₇. Jane yᵉ daughter of John Catchpole & Jane his wife was baptiz'd.

March 6 168⁶⁄₇. Thomas yᵉ son of Edward & Ann ffoord was baptized.

May 15 1687. Anne yᵉ daughter of Thomas Golder & Christian his wife was baptized.

Septemb: 4th 1687. William yᵉ son of George Sharp & Elizabeth his wife was baptized.

Septemb 11. 1687. Jane yᵉ Daughter of Thomas Rigden & Jane his wife was baptized.

Septemb 11. 1687. Mary yᵉ daughter of Richard Mihill & Mary his wife was baptized.

Jan: 15. 168⁷⁄₈. William yᵉ son of Thomas & ⁽¹⁾ . . . . Rye was baptised.

Jan: 22. 168⁷⁄₈. Anne yᵉ daughter of John Cason Esqʳ and Mary his wife was baptized.

May 13. 1688. Elizabeth yᵉ daughter of William & Anne Hambrook was baptized.

Septemb: 30 1688. Ruth yᵉ daughter of Richard & Mary Mooring⁽²⁾ was baptized.

Jan: 17: 168⁸⁄₉. Henry yᵉ son of Thomas Turner Gent: & Margaret his wife was baptized.

Feb: 24 168⁸⁄₉. Sarah yᵉ daughter of John Catchpole and Jane his wife was baptized.

March 10 168⁸⁄₉. Mary yᵉ daughter of Stephen & Mary Rye was baptized.

. . . . dafter of Edward fford An his wife was borne feberury 12 1689 baptized 24.

April 27th 1689. Augustine Mihil yᵉ son of Richard & Mary his wife was baptized.

April yᵉ 24th. Stephen & Solomon yᵉ sons of Edward & Jane Brice were baptized.

May 19th 1689. Richard yᵉ son of Richard & Mary Moore was baptized.

⁽¹⁾ " Mary." (b)   ⁽²⁾ " Moore, a stranger." (a)

May 19th 1689. Mary ye Daughter of Edward & Jane Graunt was baptized.

Septemb. 1. 1689. Mary ye Daughter of Nicholass Sadleton and ffrancess his wife was Baptized.

Decemb: 8. 1689. Elizabeth ye daughter of Thomas Vowell & Anne his wife was baptized.

feb: 2 1689. Elizabeth the daughter of George Sharp and his wife Elizabeth was baptized.

May 25 1690. Wiliam the sonn of Wiliam and Mary Pope was baptized.

Decemb. 28 1690. Benjamin the son of Thomas Rye was baptized.

May 13 1691. Mary the daughter of William & An: hambroke was baptized.

May 17 1691. Mary the daughter of Richard & Mary Myle was baptized.

July 19 1691. Susan the daughter of John & An West was baptized.

Septr. 27. Catharin the daughter of Tho. & Christian Goulder.

Sep : 27. Richard the son of Edward foord & his wife[1] was baptized.

Nov 22 1691. Wiliam the son of Rich. & Mary Moor was baptized.

Decr. 16 1691. Wiliam the son of Wm & Mary Pope was baptized.

Jan : 29 1692. Tho. ye son of Tho. ffouell & his wife was Baptized.

March 20 1692. Tho. ye son of John Cathpole & Jane his wife was Baptd.

Die eodem Edw. ye son of Eduard & Margaret Reading was baptized.

Elizab. ye daughter of Edw : & Mary Bean was Bapt.

1692.

March[2] 27 1692. Tho. the son of John Betts & Sara[3] his wife was baptized.

---

[1] " Edward & Ann Ford " (*b*)   [2] " May 27 " (*a*)
[3] " Susan " (*a*)

Aprill 17 1692. Sara[1] the daugter of George & Elizabeth Sharp was baptized.

July 31.[2] 92. John the son of Abraham Swift was baptized.

Michaelmas 92. GILBERT BURROUGH Rector.

Dec: 1. Jos. the son of Nic. & frances Sadleton was baptized.

Jan : 8. 1692. An the Daughter of Richard & An Andrews bapt.

Jan 29,[3] 92. John the son of John & Joan Andreus.

July 23 1693 : Sarah the daughter of Tho : & Mary Rye was baptized.

Oct 15 1693. Wm. ye son of John & Sarah Baits was baptized.

feb. 7 1693. Mary the daughter of Ed : & Mary Bean was baptized.

March 25. Martha ye daughter of Geo : Sharp was baptized.

1694. April 15. Isac ye son of Wm Thanet & Mary his wife was baptized.

mich : 94

Oct. 14. 1694. An the Daughter of Thomas ffouel and his wife.

Octr 27. 1695. Mildred the daughter of Stephen Hobdy & his wife was bapt.

Dec 25 1695. Ric : the son of Ric : Andrews & his wife was baptized.

Jan 5. 1695. Ben : the son of Stephen Rye & his wife was baptized.

feb : 9 1695. John the son of Jo : Betts & his wife was Baptized.

Aprile 5 1696. Rich : the son of Rich : Shrubshole & his wife was baptized.

April 15 1696. Afferay ye daughter of Rich : Mihil & his wife was baptized.

May 6. 1696. Mary the daughter of Rich : Sanders & his wife was baptized.

June 28 1696. John the son of David Holyday and his wife was baptized.

August 16 1696. An the daughter of George Sharp and his wife.

Aug. 18. 1696. Elizabeth the daughter of John & Elizabeth Mihil.

---

(1) " Susan " (a)   (2) " July 10 " (a)   (3) " Jan. 22 " (a)

Aug 30 1696. John the son of Robin & Elizabeth Eridge were baptized.

Octr. 4. 1696. Cathrain the daughter of Edward Brice & his wife was baptized.

feb : 14th 1696. David the son of Tho : Rigden & his wife was baptized.

March 17 169$\frac{6}{7}$. Tho : the son of Ed : Bean & his wife was baptized.

(apr. 4th 1697. Easter day) Aprile 11 Mathew the the son of John Betts & his wife was baptized.

Aprile 18 1697. Thomasin the daughter of John Andrews & his wife was baptized.

June 27. 1697. Mary the daughter of Wm. Kennet & his wife was baptized.

Septr 5 1697. Tho : and Sarah Camborne twins of Tho. Camborne & his wife of Denhill were baptized.

Sept 26 1697. Tho : ye son of Jo : Mihil & his wife.

Octr 9. 1697. An the daughter of Jo : Burch & his wife was baptized.

Novr. 8. 1697. Willmot the daughter of Stephen Hobday & his wife was baptized.

May 1st. Mary the daughter of Tho. ffowell junior & his wife was baptized.

May 8th. Rich : ye son of Rich : Sanders & his wife was baptized.

Aug 14 1698. Tho : ye son of Dav : Holyday and his wife.

July 24. 1698. John the son of Edw : Bean and his wife was baptized.

Oct 23 1699. Mary the daughter of Stephen Rye and his wife.

Nov 27. Tho : ye son Abraham Attwood & his wife was baptized.

Jan 8th 1699. Ed. the son of Richard Baker & his wife.

January 15th. Sarah the daughter of John Betts & his wife.

Jan : 22. Mary the daughter of Tho : Mihil & his wife.

April 2 1699. Tho. ye son of John Goulder.

June 4th 1699. Eliz. ye daughter of John Mihil & his wife.

51

Crissenings.

July 18 1699. Abigail ye Daughter of Ab: Baker & his wife.
August 2^d 1699. Ann ye Daughter of Wil: Wrath & his wife.
Septr. 3. 1699. Ann ye Daughter of James Burch & his wife.
Dec. 4th 1699. Mary ye daughter of Geo: Sharpe and his wife.
 Lady day 700.   GILB. BURROUGHS Rector.
Aprile 7 700. Sarah ye daughter of Tho. Rigden & his wife.

(. . . .) ^(1)

Sept. 30. John the son of Thomas ffowell & his wife.
the same day An the Daughter of David Holyday.
October 6. Margaret the daughter of John Bates. ^(2)
Oct: 24 1700. Tho. the son of William Wrath & his wife.
Feb: 23. W^m ye son of Wm Kennet & his wife.
Aprile 4 1701. John the son of John Mihil & his wife.
May 4 1701. Wiliam the son of Stephen Rye & his wife.
May 25 1701. Thomas the son of Stephen hobdy & his wife.
June 15 1701. Edward the son of Edward Sprat & his wife.
June 22 1701. Thomas the son of Richard Sanders & his wife.
June 29. Richard & Edward the sons of William Backer & his
 wife.
Jan: 18 1702. Eliz. ye daughter of James Burch & his wife.
March 22 170½. Mary the Daughter of Tho: Mihil.
March 29 1702. Eliz. the daughter of Ab: Atwood.
August the 2^d 1702. Mathew the son of Math. Brouning & his
 wife.
Oct 18 1702. Mary the daughter of Jo: Mihil and his wife.
feb: 2^d 170⅔. James the son of James Burch and his wife.
feb: 24 170⅔. Sarah the daughter of Edward Bean & his wife.
March 7th 1702. John the son of Rich: Baker & his wife.
March 21 1702. Geo: the son of Geo: Sharp & his wife.

---

(1) "April 7. Sam: ye son of Tho. Rye" (b) (Not in the Register.)
(2) " Betts " (b).

July 4th 1703. Elizabeth Wraith daughter of Willm Wraith & his wife.

Feb 7 1703. Sarah the Daughter of John Horton & his wife.

March 5 1703. Mary the Daughter of Tho. ffowl & his wife.

June 24 1704. Holyday the son of . . . .[1]

feb. 18 1704. Ann the daughter of Abr. Baker.

feb 28 1704. John the son of Abr. Atwod.

March 18. Susanna the daughter of Thomas Rigden.

Dec. 9th 1705. Jno. the son of James Burch.

March 3^{d.} Ann the Daughter of Isaac Whitnell.

May 13 1706. Ann the Daughter of Edward Spratt.

June 2nd. Susanna the Daughter of David Holyday.

July 4th. Amy the daughter of Edw. Bean.

Sept. 1st. Jno. the son Jno. Mihil.

Nov. 10. William the son of William Not.

1707. feb. 21. John the son of Mathew & Susanna Browning.

feb : 1707. Jno. ye son of Math : Browning.

Aprile 18 1708. Mary Goulder was baptised.

May 9th 1708. Jno. the son of Tho : Mihil.

Aug 29th . . . . [2] Holyday the son of David Holyday.

Sep^{tr} 7. Jno. the son of Ja : Burch.

Oct 10. Rich the son of Will. Pay.

Oct 31. Ed. the son of Nic. Sawkins.

170⅞. Feb 6th Ja : the son of Ja : Ansélme.

1709. June 2^d Mary the daughter of John Rye.

1709. Oct : 2nd Jno. the son of Jno. Beer.

1709. Oct : 9th Catharine the daughter of . . . . [3]

1709. March 12 Ja : the son of Nic : Sawkins.

1710. Septr 17 Ann the daughter of Will. Green & his wife.

1710. Oct 1st Tho the son of Tho : [4] Goulder & his wife.

1710. Octr. 10th Tho. the son of James Burch & his wife.

1710. Oct 29. Wm. the son of Tho Mihil and his wife.

---

[1] "John Holyday the son of David Holyday" (*b*). [2] " Thomas " (*b*).
[3] " Catherine daughter of Jn. Whitaker " (*b*) [4] " Jn." (*b*).

1710. March 11th Jno. the son of Isac Whitnell & his wife.

1710. March 11th Jane the daughter of Mathew Browninge.

1711. Aprile 29. W^m the son of Wm Kidham and his wife.

July 13. Robert the son of Tho. & Eliz. foord was baptized.

July 21. Edw : the son of of Tho. & Eliz. foord.

1712. August 19. Mary the daughter of Nicolas Sawkins & his wife.

August 29. Hen : the son of Henry Baker and his wife.

Aug 3^{d.} Mary the daughter of of Wm Kelsy & his wife.

feb : 22 17$\frac{12}{13}$ Jno. the son of Dan : Quested.

March 15 17$\frac{12}{13}$ Eliz. the daughter of Nich : Sawkins.

Aprile. 20. Rich. y^e son of Ja : Burche & his wife.

1713. Aug. 30. Rich. the son of Henry Baker.

Sept 13. Jno. the son of Isaac Whitnell.

1714. March 14 Tho. the son of Tho : ffoord and his wife.

March 1714. Tho. the son of . . . . Quested [1] & his wife.

1714. Octr 15 Mary y^e daughter of Dan. Colier.

17$\frac{14}{15}$ Jan. [2] Sarah the daughter of Nicolas Sawkins.

1715. Aprile 17. Mary y^e daughter of Dan. Quested.

Aprile 24. Ann y^e daughter of Tho. Golder.

1715. July 17 Tho. the son of Abraham Beaker [3] was baptized.

Septr. 4th. James the son of Isaac Whitnell was Baptized.

Septr. 26. Eliz : the daughter of Tho : ffoord.

Octr 6th. Susanna the daughter of Clem : Saunders Baptd.

March 4th. Dav : ye son of Jno. Beer was Baptized.

1716. Aprile 22. Edw. ye son of Hen : Baker.

(. . . .) [4]

Novr 14. Ann the Daughter of Tho : ffoord.

---

[1] " March 20 The son of Dan. Quested " (a)   [2] " Jan 12th " (a)
[3] " Baker " (a) & (b)   [4] " Oct 6 Thomas son of Abraham Baker " (a) (Not in the Register).

feb: 10. the Daughter of Tho: Mihil.

feb: 17. Mary the Daughter of Ja: Burch.

feb: 24. Tho: y^e son of Math: Browning.

March y^e 3$^d.$ Eliz. y^e Daughter of Jno. Rye.

1717. March 24 Jno. the son of Nicholas Sawkins.

April 7. Tho. y^e son of Wm Lokar.

Septr. 22. Steph. y^e son of Tho. Golder.

Octr. 27. Tho: y^e son of Ben Rye.

De^r 8$^{th.}$ Susanna y^e daughter of James Godwin.

Dec. 26. Sarah y^e daughter of Wm Hopkins.

feb: 16. Rob. y^e son of Jno. Beer.

1718. May 4th ffrancis the son of Hen: Baker.

February 1^{rst} 1718. William y^e son of Thomas & Mildred Rafe was baptized.

ffeb^r 25$^{th.}$ Elizabeth y^e Daughter of Tho. & Eliz: fford was baptized.

March 1$^{rst.}$ Edward y^e son of Mathew & Susan: Browning was baptized.

March 8$^{th.}$ Henry y^e son of James & Ann Birch was baptized.

Oct 11 1719. Thomas y^e son of Willm & Ann Buddell was baptized.

Dec 25$^{th.}$ Richard y^e son of Willm Lokar & Elizabeth his wife was baptized.

Jan^r 3^d 1719. Mary y^e daughter of Joseph & Elizabeth Sadleton was baptized.

Jan^r 31, 1719. Edward y^e Son of Daniel & Ann Coller was baptized.

Feb^r 7 1719. William y^e son of Willm & Catharine Wonstan was baptized.

March 25th 1720. Susanna ye Daughter of William & . . . . Hopkins was baptized.

April 15th 1720. Mary ye Daughter of Benjamin & Katharine Rye was baptized.

June 12. 1720. Walter ye son of Walter & Ann Hoge was baptized.

Arch-Bishop's Visitation June 16th 1720.

PETER INNES, Rector.

January ye 8th 1720. Elizabeth ye Daughter of Daniel & Elizabeth Quested was baptized.

March 12th 1720. Sarah ye Daughter of Joseph & Catharine Rye was baptized.

May 28. 1721. Robert ye son of Henry & Margaret Baker was baptized.

July 23 1721. Thomas ye son of John & Jane Kingsmell was baptized.

Augst 20. 1721. Baptized Elizabeth ye Daughter of W^m & Elizabeth Lokar.

Octob^r 8th 1721. Baptized Michael ye Son of Daniel & Ann Coller.

June 19th 1722. Baptized Stephen ye son of W^m & Catharine Wonstan.

Sept^{br} 9th 1722. Baptized Thomas ye Son of James & . . . . Godwin.

Decbr 23^d 1722. Baptized Frances ye Daughter of William & Ann Buddel.

Decb^{r.} 25th 1722. Baptized Ann ye Daughter of Joseph & Catharine Rye.

ffeb^{ry} 17th 1722. Baptized Edward ye Son of John & Mary Beer.

ffeb^{ry} 18th 1722. Baptized John ye Son of John & Mary Eltington.

March ye 8th 1722. Baptized Parnell ye Daughter of John & Parnell West.

April ye 14th 1723. Baptized Jane ye Daughter of John And Jane Pearce.

Sept^{br} ye 29th 1723. Baptized Mary the Daughter of Daniel & Ann Coller.

December 8th 1723. Baptized Ann ye Daughter of Benjamine & Mildred Pilcher.

Jany 14th 1723. Baptized John ye Son of Mr John Sabine & Ann his wife.

Augst 2^d 1724. Baptized William ye son of John & Parnell West.

Feb^{ry} 15th 1724. Baptized Edward ye Son of John & Mary Eltington.

March 21st 1724. Baptized Mary ye Daughter of John & Mary Beer.

August 22^d 1725. Baptized Elizabeth ye Daughter of Benjamin & Katharine Rye.

Augst 22^d 1725. Baptized Mary ye Daughter of John & Mary Laurence.

September ye 26 1725. Baptized Stephen ye Son of Benjamin & Mildred Pilcher.

Novemb^r 11th 1725. Baptized Richard ye Son of Daniel and Ann Coller.

November 21^{rst} 1725. Baptized Edward the Son of William & Susanna Pearson.

December 26th 1725. Baptized Ann ye Daughter of John and Mary Rayner.

July 31 1726. Baptized Abraham ye Son of Thomas and Ann Attwood.

Novemb^r 20th 1726. Baptized Mary ye Daughter of Henry and Elizabeth Cooman.

December 25th 1726. Baptized Thomas ye Son of John & Mary Eltonton.

December ye 28th 1726. Baptized Mary & Jane Twins, the Daughters of James & . . . . Godwin.

January ye 15th 1726. Baptized Elizabeth & Ann Twins the daughters of W^m & Susanna Pearson.

July ye 30th 1727. Baptized Mary the Daughter of Thomas & . . . . Davis.

August ye 13th 1727. Baptized Richard ye Son of John & Parnell West.

September ye 3^d 1727. Baptized Mary ye Daughter of John & Mary Rayner.

January ye 1st 1727. Baptized Henry ye Son of Daniel & Ann Coller.

January ye 4th 1727. Baptized Ann ye Daughter of John & Ann Sabine.

January ye 7th 1727. Baptized John the Son of Thomas & Ann Mihils.

March ye 17th 1727. Baptized Elizabeth the Daughter of John & Mary Laurence.

March ye 31st 1728. Baptized Jane ye Daughter of John & Mary Beer.

April ye 7th 1728. Baptized Mathew ye Son of William & Susanna Pearson.

June yᵉ 2ⁿᵈ 1728. Baptized Catharine Daughter of Benjamin & Catherine Rye.

ArchBishop Visited June yᵉ 2d.

PETER INNES, Rector.

June yᵉ 17ᵗʰ 1728. Baptized Jane yᵉ Daughter of Comfort and Mary Kingsmell.

May 11ᵗʰ 1729. Baptized Mary yᵉ Daughter of John & Mary Rayner.

June 22ᵈ 1729. Baptized Margaret yᵉ Daughter of James & . . . . . Godwin.

September 7ᵗʰ 1729. Baptized Elizabeth yᵉ Daughter of Henry & Elizabeth Cooman.

Janʳʸ 4th 1729. Baptized Thomas yᵉ Son of Thomas And Ann Mihils.

February 22ᵈ 1729. Baptized John yᵉ Son of John & Mary Laurence.

May yᵉ 12ᵗʰ 1730. Baptized Richard yᵉ Son of John & Parnell West.

June yᵉ 14ᵗʰ 1730. Baptized Margaret yᵉ Base born Daughter of Margaret Baker [1] Widow.

July 5ᵗʰ 1730. Baptized Alfred yᵉ son of John & Ann Sabine.

Decemᵇʳ 21ʳˢᵗ 1730. Baptized Catharine yᵉ Daughter of Chibbourn[2] & Ann Sabine.

Janʳʸ yᵉ 6ᵗʰ 1730. Baptized Benjamin the Son of James & Elizabeth Matson.

Janʳʸ yᵉ 31. 1730. Baptized Ann yᵉ Daughter of John & Mary Birch.

Septemᵇʳ· 12ᵗʰ 1731. Baptized Henry & David Twins the Sons of James & . . . . . Godwin.

Septemᵇʳ· 26 1731. Baptized Margaret yᵉ Daughter of John & Mary Beer.

Janʳʸ 2ᵈ· 1731. Baptized Mary yᵉ Daughter of William & Margaret Beer.

February 7ᵗʰ 1731. Baptized Elizabeth yᵉ Daughter of Thomas & Elizabeth Silk.

---

[1] "John Birch & Margaret Baker." (a)

[2] "Mr Chibborne Sabine." (a)

June 11$^{th.}$ 1732. Baptized Abigal y^e Daughter of John$^{(1)}$ & . . . .
Grew.

June 18 1732. Baptized Elizabeth the Daughter of Thomas &
Ann Mihils.

June 30th 1732. Baptized Ann y^e Daughter of James &·Elizabeth
Matson.

PETER INNES Rector.

October 22^d 1732. Baptized Ann y^e Daughter of William & Jane
Cook.

Nov$^{br.}$ 26 1732. Baptized Mary y^e Daughter of John & Mary
Birch.

July 29th 1733. Baptized Daniel y^e Son of Daniel & Elizabeth
Quested.

July 29th 1733. Baptized Mildred y^e Daughter of Thomas &
Wilmot Bewly.

December 10$^{th.}$ 1733. Baptized Susanna the Daughter of John &
Parnell West.

Jan^{ry} y^e 8th 173$\frac{3}{4}$. Baptized Mary y^e Daughter of Thomas &
Elizabeth Silk.

Feb^{ry} y^e 3^d 173$\frac{3}{4}$. Baptized Elizabeth y^e Daughter of Ralph &
Mary Dilnot.

March 5th 173$\frac{3}{4}$. Baptized Edward y^e Son of William &
Margaret Beer.

Jan^{ry} 26th 173$\frac{4}{5}$. Baptized Thomas the Son of Thomas &
Wilmot Bewly.

March 12th 173$\frac{4}{5}$ Baptized Sarah y^e Daughter of John & Mary
Birch.

Decemb$^{r.}$ 7th 1735. Baptized Ann y^e Daughter of Thomas & Ann
Mihils.

Decemb^r 10th 1735. Baptized Catharine y^e Daughter of Benjamin
& Elizabeth Kennet.

Jan^{ry} 25th 173$\frac{5}{6}$. Baptized Sarah y^e Daughter of Thomas &
Elizabeth Silk.

ffeb^{ry} y^e 9th 173$\frac{5}{6}$. Baptized Phillis y^e Daughter of Chibbourn
& Ann Sabine.

May the 25th 1736. Baptized Joseph the Son of John and Ann
Sabine.

---

[1] " Thos." (a)   " John." (b)

Augst 22 1736. Baptized Henry y^e Son of Henry & Sarah Baker.

ffeb^{ry} 25 173$\frac{6}{7}$. Baptized Benjamine y^e son of William & Margaret Beer.

March 23 173$\frac{6}{7}$. Baptized Elizabeth the Daughter of John & Mary Birch.

Ap^r y^e 24 1737. Baptized William y^e Son of John & Mary Laurence.

Augst 17th 1737. Baptized John y^e Son of John & Joanna Claringbole.

ArchBp.'s primary Visitation July 21^{rst} 1737.

Jan^{ry} 22 173$\frac{7}{8}$. Baptized Catharine y^e Daughter of Richard & Elizabeth Carden.

Octo^{br} 24 1738. Baptized Wilmot y^e Daughter of Thos· & Wilmot Bewly.

Dec^{br} 27 1738. Baptized Mary y^e Daughter of Chibbourn & Ann Sabine.

Jan^{ry} 6th 173$\frac{8}{9}$. Baptized Thomas y^e Son of Ralph & Mary Dilnot.

March 11 173$\frac{8}{9}$. Baptized Nicholson y^e Son of John & Joanna Claringbole.

March 12 173$\frac{8}{9}$. Baptized Mary y^e Base Born Daughter of Elizabeth Gasking.

Ap^r 22. 1739. Baptized Stephen the Son of John & Mary Laurence.

Ap^r· 29. 1739. Baptized W^m y^e Son of Stephen and Ann Knight.

Ap^r· 29. 1739. Baptized Sarah y^e Daughter of Henry & Sarah Baker.

Ap^r· 29. 1739. Baptized Esther y^e Daughter of Daniel & Mary Woollett.

August 26 1739. Baptized William y^e Son of William & Margaret Beer.

September 30 1739. Baptized John the Son of Thomas & . . . . Ashby.

October 14th 1739. Baptized Stephen y^e Son of Stephen & . . . . Brett.

March 5th 17$\frac{39}{40}$. Baptized Esther y^e Daughter of John & Mary Birch.

Ap^r· 13th 1740. Baptized William y^e Son of William & Elizabeth Fuller.

Septemb^r 1st 1740. Baptized Ann y^e Daughter of Mr Chibbourn Sabine & Ann his wife.

Octr 26th 1740. Baptized Thomas y^e Son of John & Mary Laurence.

Nov^{br} 9th 1740. Baptized John y^e Son of Stephen & Ann Knight.

Nov$^{br.}$ 23. 1740. Baptized W^m y^e Son of Rich. & Eliz: White.

Jan^{ry} 4 1741. Baptized Stephen y^e Son of Tho$^{s.}$ & Wilmot Bewly.

Aprill 5 1741. Baptized Elizth: y^e Daughter of John & Margaret Rafe.

Apr. 22 1741. Baptized Ann the Daughter of Henry and Sarah Baker.

ArchBishop's 2^d Visitation. Held June 16 1741.

PETER INNES Rector.

Septbr 27 1741. Baptized Sarah y^e Daughter of James & Elizabeth Pingle.

Oct^{br} 18 1741. Baptized Thomas Bryan y^e Son of John & Joanna Claringbould.[1]

Jan^{ry} 19 174$\frac{1}{2}$. Baptized Elizabeth y^e Daughter of Richard & Sarah Maine.

Augst y^e 8th 1742. Baptized Hannah y^e Daughter of John & Mary Birch.

October y^e 31^{rst} 1742. Baptized Mary y^e Daughter of Stephen & Ann Knight.

Jan^{ry} 30 174$\frac{2}{3}$. Baptized Ann y^e Daughter of John & Mary Laurence.

May 29 1743. Baptized Sarah the Daughter of Edward & Sarah Baker.

Sep$^{t.}$ 30 1743. Baptized Mary y^e Daughter of Richard & Elizabeth White.

Dec^{br} 29 1743. Baptized Joanna y^e Daughter of John & Joanna Claringbould.

Ap^r 23 1744. Baptized Ann y^e Daughter of Thomas and Elizabeth Law.

---

[1] "Nicholson." (b) In the Register "Nicholson" has been crossed out and "Claringbould" substituted.

May 13 1744. Baptized Mary ye Daughter of Ambrose & Elizabeth Coller.

June 3 1744. Baptized Robert ye Son of Robert & Elizabeth Butler.

June 24 1744. Baptized Susanna ye Daughter of Stephen & Ann Knight.

Jan^{ry} 20th 1745. Baptized James ye Son of John & Mary Birch.

July the 7th 1745. Baptized Richard ye Son of Richard & Elizabeth White.

July the 28th 1745. Baptized Richard ye son of John & Mary Laurence.

ffebruary ye 2^d 1746. Baptized John ye Son of John & Mary Cullen.

ffebry 16 1746. Baptized Parnell ye daughter of John & Elizabeth Hogben.

PETER INNES Rector.

[*End of the Baptisms in the first Register Book.*]

[*SECOND REGISTER BOOK.*]

BAPTISMS.

February[1] 17th 174⅚. Baptized Elizabeth yᵉ Daughter of Thoˢ Law lately deceas'd & Elizabeth his wife.

March 3ᵈ 174⅚. Baptized Richard yᵉ son of Thomas & Margaret Wood.

March 6th 174⅚. Baptized Jane the daughter of John & Joanna Claringbould.

May 4th. 1746. Baptized John yᵉ son of Thomas & Elizabeth Friend.

May 18. 1746. Baptized James yᵉ son of Richard & Mary Birch.

Augˢᵗ yᵉ 17: 1746. Baptized Sarah yᵉ daughter of Ambrose & Elizabeth Coller.

Augˢᵗ yᵉ 31 1746. Baptized William yᵉ son of Henry & Sarah Johnson.

Novᵇʳ yᵉ 2ⁿᵈ 1746. Baptized Valentine yᵉ son of Robert & Elizabeth Butler.

Decᵇʳ 11th 1746. Baptized Jane yᵉ daughter of Thomas & Sarah Gray.

Apᵣₗ 12 1747. Baptized John yᵉ son of Stephen & Elizabeth Sutton.

May 31 1747. Baptized Martha yᵉ daughter of John & Mary Birch.

June 14 1747. Baptized William yᵉ son of John & Elizabeth Hogben.

July 23 1747. Baptized Thomas yᵉ son of Edward & Jane Ford.

March 4 1747-8. Baptized Richᵈ Davison the son of John & Joanna Claringbould.

March 13 1747-8. Baptized Ann yᵉ daughter of Richard & Elizabeth Castleden.

March 27th 1748. Baptized Mary yᵉ daughter of Abraham & Elizabeth Baker.

---

[1] " December." (*a*) & (*b*)

Aprill yᵉ 3ʳᵈ· 1748. Baptized Ann yᵉ daughter of Richᵈ & Eliza beth White.

July 29 1748. Baptized Thomas Watkinson, The son of Thomas Turner Junʳ Esqʳᵉ, and Margarett his wife.

PETER INNES, Rector.

Augˢᵗ 14 1748. Baptized Elizabeth yᵉ Daughter of William & Mary Pettit.

ffebʳʸ 9th 1748-9. Baptized Margarett yᵉ Base Born Daughter of . . . . & Elizabeth Lockar.

March 12 1748-9. Baptized Mary yᵉ daughter of Robert & Eliza-beth Butler.

March 19 1748-9. Baptized John the son of John & Elizabeth Munns.

Apʳ· 12 : 1749. Baptized Robert yᵉ Son of Edward & Jane Forde.

July yᵉ 2 1749. Baptized Danel yᵉ Son of Stephen & Elizabeth Sutton.

July yᵉ 30 1749. Baptized Richard the Son of John & Elizabeth Hogben.

Edward son of John & Elizabeth Beer was Bapt. Novʳ· ye 12 1749·

March yᵉ 11 1749-50. Baptized Henry the son of John & Ann Mihles.

Thomas son of Richard & Elizabeth Caselden bapt. March 25 1750.

Robert the son of Thomas & Elizabeth Friend baptizᵈ April ye 8ᵗʰ 1750.

Octʳ 21ˢᵗ 1750. Elizᵗʰ daughter of Henry and Elizᵗʰ Castleden.

BRYAN FAUSSETT, Curate.

Feb : 17 1750/1. Baptized Mary yᵉ Daughter of John & Mary Birch.

Feb. 24 1750/1. Baptized John yᵉ son of Henry and Susan Bushel.

Feb 28 1750/1. Baptized Edward son of Edward and Jane Ford.

March 3. 1750/1. John the son of William and Anne Cullen was baptised.

March 27ᵗʰ· 1751. Elizabeth yᵉ daughter of Daniel and Mary Smith was baptized.

April 7 1751. John the son of John & Elizabeth Mutton was baptised.

July 14 1751. Mary ye Daughter of Richard Elizabeth Casselden was baptized.

B. FAUSSETT, Curate.

1751.

September ye 29th. 1751. Anne ye daughter of Stephen and Elisabeth Sutton was baptised.

November ye 3d 1751. Susanna ye daughter of John and Susanna Marsh was baptised.

1752.

February ye 9th. 1752. Richard the son of John and Ann Mihles was baptised.

February ye 16th 1752. John the son of Thomas & Elizabeth Browning was baptised.

February yn 23, 1752. John the bastard son of James Church and Ann Birch was baptised.

March ye 1st 1752. Margaret ye daughter of John & Elisabeth Beer was baptised

May ye 24 1752. Mary ye daughter of Henry and Elisabeth Casselden was baptized.

May ye 31st. 1752. John ye son of John and Elisabeth Mutton was baptised.

August ye 2d. 1752. James the son of Richard & Hannah Ratley was baptised.

August ye 2d. 1752. John ye son of Thomas & Sarah Goulder was baptised.

Novr 5. 1752. John ye son of Daniel and Mary Smith was baptised.

December ye 28th 1752. Carolina the daughter of Edward and Elisabeth Bean was baptised.

February 25 1753. Susanna the daughter of Richard Saunders and Anne his wife was baptised, and Margaret the daughter of Richard Baker and Mary his wife was baptised.

March ye 4th. 1753. Thomas the son of Henry and Susan Bushell was baptised.

1753. April ye 12th. Bryan ye son of the Reverend Bryan Faussett Curate of this parish and Elisabeth his wife was baptised.

April yᵉ 29ᵗʰ· 1753. Martha yᵉ daughter of Thomas and Margaret Castleden was baptised.

July 1. 1753. William yᵉ Son of Thomas & Elisabeth Mihles was baptized.

Sept : yᵉ 6ᵗʰ· Martha yᵉ daughter of Richard and Elizabeth Casselden was baptised.

B. FAUSSETT, Curate.

November yᵉ 11ᵗʰ· 1753 Thomas yᵉ son of Thomas & Ann Browning was baptised.

1754.

February yᵉ 17. 1754. Daniel yᵉ base born son of Daniel Quested and Elizabeth Whitehead was baptised.

February yᵉ 24ᵗʰ 1754. Henry yᵉ son of Henry and Elizabeth Castleden was baptized.

February yᵉ 24ᵗʰ· 1754. Sophia yᵉ daughter of John & Elisabeth Mutton was baptised.

March yᵉ 3ʳᵈ 1754. Chibborne yᵉ Base born son of Catherine Sabine was baptised.

March yᵉ 24ᵗʰ· Richard yᵉ son of John & Elisabeth Beer was baptised.

April yᵉ 28ᵗʰ· 1754. Mary yᵉ daughter of Stephen and Elisabeth Whitnall was baptised.

April 28. 1754. Henry the Son of John & Susanna Marsh was baptised.

May yᵉ 19ᵗʰ· 1754. Thomas the Son of Thomas and Elisabeth Browning was baptised.

September 15 1754. Mary yᵉ Daughter of Valentine and Elisabeth Makey was baptised.

October yᵉ 6ᵗʰ· 1754. Sarah yᵉ Daughter of Thomas and Elisabeth Mihles was baptised.

November yᵉ 3ᵈ· Richard yᵉ Son of James and Mary Smith was baptised.

November yᵉ 17ᵗʰ· Michael yᵉ Son of Richard and Elisabeth Casselden was baptised.

March 12 1755. Edward yᵉ son of Edward and Elisabeth Bean was baptised.

July yᵉ 20ᵗʰ 1755. Sarah yᵉ Daughter of John & Elisabeth Mutton was baptised.

September 14 1755. Henry yᵉ son of Henry & Mary Richards was baptised.

September 28ᵗʰ 1755. Matthew yᵉ son of Thomas and Elisabeth Browning was baptised.

March 14ᵗʰ· 1756 Sarah yᵉ Daughter of Thomas and Sarah Goulder was baptised.

BR. FAUSSETT, Curate.

———

WILLIAM BARRETT, Curate.

August 8ᵗʰ· 1756. Thomas yᵉ Son of Thomas and Mary Page was baptized.

September 5ᵗʰ 1756. John yᵉ Son of John and Susanna Marsh was baptised.

WILLIAM BARRETT, Curate.

Sep 26ᵗʰ 1756. Elizabeth yᵉ Daughter of Thomas & Elizabeth Browning was baptized.

Oct 31ˢᵗ 1756. James yᵉ son of John & Elizabeth Beer was baptized.

Novʳ: 21ˢᵗ 1756. Sarah yᵉ daughter of Thomas and Judy Godding was Baptized.

Novʳ· 25ᵗʰ 1756. Thomas yᵉ Son of Thoˢ· and Elizabeth Mihles was baptised.

Febʸ 4ᵗʰ 1757. Sarah daughter of Richard & Elizabeth Castleden was baptized.

July 17ᵗʰ· 1757. Sarah yᵉ daughter of Valentine & Elizabeth Makey was baptised.

Aprill 16ᵗʰ 1758. Susannah yᵉ daughter of Thoˢ & Sarah Phinees was baptised.

May 14ᵗʰ 1758. Eleanor daughter of John & Elizabeth Mutton was baptized.

May 28ᵗʰ 1758. Elizabeth daughter of Stephen & Ann Lucas was baptized.

July 23ʳᵈ 1758. Ann yᵉ base born daughter of . . . Keler & Catharine Sabine was baptized.

August 20ᵗʰ 1758. Mary yᵉ daughter of Daniel & Mary Smith was baptized.

September 10th 1758. Benjamin ye son of George & Mary Rigden was baptized.

September 17th 1758. Thomas ye son of Edward & Sarah Baker was baptized.

Decr. 31st 1758. Jane ye daughter of John & Susanna Marsh was baptized.

March 11th 1759. Edward ye base born son of Edwd Jorden & Ann Baker was baptized.

March 25^{tn} 1759. Mary⁽¹⁾ ye daughter of Edwd & Margaret Beer was baptized.

June 3rd 1759. Elizabeth daughter of Abraham & Elizabeth Baker was baptized.

July 29th 1759. John son of Thos. & Elizabeth Mihles was baptized.

Augt. 26th 1759. Thos. ye Son of Thos. & Elizabeth Browning was Baptized.

Jan^{ry} 20th 1760. Elizabeth daughter of John & Elizabeth Mutton was baptized.

Jan^{ry.} 27th. 1760. John son of John & Rachel Dillnot was baptized.

WM. BARRETT, Curate.

March 30th 1760. William ye son of Thom^{s.} & Judy Godding was baptized.

April 13th. 1760. John son of Ric^d & Elizabeth Castleden was baptized.

August 10th 1760. Thomas son of Thomas & Sarah Finnis was baptized.

August 17th. 1760. John ye son of John & Jane Murrell was baptised. belonging to ye Camp.

August 17th 1760. William son of Thomas & Mary Page was baptized.

August 24th 1760. John son of John & Mary Hudson was baptized. belonging to ye Camp.

Octr. 5th 1760. John son of Joseph & Margaret Wright was baptized. belonging to ye Camp.

Decr. 20th. 1760. Martha daughter of John & Susannah Marsh baptized.

(1) "Ann." (b) "Mary." (a)

May 10th 1761. Mary daughter of Thom^{s.} & Ann Kingsmill was baptized.

May *17*⁽¹⁾ 1761. Sarah daughter of Daniel & Mary Smith was baptized.

(.   .) ⁽²⁾

Novr. 8th 1761. William Son of John & Sarah Horton was baptized.

Nov. 22^{ud} 1761. William son of John & Elizabeth Mutton was baptized.

Decr. 13th 1761. Ann daughter of Thom^{s.} & Sarah Goulder was baptized.

Jan^{ry.} 10th 1762. John son of Ric^d & Mary Belsey was baptized.

March 7th. 1762. Willm. son of Edwd. Margaret Beer was baptized.

April 11th. 1762. Willm. son of James & Ann Williams was baptized.

Augt. 29th 1762. Marcey ye daughter of Ric^d & Eliz^{th.} Castleden bap^{td.}

March 27th 1763. Elizabeth ye base born daughter of Stephen Finn jun^{r.} & Elizabeth Whitehead was baptized.

Augt 7th. 1763. Gibbon son of Gibbon & Margaret Lad was baptized.

Sept 4th 1763. Sarah daughter of John & Mary Williams was baptized.

Oct 3rd 1763. William son of Henry & Elizath Spaine was baptized.

WM. BARRETT, Curate.

1763. Novr 27. Mary the daug^r of James & Ann William.

Dec 25th. Elizabeth Daughter of James Brooks and Elizabeth his wife.

1764. Jany. 29th. Sarah daughter of Thomas & Sarah Finnes was baptized.

———

W. TASWELL, Curate.

Feby 26. William son of Richard and Mary Ratley was baptiz'd.

---

(1) " May 14th " *(a)* & *(b)*

(2) " Sept 6th 1761. William son of Thomas and Elizabeth Brisley was baptised." *(a)* (Not in the Register.)

March 11th. Edward son of Thomas and Ann Brisely was baptiz^{d.}

April 15th. Edward and Elizabeth base born Children of Edward Ruttly and Elizabeth Browning were baptiz'd.

May 27th. James son of Thomas Godwin and Judith his wife was baptiz^{d.}

June 24th. John son of John and Elizabeth Mutton was baptized.

August 19th. Jane daughter of Thomas Castle and Elizabeth his wife was baptized.

Octo^{br} 25. Elizabeth daughter of William Knight and Mary his wife was baptiz'd.

H. Fox, Curate.

1765.

Jany 20. Thomas son of Gibbon and Margaret Lad was baptized.

Jany 27. Richard son of Richard and Elizabeth Castleden.

March 10th. Henry son of John & Elizabeth Mutton.

May 5th. Elizabeth daughter of Thomas and Sarah Finnis.

H. Fox, Curate.

1765. May 19. John the son of Ingram and Elizabeth Swain.

June 9th. John son of John and Sarah Horton.

July 22^{d.} Thomas son of James & Elizabeth Brooks.

September 22 1765. Sarah daughter of Henry Harnett and Jane his wife was baptized,

Nov 3 1765. James son of James & Ann Williams was baptized.

1766.

Decem^{br} ye 22nd. John Baseborn son of John Wood and Elizabeth Webb was baptized.

May 11th. Elizabeth daughter of Richd Keeler and Martha his wife was baptized.

June y^e 1st. Richard son of Wm White and Martha his wife was baptiz'd.

June y^e 1st. Robert son of John Mutton and Elizabeth his wife was baptized.

August 24. Elizabeth daugh^{tr.} of John Finnis and Mary his wife was baptiz'd.

Octr 5$^{th.}$ Thomas son of John & Elizabeth Mutton was baptiz'd.

Nov^{br} 2$^{nd.}$ Elizabeth baseborn daughter of John Butler & Sarah Beer was baptiz'd.

1767. Feby 8$^{th.}$ Susannah daughter of Gibbon & Margaret Ladd was baptized.

Feb^{ry} 18$^{(1)}$ John son of Peter & Mary Jacob was baptiz'd.

March 29 : John son of W^m & Mary Knight was baptiz'd.

W. TASWELL, Curate.

Nov^{br} 8$^{th.}$ Tho$^{s.}$ son of James Williams and Ann his wife was baptiz'd.

1768. May 14$^{th.}$ Thos: son of John Horton & Sarah his wife was baptiz'd.

28th Aug$^t.$ Tho$^{s.}$ son of John & Elizth Mutton was baptized.

23 Oct$^r.$ Ann daug^{tr} of Ja$^{s.}$ & Elizth Brookes was baptised.

30$^{th.}$ Jane daug^{tr} of John Price and Sarah Church was baptized.

1769. 1 Jany. Saml son of Peter & Mary Jacob was baptized.

JOHN NAIRN was inducted into this Rectory Feb. 13.

March 23. Sarah d$^r.$ of Tho. White and Mary his wife was baptiz'd.

9 Ap$^l.$ Elizth Daug$^r.$ of Edw'd & Sarah Beer.

May 14$^{th.}$ John son of John Wood & Sarah his wife was baptiz'd.

July 30. Harrison son of Thomas & Mary Page was baptized.

September 24$^{th.}$ Alexander son of James & Ann Williams was baptiz'd.

1770.

June 3. Mary daughter of Thomas White and Mary his wife.

June 10$^{th.}$ Mary daughter of John Mutton and Elizabeth his wife.

July 8$^{th.}$ Mary daughter of Sawyard & Hester Simpson.

October 7$^{th.}$ John son of James & Elizabeth Brooks.

1771.

1771. February 17. Smith son of William & Elizabeth Mutton.

---

[1] " Feb. 15$^{th.}$" (a)

Feburary 17. Elizabeth base born daughter of Ann Sutton.

April 28. William son of Peter & Mary Jacob.

August 18. Ann daughter of William & Mary Dawkins.

October 13. Susanna daughter of John and Susanna Finch.

October 27. Halke son of William & Abigail Ellen was privately baptized & received into the Church 28th of June, 1772.

JOHN NAIRN, Rector.

1771.

1771. November 17th. John son of James & Ann Williams.

November 24. Thomas son of John & Mary Finnis.

1772.

1772. January 1. Thomas son of Thomas Watkinson Payler* Esqre & Charlotte his wife was privately baptized, and was received into the Church 13th of January.

January 12. William son of Thomas & Mary Laurence.

February 2. Christopher son of John & Sarah Wood.

April 12. George, son of James & Mary Pritchard.

July 3. Ralph, son of John & Elizabeth Mutton.

August 9. Mary daughter of Richard & Martha Keeler.

September 27. Elizabeth daughter of Richard & Mary White.

Novembr: 29. Ann daughter of Thomas & Mary White.

December 13. Michael base born son of Mary Hopkins.

1773.

1773. March 14. Mary daughter of Thomas & Mary Mutton.

April 11. Richard son of James & Elizabeth Brooks.

April 18. Mary daughter of Richard & Mary Pierce.

June 27. Edward son of John & Mary Castle.

August 22d. Richard son of Richard & Margaret Rose.

October 2. Charlotte Clare daughter of Thomas Watkinson Payler Esqre & Charlotte his wife.

---

* The Turners of Ileden assumed the name of Payler, about the middle of the 18th century.

October 10.   Henry son of James & Ann Williams.

Novemb^r 28.   Ann daughter of William & Ann$^{(1)}$ Pearse.

December 19.   Elizabeth daughter of John & Elizth Mutton.

1774.

1774.   February 20.   Elizabeth, daughter of William & Abigail Ellen.

March 20.   Jesse, son of Francis & Ann Pilcher.

April 24.   Elizabeth Ann, daughter of Peter & Mary Jacob.

May 1.   Ann, daughter of James & Elizabeth Mutton.

May 1.   John, son of Edward & Sarah Beer.

June 5.   Edward, son of George & Parnell Newport.

June 19.   Harriot, daughter of Thomas & Mary White

July 10.   Maria, daughter of John & Mary Finnis.

Aug. 21.   Sarah, daughter of Richard & Mary Pierce.

Octob^r 23.   John, son of Thomas & Mary Mutton.

November 20.   Richard, son of Richard & Mary White.

JOHN NAIRN, Rector

1775.

1775.   July 6.   Sarah, daughter of John & Sarah Horton.

July 30.   John, son of Joseph & Catherine Best.

Aug 20.   Thomas son of George & Parnell Newport.

Octob^r 1st Michael, son of James & Elizth Brooks.

October 29.   Pleasant, daughter of James & Elizth Mutton.

1776.

1776.   March 7th William, son of Thomas Watkinson Payler Esqre and Charlotte his wife.

March 17.   Ann, Daughter of John & Mary Castle.

April 21.   Thomas, son of Richard & Martha Keeler.

April 21.   Jane, daughter of Thomas & Mary White.

July 7.   Thomasine, daughter of John & Mary Finnis.

July 28.   Sarah, daughter of John & Sarah Munns.

---

(1) " Mary." (b)   In the Register " Mary " has been erased and " Ann " substituted.

August 25. Catherine daughter of John & Sarah Mitchison.

October 6. William, son of Peter & Mary Jacob.

1777.

1777. February 16th. Edward, son of Edward & Mary Browning.

February 23. Edward, son of Richard & Mary White.

March 16th. William, son of William & Ann Pearce.[1]

March 23. James, son of James & Elizabeth Mutton.

March 30. Elizabeth Susan, daught^r of Thomas & Mary Newport.

November 7. Henry Watkinson, son of Thomas Watkinson
Payler Esqre & Charlotte his wife.

1778.

1778. March 29. Mary daughter of John & Sarah Wood.

April 12. Ann, daughter of Edward & Sarah Beer.

April 26. Joseph, son of James & Elizth Brooks.

May 24. Joseph, son of Joseph & Catherine Best.

June 14. John son of Francis & Ann Pilcher.

Aug. 23. James William base born son of Alice Pritchard.

November 8th. Ann, daughter of Joseph & Catherine Boughton.

December 27th. Augustin son of Austin & Ann Spain.

1779.

1779. March 28th. Abraham, son of William & Susanna Wilkes.

April 4th. John son of James & Elizabeth Mutton.

JOHN NAIRN, Rector.

1779. May 16. Ann, daughter of Thomas & Elizth Bailey.

May 30. Henry, son of John & Mary Castle.

September 12. Bartholomew, son of Bartholomew and Mary
Collard.

September 18. Francis Richard, son of Thomas Watkinson
Payler Esqr. and Charlotte his wife.

October 3. Catherine, daughter of Joseph and Catharine Best.

---

[1] " Richard & Mary Pierce." (a) & (b) . . also thus originally in
Register, but erased.

1780.

1780. January 2. William, son of Henry & Mary Collison.

February 6. John, son of George & Parnel Newport.

March 19. John, son of Richard & Mary White.

May 7. Frances, daughter of Edward & Sarah Beer.

October 1. Charlotte, daughter of James & Elizth Brooks.

October 8. John, son of James & Elizabeth Mutton.

Novr. 26. William, son of William & Elizabth Dine.

1781.

1781. Febr. 18. Mary, daughter of Richard & Mary Sutton.

Febr. 18. Winefrid, daughter of Bartholomew & Mary Collard.

Febr. 25. Hannah, daughter of Austin & Ann Spain.

March 6. Thomas, son of Edward & Mary Ford.

March 18. James, son of William & Ann Pearse.

July 15. William, son of William & Ann Oyns.

October 9th. Jemima Margaret, daughter of Thomas Watkinson
Payler Esqr. and Charlotte his wife.

1782.

1782. Jan 22. William, son of Peter & Ann Barron, vagrants.

March 24. John, son of Thomas & Elizabeth Davis.

April 7. Sarah, daughter of James & Elizth Brooks.

May 12. Caroline, daughter of John & Carol^{ne} Robins.

Aug 25. Edward, son of Thomas & Ann Ford.

Oct. 5. George, son of George & Parnell Newport.

Oct^{tr.} 27. Elizabeth, base born daughter of Lucy Hollams, by
John Gilbert the reputed Father.

JOHN NAIRN, Rector.

1782. Novr 24. Ann daughter of Edward & Anne Browning.

1783.

1783. March 2^{d.} Richard, son of Richard & Mary Sutton.

May 25. Robert son of Edward & Mary Ford.

June 22. Charlotte, daughter of Austin & Ann Spain.

July 13. Elizabeth, daughter of John & Elizth Collar.

Stamp Act. Oct 2^{d.}

October 5. William, son of Thomas & Mary Sladden.

October 10. Thomas, son of Thomas & Ann Ford.

1784.

1784. May 2. Mary daughter of William & Grace Couchman.

May 23. Isaac, son of James & Elizth Brooks.

Aug 8. Carolina, daughter of John & Caroline Robins.

Octr 10. Elizabeth, daughter of John & Elizth Smith.

1785.

March 20th. Richard Charles, son of George & Ann Collar.

June 12. Thomas, son of Thomas & Elizabeth Browning.

Aug 14. Robert, son of Thomas & Ann Ford.

Octr 2. Ann, daughter of John & Ann Stone.

Novr. 27. Mary, daughter of James & Eliz. Mutton.

John Anthony Payler, see the Page next to the Marriges in this book.*

1786.

1786. Janr 15. Robert, son of William & Ann Oyns.

April 23. John, son of John & Elizabeth Collar.

April 29. Edward, son of Richard & Mary Sutton.

May 21. Grace, daughter of William & Grace Couchman.

May 28. George son of Thomas & Mary Slodden.

June 11. John, son of James & Sarah Greenstreet.

Nov. 19. John son of John & Sarah Dine.

1787.

1787. May 11. Sarah, daughter of George & Sarah Castle, privately baptised & Received June 3^{d.}

June 10th. William, son of James & Elizabeth Brooks.

July 15. William, son of John & Caroline Robins.

* See Memoranda at the end of the Baptisms.

1788.

1788. March 30th. William, son of John & Eliz. Atwood.

July 20. Sarah, daughter of Thomas & Ann Ford.

August 1st. Ann, daughter of George & Ann Richford was privately baptised & received Aug. 10th.

October 12. Charlotte, daughter of John & Sarah Dine.

October 21. Elizabeth, daughter of William & Elizabeth Sutton.

JOHN NAIRN, Rector.

1789.

June 21. George, son of John & Maria Laurence.

July 21. James son of John & Caroline Robins.

1790.

1790. January 2^{d.} Stephen, son of Austin & Ann Spain.

February 14. Sarah Ann, daughter of George & Ann Jemmet.

June 6. John, son of Philip & Susanna Norton.

1791.

1791. March 6. James, son of John & Sarah Dine.

March 15. Sarah, daughter of John & Mary Sutton.

April 10. Thomas, son of Thomas & Mary Green.

June 12. William, son of Nicholas & Mary Whitaker.

September 21. Sarah, daughter of John & Caroline Robins.

October 2. John, son of John & Elizabeth Wood.

Decr 18. Elizabeth, base born daughter of Elizabeth Wood by Edward Harnet.

1792.

Jan. 8^{th:} Gibbon Ladd, base born son of Sarah Terry, by Gibbon Ladd.

April 1. James, son of James & Ann Covenny.

May 20. William, son of John & Ann Pilcher.

August 19. John, son of George & Ann Richford.

October 21. Ann, daughter of John & Elizabeth Collar.

Nov. 25. Mary, daughter of Thomas & Ann Ford.

Nov. 25. Elizabeth, daughter of Robert & Alice Mutton.

1793.

February 24. Mary Ladd, base born daughter of Sarah Terry by Gibbon Ladd.

March 24. Mary, daughter of Thomas & Mary Green.

April 28. William, son of John & Sarah Dine.

May 1. John, base born son of Ann Smithson, by William Rye.

June 30. Thomas son of John & Elizabeth Wood.

September 8. John, son of John & Ann Pilcher.

November 10. Elizabeth, daughter of Thomas & Sarah Ellen.

1794.

January 5th. Charlotte daughter of John & Elizabeth Kennett.

Febr. 16. William son of George & Parnel Newport privately baptized received April 12th.

Febr. 25. Mary & Elizabeth, Twin daughters of William & Mary Philpot, privately baptized. Elizabeth was Received June 1st. Mary died.

JOHN NAIRN, Rector.

1794.

1794. April 12. Sarah, daughter of William & Sarah Castle.

May 4. Thomas, base born son of Elizabeth Wood.

May 18. Charlotte, base born daughter of Mary Kingsmill.

May 18. Charlotte, daughter of John & Eleanor Philpot.

June 29. Michael, son of Michael & Eleanor Stupple.

June 29. Thomasine, daughter of Andrew & Anne Holman.

July 20. John, son of Richard & Ann . . . . White.

October 9. Hannah, daughter of Thomas & Hannah May.

December 14. Anne, daughter of Bartholomew & Mary Collard.

1795. February 1st. John Hanley, son of Thomas & Sarah Holmes.

February 1st. James, son of John & Elizabeth Fagg.

February 8. Sarah daughter of Thomas & Mary Green.

March 8. Thomas, son of John & Carolina Robins.

March 22. Henry, son of John & Elizth Atwood.

August 2. Mary, daughter of John & Elizabeth Collar.

October 18. John Marsh, son of Christopher & Mary Wood.

October 25. George, son of John & Eleanor Philpot.

December 6. Thomas Terry, base born son of Cecilia Jordan by Thomas Terry.

1796.

Jan 17th. George, son of Thomas & Hannah May.

Septr 4. Thomas, son of Thomas & Sarah Holmes.

Septr 4. Mary, daughter of John & Sarah Dine.

Novr 27. Edward, son of John & Eleanor Philpot.

1797.

January 4th. Edward, son of John & Elizabeth Atwood, privately baptised Received Jan. 17. 1797.

April 2. Charlotte, daughter of George & Mary Rye.

May 4th. Sarah, daughter of Edwin Humphry Sandys Esqr and Helen his wife was privately baptised. Received the 16 of June.

May 21. Alice, daughter of Thomas & Elizabeth Couchman.

July 6. Valentine, son of Valentine & Sarah Ellen.

Sept. 10. James, son of Thomas & Hannah May.

1798.

Jan 7. William, son of John & Elizabeth Collar.

Feb. 18. Michael base born son of Sophia Rowland.

March 18. John, son of John & Eleanor Philpot.

April 22. John, son of John & Mary Savage.

June 17. George, son of Thomas & Ann Ford.

1799.

March 17. Edward son of Thomas & Hannah May.

March 17. Gregory, son of Thomas & Elizab^{th.} Couchman.

JOHN NAIRN, Rector

April 28. Mary, daughter of John & Eleanor Philpot.

June 16. James son of John & Elizabeth Atwood.

August 5. William, son of William & Mary Bradbury, of the 3rd Reg^{t.} of foot Guards.

August 25. Margaret, daughter of John & Ann Rogers, of the 4th of Foot.

Sept. 4. John, son of John & Mary Swiney of the 4th Reg^{t.} of Foot.

Sept. 9. Catherine, daughter of John & Charlotte Williams of the Ninth Reg^{t.} of Foot.

Octr. 6. Martha, daughter of Edward & Ann Browning.

Nov. 10. Thomas, son of Robert & Sarah Fetherston.

Nov. 12. John, son of Edwin Humphry Sandys Esqr. and Helen his wife.

Decr. 8. George, son of George & Charlotte Maytam.

Dec. 22. John, son of Benjamin & Sarah Mutton.

1800.

Feb. 9th. Ann, daughter of William & Elizabeth Williams.

March 23. Thomas, son of Edward & Mary Mutton.

May 11. Harriet, daughter of John & Eleanor Philpot.

June 22. Charlotte, daughter of Thos. & Hannah May.

Sept. 14. James, son of Henry & Winefred Maxted.

Decr. 28. Sarah, daughter of William & Elizabeth Beer.

1801.

Jan 16. Catherine, daughter of John & Elizabeth Collar.

Feb^{r.} 8. Henry, son of John & Hannah Mutton.

Febr. 23. William, son of Thomas & Sarah Ellen.

April 23. Thomas, son of John & Ann Brooks.

August 9th. James, son of John & Elizath Atwood.

Novr. 15. George, son of John & Sarah Warburton.

Decr. 3. George, son of
Decr. 3. Susanna, daughter of } Finnis & Dinah Bowes.

Decr. 27. Henry, son of Rich^{d.} & Mary Maxted.

1802.

Febr. 21. Mary daughter of Richard & Eliz. Rose.

JOHN NAIRN, Rector.

1802.

Febr. 28.   Michael, son of John & Eleanor Philpot.

1803.   Jan 23.   John, son of William & Eliz^{th.} Williams.

March 6.   Maria, daughter of William and Elizabeth Beer.

March 9.   John, son of John & Hannah Mutton.

May 1.   Thomas, son of John & Sarah Warburton.

October 2.   John, son of Edward & Abigail Browning.

December 20.   Sarah, daughter of Halke and Pleasant Ellen.

1804.

Jan^{ry} 1.   John, son of Edward & Ann Keeler.

January 29.   Elizabeth & Sarah daughters of John & Elizabeth. Atwood.

June 3.   Ann, daughter of William & Jane Sawkins.

June 24.   Sarah, daughter of Francis & Ann Pilcher.

Aug 12.   Sarah, daughter of James & Martha Twig.

Aug 19.   George, son of George & Elizabeth Wood.

Sept 2.   John son of John & Ann Hersefield, of sixty-first Regiment.

Sept. 2.   Sarah Eliza—daughter of John and Sarah Turner, of the Guards.

October 8.   James, son of James & Elizabeth Norman of 53^d Regt.

December 2.   Stephen, son of John & Eleanor Philpot.

1805.

March 14.   Sarah, daughter of John & Sarah Warburton.

March 17.   Catherine, daughter of Thos. & Mary Morriss.

May 26.   William, son of John & Ann Newport.

June 18.   Mary daughter of John & Elizth Atwood.

Aug 11.   Edward, son of John & Hannah Mutton.

1806.

Jan 1st.   Sarah, daughter of George & Elizabeth Wood.

JOHN NAIRN, Rector.

1806. March 9th. John, son of W^m & Elizabeth Fisher.

March 23rd. John son of W^{m.} & Charlotte Pilcher.

April 6. William son of George and Elizabeth Benefield.

July 8th. Robert, son of Robert & Sarah Gardner.

CHARLES HUGHES, Curate.

Septr. 28. Henry son of William Henry and Elizth Pritchard (late Elizth Crowe, Sp^{r.}) was born Sept 6 : bapt^d Sept 28 : 1806.

William Henry son of William & Elizth Beer (late Elizabeth Featherstone Spin^r) was born April 14th 1805 and baptized October 6th 1806.

Mary daughter of Richard & Rachel Shirley (late Rachel Mutton Sp^r) November 2^d 1806.

Thomas Egerton son of the Revd Cooper Willyams & Elizabeth his wife (late Elizth Snell Spinster) born Sept. 29 1806 & baptized November 24th 1806.

1807.

Edward son of Edward & Martha Ford (late Martha Dixon Spinster) was born Feb. 16th privately bapt^d Feb. 20th & received into the Church March 22^d 1807.

John son of John & Susannah Robins (late Susannah Hogbin Spinster) born March 31. Baptized April 19th 1807.

Thomas son of George & Sarah Philpot (late Sarah Bushel Sp^r) born April 15 baptized May 3^d 1807.

Hester daughter of John & Eleanor Philpot (late Eleanor Rousel) born March 20th priv^{ly.} baptized June 12th and received into the Church Aug. 9th 1807.

Elizabeth daughter of William & Elizth Beer (late Elizth Featherstone) born May 10th. Baptized June 21 1807.

COOPER WILLYAMS, Rector.

Edward son of Edward & Abigail Browning (late Ab^l : Walker) born Aug. 5th priv^{ly} baptized Augt 6th rec^d into ye Church Sep 13 1807.

Richard son of Robert & Sarah Gardner (late Sarah Brice, Spinster) born Augst 3^d baptized Octr 1st 1807.

James son of George & Elizabeth Wood (late Elizth Mexted) born Sepr 18 baptized Octr 9th 1807.

H

Elizabeth daughter of Robart & Mary Beek (late Mary Epps) born Aug^st 14th baptiz^d Octr 11. 1807.

James son of John & Hannah Mutton (late Hannah Brise Sp^r·) born Oct 15. Baptized Novr 8th 1807.

John & Edward Twin sons of George & Elizabeth Newport (late Eliz^th Blake Sp^r) born Decr 9th priv^ly baptized Dec 10th 1807.

1808.

Charlotte daughter of W^m & Charlotte Pilcher (late Charlotte Clayson) was born Jany 1st 1808 baptized Jan^ry 31 1808.

Mary daughter of Thomas & Elizabeth Shrubsole (late Eliz^th Gold, Spinster) born Dec. 14th 1807 baptized March 6. 1808.

John son of George & Elizabeth Newport (late Eliz^th Blake Sp^r) was born Dec 9th 1807 baptized May 22^d 1808.

Edward son of Susannah Codham (reputed Father Richard Langford) born Oct·: 8, baptized Nov 13 1808.

William son of George & Sarah Philpot (late Sarah Bushel Sp^r) born Octr 26 baptized Nov 27, 1808.

1809.

Thomas & John Twin sons of Edward & Martha Ford (late Martha Dixon Sp^r) born Nov. 14 1808, Bapt. Jany 1 1809.

Sophia daughter of John & Eleanor Philpot (late Eleanor Rousel Spinster) born Nov 17, 1808, bap. Feb. 19 1809.

Sarah daughter of Thomas & Mary Minter (late Mary Johnson Sp^r) born Jan^r· 3^d baptized Feb^r 12, 1809.

William son of Robert & Sarah Gardner (late Sarah Brice Sp^r) born June 4th priv^t· baptized June 15th Rec^d into the Church, Nov. 23.

COOPER WILLYAMS Rector.

1809.

John Vyner son of the Revd Cooper Willyams and Elizabeth R. his wife (late Elizabeth R Snell Spinster), was born July 14th baptiz^d priv^ly July 23 and received into the Church Sept. 19, 1809.

Maria daughter of William & Elizabeth Codham (late Elizabeth . . .) Born July 30th bapt^d Aug. 20th·

Thomas son of Robert & Mary Beek (late Mary Epps Sp^r) born Aug^st· 17th priv^ly bap^td Aug 22 1809.

Mary Ann daughter of William & Mary Wild (late Mary May-
tham Sp^r) born Augst 19th baptized priv^{ly} Augst 22^d, rec^d into
ye Ch. Sept. 3^d.

John son of John & Frances Willis (late Frances Rickwood Sp^r)
priv^{ly} baptized October 3^d 1809.

Amelia daughter of William & Elizabeth Beer (late Eliz. Featherstone Sp^r) born Sepr 28th baptizd Oct 29.

William son of John & Mary Eareth (late Mary Reeve Sp^r), born
Sepr 22^d. baptized November 5th.

William son of William & Charlotte Rye (late Charlotte Dines
Sp^r) born Oct 20th baptizd Nov. 19. 1809.

Belinda daughter of William & Sarah Reynolds (late Sarah
Hamms, Spinster) born Nov 14th baptizd Dec 10th 1809.

1810.   1810.

Mary Ann daughter of William & Charlotte Pilcher (late Charlotte
Clayson Spinster) born Jan^{ry} 26, Bap^{td} March 4th 1810.

Stephen son of John & Elizth Fagg (late Eliz^h Cleveland, Sp^r)
born March 19th baptized May 13, 1810.

COOPER WILLYAMS, Rector.

Elizabeth daughter of William & Mary German (late Mary Mutton
Sp^r) born Jan 9, priv^{ly} bap^{td}. Jany 23^d, Rec^d into the Church
June 24th 1810.

Charlotte, daughter of Thos & Elizth Shrubsole (lat Eliz. Gold:
Sp^r) born Feb. 1st, priv^{ly} bap^{td} Feb 9th, rec^d into the Church
July 8, 1810.

Elizabeth daugh^t. of John & Eleanor Philpot (late Eleanor Russel,
Sp^r) born Augst 17th baptiz^d Sept 9, 1810.

William son of Richard & Jane Tumber (late Jane Luke Sp^r) born
July 14th bapt^d Nov 25 1810.

1811.   1811.

Sarah daughter of Robert & Sarah German (late S. Brice Sp^r) born
Novr 19. 1810. Bapt Jan 2 1811.

Eliza daughter of W^m & Elizabeth Codham (late E. Philpot Sp^r)
born Oct 17, 1810, bap^{td} Jan 27, 1811.

Mary daughter of Thomas & Rebecca Ford (late R. Barton Sp^r)
born Decr 20th 1810, baptized. Feb 3^d 1811.

Caroline daughter of George & Sarah Philpot (late S. Russel, Sp^r)
born Jany 26, baptized Feby 24. 1811.

Mary daughter of John & Elizabeth Dines (late Spain) born May 7ʰ 1811, privˡʸ bapᵗᵈ May 11 recᵈ into the Church June 23ᵈ·

Robert son of Edward & Martha Ford (late M. Dixon Spʳ·) born May 23ᵈ : Baptized June 23ᵈ 1811.

Charlotte daughter of John & Elizᵗʰ Fagg (late Cleveland Spʳ) born May 9ᵗʰ Bapᵗᵈ· July 7. 1811.

John, son of Richard & Charlotte Rye (late Dines Spinʳ) born July 4. baptᵈ Aug 4. 1811.

Sarah, daughter of John & Mary Eareth (late Reeve Spinster) born July 18ᵗʰ, Baptᵈ Aug 18 : 1811.

Elizabeth base born daughter of Alice Rutherford spinster, The Father unknown, baptized Aug 18, 1811.

Sarah daughᵗʳ of John & Hannah Mutton (late Brice Widow) born Aug. 1. baptized Sept 1 : 1811.

Henry son of Willᵐ & Charlotte Pilcher (late Clayton Spʳ) baptᵈ Oct. 10 1811.

COOPER WILLYAMS, Rector.

1812.

Mary daughter of Wᵐ & Mary German (late Mutton Spʳ) born Jan 9. baptized. Jan 19 1812.

Eliza Ann[1] daughter of Edmund & Mary File (late Pilcher) born Feb 13. baptized March 8, 1812.

Thomas son of Thos & Elizᵗʰ Shrubsole born Feb. 11. Bapᵗ· March 22.

Edward son of Henry & Sarah (late Spencer) born June 2ᵈ· Baptizd July 5ʰ· 1812.

COOPER WILLYAMS, Rector.

[*End of the Baptisms in the Second Register Book.*]

[1] " Elizabeth File." (*a*).

[The following Memoranda are found in this Second Register Book ; one on the fly-leaf of the book, the other on the page preceding the Marriages.]

Mem. * Charles Vincent son of · · · this Parish was baptized
at Wymenswold Church Febury 2' 1777 by John Nairn.

Mem.   Baptized.

1785. August 12th John Anthony, the son of
Thomas Watkin Payler Esqr & of
Charlotte his wife was born the 7th &
baptised this Day.
The above is a true copy taken from the Register
of Baptisms, belonging to the Parish of Walcot
in the City of Bath. Witness the hand of
JOHN SIBLEY, Rector.

The above is a true copy of a certificate received
from Tho : Watkinson Payler Esqr of Ileden,
By JOHN NAIRN, Rector of Kingston.

---

* " Charles Vincent Joles son of Nathaniel & Anne Joles baptized
Feb 2^u 1777 " *Wymynswold Register.*

MARIADGES 1558.

Julye 1558.

1558.　12 daye were maryed Ralfe Mare
　　　　& Ursula Moore anno supra :

November.

25 daye were maryed Richard Turner
　　& Anne Nethersole anno Supra :

Novembris 1560.

1560.　6 daye were maryed Nicholas Slowman
　　　　& Alce Hobdaye anno supra :

Maye 1561.

1561.　6 daye were maryed John Boulton
　　　　& Elinor　.　.　.　anno Supra :

Novembris.

20 daye was Maryed Michaell Baker
　　& Adrian Keyse anno supra :

November : 1563.

1563.　24 daye were maryed John Rugley
　　　　& Margerye Bartun anno supra :

January 1564.

1564.　30 daye were maryed Thomas Hopkine
　　　　& Jone Marche anno supra :

Aprell 1565.

1565.　10 daye were maryed William Moone[1]
　　　　& Alice Rugley anno supra :

June.

1 daye were maryed John Wilcocke[2]
　　& Alice Lockewood anno supra :

---

[1] " Grome." (*a*)　　　　[2] " Johannes Wylcoke, clericus." (*a*)

July.

17 daye were maryed Thomas Milborne
& Alice Gould anno Supra :

30 daye were maryed William Sampson
& Annis Wood anno supra :

November.

26 daye were maryed John Browninge
& Jone Rugleye   Anno Supra :

Maye 1567.

1567. 28 daye were maryed Robert Sturdye
& Gylian Lucke   anno supra :

November.

24 daye were maryed James Sayer
& Jone Ruglye   anno supra :

October 1568.

1568. 21 daye were maryed John Pette
& Jane Coolinge.   anno supra :

Maye 1571.

15 daye were maryed Thomas Hopkine
& Elizabethe Harffeild   anno supra

ROBBE. BASSOCKE * ⎫ ChurchWardens.
JOHN HOPKIN   ⎭

September 1571.

1571.   6 daye were maryed Thomas Hall
& Anne Gould   anno Supra :

September 1574.

1574. 20 daye were maryed william Gould
& Jone Barton   anno supra :

(. . . . .)[1]

---

* See footnote, page 2.
[1] "28th October   Wyllm. Wyer & Annis Rugleye." *(a)* (Not in the
Register.)

Julye 1575.

1575. 4 daye were maryed Thomas Peerce
& Margaret Rayner   anno supra :

November.

24 daye were maryed John Nethersole
& Alice Chapman   anno supra :

October 1576.

1576. 22 daye weare maryed Robert Rugley
& Margarett Ditton   anno supra :

Maye 1577.

1577. 11 daye were maryed Nicholas Beageant
& Marye Boykett   anno Supra :

September.

30 daye were maryed Andrew Johnson
& Isabell Younge   anno supra :

Januarye.

20 daye were maryed Nicholas Bunce
& Samuell Chourthop   anno Supra :

November 1578.

1578. 27 day weare maryed Elyas Boykett
& Bettris Scarlett   anno supra :

November 1579.

1579. 16 daye were maryed Thomas Mughole
& Jone Nicholas widowe   anno supra

ffebruarie.

15 daye were maryed John Christian
& Alice Sweetinge   anno supra :

June 1580.

1580. 27 daye were maryed John Gyles
& Agnis Hopkine   anno supra :

July 1581.

1581. 31 daye were maryed Anthony Mason
& Margaret Prestod[1]   anno supra :

October.

30 daye were maryed John Rickard
& Isabell Johnson[2]   anno supra :

November 1583.

1583. 12 daye were maryed Gilberd Morris
& Alice Hatche   anno supra:

ffebruary.

13 daye were maryed John Stokes
& Patience Nethersole   anno supra

ROBBE. BASSOCKE } Church Wardens.
JOHN HOPKYN }

October 1586.

1586. 17 daye were maryed Thomas Newstreate
& Marye Hilles   anno supra :

October 1587.

1587. 9 daye were maryed Richard Rugley
& Dorytie Danyell   anno supra :

10 daye weare maryed John Quilter
& Anne Austen   anno supra :

Maye 1588.

1588. 16 daye were maryed John Churchman
& Alice Swinford widow   anno supra

June.

3 daye weare maryed Vincent Nethersole
& Elizabethe Denne   anno Supra :

October 15.

6 daye were maryed Thomas Epps
& Jayne Serieante [3]   anno Supra :

---

[1] " Widow." *(a)*   [2] " Widow." *(a)*   [3] " Sergen." *(a)*

The same daye also were maryed Edward
Chambers & Elizabeth Dale   anno supra:

November.

29 daye were maryed John Blasht
& Marye Rugley   anno Supra:

January.

20 daye were maryed George Wayte
& Margery Johnson   anno Supra:

June 1589.

1589. 30 daye weare maryed George Milles
& Marye Wilsford [1]   anno Supra:

September 1591.

1591. 11 daye weare maryed Edmond Tristram
& Pleasante Bunce widow   anno supra

Maye 1592.

1592. 16 daye weare maryed Henry Carpenter
& Jone Hogbeane   anno supra:

October.

5 daye were maryed William Swifte [2]
& Marye Philpott   anno Supra:

30 daye were maryed Thomas Seryven
& Jone Labanne   anno supra:

Aprell 1593.

30 daye were maryed John Coorte
& Ursula . . . [3]   anno Supra:

September.

13 daye weare maryed Mathew Whitinge
& Mary Thompson   anno supra:

ROBBE BASSOCKE } Churchwardens.
JOHN HOPKYN

---

[1] " George Willes & Maisteris Mary Wilfoorde." *(a)*
[2] " Mr. William Swift." *(a)*   [3] " Ursula . . . widow." *(a)*

October 1593.

1593. 20 daye were Maryed Richard Brigge
& Ellyne Audley   anno Supra:

November.

19 daye were maryed Mathew Browninge
& Wenefrethe Kember   ā supra:

26 daye were maryed John Stace and
Elizabethe Hogben   anno Supra

June 1595.

1595. 30 daye were maryed Robert Bassocke
& Alice Younge[1]   anno Supra:

Aprell 1597.

1597. 21 daye were maryed John Sergeant
& Alice Winter[2]   anno supra:

August.

8 daye were maryed william Mershe
& Agnis Odleye   anno supra:

September.

21 daye were maryed John Curlinge
& Margarett Cooke   anno Supra:

26 daye were maryed Thomas Sturges
& Mary Hogben   anno supra

October.

10 daye were maryed Thomas Browninge
and Alice Knott   anno supra.

* By me JHN HASTLYN, p'son.

ROBERT BASSOCKE Churche Warden.

JOHN HOPKYN church warden.

1599. Julye. 16 daye was married Rycharde Lawrence and
Annie Woode.

---

[1] "Widow." (a)   [2] "Widow." (a)
* See footnote on Page 22.

1600. Septeb: 25 Nicholas Weevel & Anne Rugley were married.

Septeb: 30 day were married William Nookes and Anna Duninge.

Novb: 6: Were married Thomas Tanton of Elam, & Annïs Wood of this p*ar*ishe.

1602. July 5 day was maried Margaret Douninge to Richarde Rugley.

The 15 of ye same moneth were maried John Sterlinge & ursilla Courte.

1603. Octob 13 Were maried Richard Sayer and Euerell Maye.

Octob 17 were maried Gregory Smithsonne And Mary Rugley.

An: 1605.

November: 18. were maried Thomas George & Mildred Hopkin.

An: 1606.

June 16. were maried Avery Sabin & Ann Denn.

July 7. were maried Timothy Iniester & Marget Rugley.

Octob. 27. were maried Edwarde Dadd & Nicholan Drilande.

Novembr. 23 were maried Richarde White, & Ann Murton.

An. 1607.

June 22 were maried { Robert Pierse.
Jone Mason.

January 17. were maried { John Simons.
Marget Rickwoode.

An. 1608.

Septembr. 12. were maried { John ffells.
Jane Dale.

Octob. 2. were maried { Thomas Partriche.
Elsabeth Pierse.

Octobr 31 were maried { Richarde Wrathe.
Marye Craye.

The same day were maried { John Cullen.
Jone Rugley.

Octobr. 8 were maried { James Sayer.
Elsabethe Cooman.

Visitat. Octob: 10.

Febru : 3. were maried { George Crickman.
{ Joane Marshe.

An. 1610.   Visitat. April 24.

July 2. were maried { Edward Browinge.
{ Marget Young.

Visitat. Sep. 25.

Novebr. 5. were maried { Daniel Rugley.
{ Barbara Paramoure.

January. 31. were maried { John Rickwoode.
{ Joane Lewes.

An. 1611 March 31. were maried { Richarde Hopkin.
{ Ann Rigden.

April 4. were maried { Edwine Auger, gent.
{ Mary Gibbon.

February 9. were maried { John Clarke.
{ Ann Johnson.

Visitat, 28 April.

Octob : 8 were maried { Vincent Lawrence.
{ Jane Cray.

An : 1613.

April. 15 were maried { Thomas Birde.
{ Marget Dale.

Visitat. 21 of April.   An : 1613.

Visitat. Septemb. 28.

Novemb : 8 were maried { Paule Browninge.
{ Elsabethe Chackson.

Noveb : 15 were maried { Vincent Cray.
{ ffrancis Brett.

January 14 were maried { Samuel Morton.
{ Jane Amies.

An : 1614.

Visitat. April 30.

Visitat. Sep : 28.

Noveb : 21 were maried { Thomas Golde.
{ Elsabethe Harries.

February 20 were maried { Edward Sanchy.
{ Marget Watson.

Visitat. April 10.   An : 1616.   Visitat. Octob 1.   An : 1616

An : 1617. Visitat. April 30.

September 14. were maried {John Trappam.
{Joane Peirse.

Visitat. Octob : 3.

Visitat. April 14. An : 1618

Septemb 28 were maried {James Buckhurst.
{Marget Gibbon.

Visitat. y⁰ 1 of October. an. supra.

June 8 were married Thomas Kingsmeel. Ann Younge.

Visitat. yᵉ 27. of Sep : an. 1619.

November 22 were maried William Binge.
Ann Danton widdow.

Noveb : 25 were maried {John Everden.
{Jane Rugley.

ffebru : 28 were maried. {Nicholas Barbar.
{Mary Younge.

An : 1620.

Novemb : 2. were maried. {Matthewe Shoveler.
{Joane Giles.

Novemb : 20 were maried. {William Sally.
{Dionise Mughole.

Visitat. yᵉ 10 of April.

An 1621. April 30 were maried {George Beane.
{Sara Chackffield.

Visitat. Sep : 28.

Noveb : 19 were maried {Herbert Boyce.
{Mary Bassocke.

March 4. were maried. {Edward Toddys.
{Marget Rigden.

An : 1622.

Nouember 18 were maried. { James Courte.
{ Elsabethe Sayer ⁽¹⁾

An : 1623 Visitations yᵉ 23 of September.

January 19 were maried {Nicholas Furnley.
{Ann Boughton.

⁽¹⁾ " Widow." *(b)*

An 1624.

Septemb: 24. were maried { Nicholas Paramore.
Martha Mershe.

Visitat. Sep : 30.

Novemb. 1 were maried { Thomas Herset, alias Hastifer.
Mary Cullen widdowe.

December 30 were maried { Richard Osborne.
Elizabeth Benchkin.

ffebruary 1. were maried { John Boyket.
Amy Smithe.

Visitat. April 28.

An. 1626. October 16 were maried { John Cooper.
ffrancis Elgar.

October 22 were maried { John Rickwood.
Marget Browninge.

An : 1627.

October 15 were maried { Stephan Kingsmeel.
Elsabethe Denn.

The same day were maried { William Wrathe.
Ann Philpott.

An : 1628. ffebruary 8 were maried. { Henry Stoubridge.
Mary Sucket.

An : 1629. March 31. were maried { William Fagg.
Mary Osborne.

May 1. Were maried { Thomas Apricharde.
Mary Soome.

1630. Apil 26. were maried { Robert Medmer.
Elsabethe Hunte.

1632. Novemb. 26 were married { Searles Proud gent.
Anne Denne gent.

Novemb 29 were married Edward Baldrie & Dorothy Question.

ffebruary : ye seventh were married John Hogben & Ann Harnett.

1633. November the 14th were married John Maurice & Jane Alleyne.

1634. May the 12th were married John Hopkin & Anne Butcher.

Novemb. the 3d were married Richard Mihēll & Mildred Danton.

Novembr ye 10th were married John Browne & Elizabeth Mihell.

1635. October the 15th were married John Starling & Mary Alleyn.

December the i were married Robert Browning & Martha Crickman.[1]

1636. May the 5th were married William Browning & Sara Murrey.

August the 7th were married Peter Free & Elizabeth Yeomans.

October ye 4th were marryed John Spayne & Susan Spayne.

November the 6th were marryed Thomas Budds & Mary Mihell.

1637. Apryll ye 17^{th [2]} were marryed William Gould & Judeth Read.

1638. October ye 25th were marryed Thomas Bakar & Sarah Pittock.

Novemb : ye 1st were marryed John Browne and Elizabeth Early.

1639.

1640. Septemb : ye 28th were marryed William Waddall & Elizabeth Yongue.

Octob. ye 20th were marryed Thomas Rye & Amye Dixon.

ffebruary ye 11th were marryed William Hopkin & Margrett Rofe.

1641. September ye were marryed Thomas Homesby & Susan Cheyton.

1642. Septemb : ye 26th were marryed Danyell Ovell and Mary Neame.

· 1648. Octob ye 9 were married Vincent Rickwood and Mary Dadd.

Novemb. ye 2 were married Stephen Maple and Elizabeth Cranbrooke.

1653. March ye 12 were married John Dixon of Barham and Margarett Wood of Kingston by the magistrate Mr Thom : Scott of Canterbury Justice of peace according to ye late Act of parliament Morris Browne and Rich : Wood of Barham being present to wittness ye same.

1655. 21 of Novmber was baptized Elisabeth haiward the dafter of Arter hayward *and* Elisabeth his wife.

1657. february ye 16 were married Hercules Hills of ye parish of St Lawrence in ye Ile of Thanett & Sarah Wood of ye parish of Kingston . ye bands having beene published 3 severall lords days and nothing obiected against yem.

p^r me NIC. DINGLEY. Register.

---

[1] " Critman." *(b)*   [2] " April 13th. " *(a)*

Nouember the i was baptised Authur haywood y^e sonne of Authur Hayward & Elizibeth his wife.

165?. Aprill y^e 22 were married Robert Turner of y^e parish of Kingston & Ann Cooper of y^o parish of Eastry yeir bands having beene published 3 markett days in ye city of Canturbury according to ye late act for publishing.

pr me NIC : DINGLEY Reg$^{st.}$ parochiœ de Kingstone.

June ye 27 1659 were married Andrew Wanstall & Elizabeth Trapps both of y^e parish of Kingston yeir bands having published three lords days in y^e parish church of Kingstone.

1660. May 31 were married in y^e parish church of Kingston Willia*m* Newman of Canturb. and Grace Partridge his wife.

(. . . . . . .) [1]

1662. Feb 21. were married Thomas Readwood & Elizabeth Verrier by licence fro*m* ye court.

NIC. DINGLEY Rector ibid.
RICH. WOOD Churchwarden.

Jan 23 1664 were married Willia*m* Marsh of Barham and Mary Masterson of Kingston.

May 25 were married Abraham Attwood & Ann Tallis.

May 28 of the same yeare were married Vincent Draper and Ann Gold.

June ye 25th of the same yeare were maried Richard White and Ann Mihill.

June ye 27 of the same yeare were married Henry Marsh Gent. & Mrs Leah Ady, [2] by License from the Court.

1666. October 9. of ye same yeare were married Gualter Laker of Chillam & Mary Brenchley of Kingston.

February 14. were married Gabriell Honnifold Esqre[3] & Margarett Swann of Canturbury by licence from ye court.

August ye 20 1667 were married Thomas Marsh. gent : of ye city of Canturbury & M^s Francis Buck of Waltham by licens from ye court.

---

[1] " 1661 Oct 6. was married William Mihill & Elizabeth his wife." *(a)* (Not in the Register.)

[2] " Henry Marsh gent. of Kingstone & Leah Ady gent. of Denton." *(a)*

[3] " Gabriell Honnifold of Eastwell, Esqr." *(b)*

1668. Septemb. 24 were married John Foreman & Mariory Ruck of ye parish of Elham by lycense from ye court.

    Nic Dingley Rector . . . . Churchwarden.

1668 were married Tho : Feux of Barham and Christian Rickwood.[1]

1669. Octob. 21 of ye yeare were married John Soale & Susanna Turner.

1670. Octob^r ye 4 of ye same yeare were married Thomas Sayer and Joane Question.[2]

Octob^r· ye 20 were married John Kingsmell & Margarett Power of Patrixbourne.

Thomas Maxtead and Mildred Mihill both of Kingstone were married May 11 1674.

Thomas Browne and Mary Cheeseman both of Kingstone were married October 9 : 1676.

John Baker of Barham and May fford of Kingstone were married Aprill 9 1678.

Richard Mihill & Mary Brensley both of Kingstone were married July 25 1678.

Nicholas Pilcher } of Kingston were married ffebr : 6th 1683.
Hannah Talis

1684. Tho. White of Bridge } were married Ap^r· 10th· 1684.
Sarah Ford of Kingston

Jan 20 1688. Richard Moore & Mary Reed both of this Parish were married.

April 26 1691. James ford of Kingston Elisabeth Taylior were married.

Nov 5 1693. Wiliam Thanet & Mary Sharp of Kingstone was married.

Octr 7 1694. Stephen Hobdy & Everherd Sayer.[3]

  Visitat. Octr. 7 1695

Octr 15 1695. James Burch & An : Mihil was married.

Nov 10 1695. John Mihill & Elizabeth Taylior were married at Canterbury.

May[4] 1698 Tho : and Mary Mihil were married.

Lady day 700. Gilb : Burroughs Rector.

---

[1] " Of Kingstone." *(a)*   [2] " Joane Questhead." *(b)*
[3] " Everard Sayer." *(b)*   [4] " May 16." *(a)*   " May 14." *(b)*

June 24 1700.   Ric. Keeler Eliz. Cuelern.[1]

Nov. 12 1700.   Thomas Chapman & Elizabeth Gold were maried.

Married.

May 15 1701.   John Andrews & Abigail Jull were married.

Oct 5. 1701. { John Vyle & Eliz : Green. / Mathew Browning & Susan fox.

Oct 11 1702.   Rich. Richfoot Ann Draper.

Oct 3 1703.   Allman Turner & Mary Brice.

Oct 12 1707.   Will. Weeks & ye widow ffowell.

Decr 2 1707.   Will. Pay & Eliz. Hopkin.

Jan : 13 1709.   Ed : ffrank & Mary Stuple.

June 27 1710.   Will : Kiddam and Mary Low.

feb : 4th 17$\frac{10}{11}$.   James and Eliz : sharp.[2]

Aprile 8th·   Henry Baker and Mary Clement.

1714.   Aug 2^d Jn° Welbank & Eliz : Goulder.

1714.   Dec. 20 Will : Homes and Ann Weeks.

PETER INNES succeeded y^e Revd Mr BURROUGHS in ye Liveing of Kingston Octr ye 15th 1718.

1720.   March 31^rst Walter Hoge & Ann Gundy both of Kingston were married by Licence.

1722.   March 25th Thomas Golder & Elizabeth Fox both of Kingston were married by Banns.

1722.   January ye 7th Married Edward Brensley and Everell Hobday both of Kingston by Banns.

1724.   December ye 24th married John Robinson of Bridge & Hanna Talpot[3] of St. Margarets Cant : by License.

1728.   Sep^tr ye 22 Married Stephen Maple & Ann Whitnel.

1728-9.   ffeb^ry 17th Married Daniel Coller & Ann Hogben.

1729.   Novemb^r 9th Married Joseph Webb & Mary White.

---

[1] " Richard Kiddar & Elizabeth Curlane." *(a)*   " Richard Keeler & Elizabeth Curloin." *(b)*

[2] James Sharpe & Eliza Sharpe. *(a)*   " Henry Pilcher & Elizabeth Sharpe." *(b)*

[3] " Widow." *(a)*

1730. Octob^r 7th Married John Shelley & Jane Davis.

1732. May 17th Married John Wraith & Elizth: Hogben.

1732. Octob' 5th Married George Pettit & Susanna Adams.

1732. Octob^r 29 Married Thomas Bewley & Wilmot Hobday.

1732. Nov^{hr} 10th Married Vincent Safary & Ann Neams.

1733. July 8th Married Thomas Baker & Jane Lot.

1733. October y^e 8th Married Mr Thomas Stringer of Maidstone (B) & Mrs Susanna Innes of Kingston (Sp) By Licence.

1733. Octobr. 19th Married Mr George Walker of Faversham (B) & Lydia Smith$^{(1.}$ of *Linx*sted* (S.) By Licence.

1733/4. Jan^{ry} the 4th Married George Oldfield (B) & Sarah Hopkins (S) both of Elham by Licence.

1734. July the 3^d Married Thomas Finnis of St Mary Dover (B) & Elizabeth West of y^s Parish (sp).

1734. Sept^{br} 28th Married Nicholas Deal & Ann Friend.

1734. Sept^{br} 29^h Married George Hills & Hannah Tyrrill.

1736. Sept^{br} 30 ' Married John Claringbull & Joanna Nicholson both of Canterbury by License.

1737. Sept^{br} 20th Married Valentine Wellard & Mary Golder.

1737. Octr 11^t Married Wm Bush & Mary Russell.

1738. July 8th Married Henry Mills & Sarah Turner.

Sept 30^t 1738. Married John Morris & Eliz. Horton.

Apr^l 23 1739. Married Edward Baker & Sarah Streeting.

May 9th 1739. Married Daniel Rofe & Elizabeth Saddleton by Licence.

Dec 10 1739. Married Wm Stokes & Anne Sabine.

Dec 24 1739. Married Robert Sprat & Mary Dadson.

Jany 6 1739-40. Married Richard White & Elizth Buddell.

June 29 1740. Married John Champkin & Rachel Wrakes both of Elmested by Licence.

Sept^{br} 21 1741. Married James Pingle of Eythorn & Elizabeth fford of y^s Parish by Licence.

Oct^{br} 1 1741. Married Isack ffox of ye Parish of Swinfield & Eliz : Baker of y^s Parish by Banns.

---

(1) " Mrs. Lydia Smith." *(a)* * " Lynsted " (Marriage Licence).

Oct^{hr} 11 1741.   Married John Church of Lower Hardres & Sarah Hopkins of y^s Parish by Banns.

Oct^{hr} 31 1741.   Married Thomas Birch of the Parish of Barham & Elizabeth Dadson of y^s Parish, By Banns.

Nov 18: 1743.   Thomas Laws & Elizabeth Sabine, Both of this Parish by Banns.

ffeb^{ry} 9^h 1744.   Married John Bean of this Parish & Rebecca Hogben of Stelling Parish By Licence.

October ye 15th1744.   Married John Hogben & Elizabeth Finns.

April 19 1745.   Married Wm Homes & Mary Beer, Sojourners.

Augst. 7th 1745.   Married Abraham Baker & Elizabeth Quested, both of this Parish by Banns.

Oct^{br}2. 1745.   Married George Pilcher & Margaret Browning.

Ocs 10 1745 Married Edward fford & Jane Sprat.

March 2^d 1745/6.   Married Thomas Collar & Sarah[1] Brockman.

[*End of the Marriages in the first Register Book.*

---

[1] " Mary." *(a)*

MARRIAGES.

[*SECOND REGISTER BOOK.*]

Aprill 10th 1746. Married Philip Lemon & Margaret Minter by License.

May 18th 1746. Married Edward Browning & Parnell West by Banns.

July ye 6th 1746. Married John Clark & Alice Watson both of St. Andrews Cant. by License.

July ye 22^d 1746. Married William Monro & Jane Tunbridge by Licence.

May ye 21st 1747. Married Richd. Castleden and Elizabeth Law by Banns.

Ap^{r.} 25. 1748. Married Wm. Pettit of ye Parish of Chillenden & Mary Laurence of this Parish by Banns.

Dec^{br} ye 26. 1748. Married William West and Eleanor Renolds both y^s Parish, by Banns.

Augst 27th. Married Thos Hills of the Parish of Sandwich and Mary Kingsford of Ash. by License.

March ye 18 1749. Married John Marsh of the parish of Bishopsbourne & Susanna Arnold of this Parish by Bans.

Octr 2^d 1750. Married Wm. Kingsford of the Parish of Lydden & Eliz: Ellenden of this parish by Banns.

Octr ye 18 1750. Thomas Browning & Eliz: Palmer were married by Banns.

BR. : FAUSSETT, Curate.

Nov: ye 1st 1752. Thomas Browning and Ann Hogbin both of this Parish were married by Banns.

Oct: 11. 1753. John Smith and Elizabeth Hall, both of this Parish were married by Banns.

BRYⁿ FAUSSETT, Curate.

[*End of Marriages in the Second Register Book.*]

MARRIAGES.

[*1775*—*1812*.]

1755. Sep 28. Daniel Quested. & Martha Tatnall, of Minster, Thanet, by Licence.

1756. Nov. 14. Thomas Browning &. Elizabeth Mihils.

1757. Oct. 19. John Fagge (Yeoman†) of Barham, & Mary Stokes (of Nethersole in this Parish†).

1759. Oct. 24. Thomas Court & Catharine Sabine, by Licence.

1760. Feb. 14. Thomas Kingsmill. w. (Yeoman†) & Ann Neam.

1760. Ap. 20. Abraham Whitnall of Barham & Susannah Sharpe.

1761. Dec. 29. Thomas Castle & Elizabeth Sprat by Licence.

1762. Jan 10. James Williams & Ann Birch.

1762. Oct. 19. Gibbon Ladd of Wotton & Margaret Godden.

1763. Ap. 16. Henry Spaine & Elizabeth Mutton.

1763. Aug 23 Henry Attwood of Upper Hardres & Susannah Simpson.

1763. Nov. 24. Richard Ratclif w. & Mary Sabine, by Licence.

1763. Dec. 6. James Brooks of Adisham & Elizabeth Lawes.

1764. Ap. 5. John Mutton & Elizabeth Dilnot, by Licence.

1764. Oct. 7. Edward Ruttley, St Mary's Dover & Elizabeth Browning, w.

1765. Oct. 26. Daniel Smith & Alice Mutton.

1765. Oct. 31. William Laurence of Bridge & Sarah Church.

1766. Dec. 22. James Chapman & Elizabeth Stewart.

1768. May 25. Michael Fox, & Judith Sutton.

1768. June 7. John Pilcher, w. & Ann Atwood, w.

---

* The Marriages from this point down to 1837, when the present form of Registration commenced, are copied from the two Register Books as ordered respectively by 26. George II. (1754) and 52. George III. (1812). They are here given with the following abbreviations :— the names of witnesses and of the officiating Clergy are omitted ; residence is only stated when either of the persons was from another parish ; when not specified as "by license," the marriage was "after banns"; the letter w. after a name signifies widower or widow.

† From the Register of Banns.

1769. Jan. 21. John Wood. w. & Jane Mutton.

1769. Sept. 30. William Wellard of Adisham & Elizabeth Rye.

1769. Oct. 17. Edward Kemp of Upper Hardres & Hannah Keeler.

1769. Nov. 4. Thomas Beer & Elizabeth Swain, w.

1769. Dec. 26. Richard Arnold of Goodnestone & Elizabeth Safery.

1770. May 26. William Mutton & Elizabeth Smith.

1770. Oct. 6. Thomas Barrett & Sarah Browning, by Licence.

1770. Oct 13. Henry Ellet of Ospringe & Mary Terry.

1772. Aug 31. Richard Thomas of Barham & Susanna Chandler.

1773. Feb. 16. Richard Rose & Margaret Baker.

1773. May 29. Joseph Cobb of Patricksbourn & Sarah Sutton.

1774. Jan. 22. George Newport of Acris & Parnell Browning—a minor, with consent of her Father Edward Browning, by licence.

1774. Oct 12. James Pearse of Nonington & Mary Rogers.

1775. March 16. Joseph Higgens of Barham & Mary Toms, by Licence.

1775. May 4. William Pout w. of St Mary Bredman, Canterbury & Mary White, by Licence.

1775. Sept. 26 Robert Ford & Ann Shaw of Wymenswold.

1776. Aug 12. William Halladay of Chilham & Ann Nash, by Licence.

1776. Oct. 12. Austin Spain & Ann Lawrence.

1776. Nov. 7. John Sargent Stonham of St Margaret, Canterbury & Mary Hobday, by Licence.

1779. March 6. William Wraight of Barham & Mary Smith.

1779. March 17. Henry Collison & Mary Beer, by Licence.

1779. Ap. 5. James Beer of Ripple & Mary Bottler.

1779. Aug 22. William Makey of Nonnington & Ann Rigden, by Licence.

1779. Oct. 14. Edward Ford & Mary Belsey.

1779. Dec. 9. Charles Nairn of Cranbrook Esqre & Philadelphia Balderstone, by Licence.

1779. Dec. 18. William Dine & Elizabeth Baker.

1781. Nov 12. John Argar of Elham & Mary Fordred.

1782. Ap. 27. Thomas Ford and Ann Green.

1783. May 26. Stephen Dunguy & Frances Webb.

1783. Dec 31. Henry Mummery & Elizabeth Elgar, by Licence.

1785. Nov. 20. Thomas Worringham & Hannah Castle.

1786. Aug 13. John Dine & Sarah Castle.

1786. Sept. 23. Edward Kelson of Kensington, Middlesex & Susanna Brumhead by Licence.

1786. Sept. 26. Robert Beal of Barham & Ann Holness.

1788. Oct. 14. John Tyrrell of Barham & Ann Kemp.

1789. May 19. Henry Sutton & Ann Castle of Barham.

1789. Dec. 27. William Marshal of Elham & Elizabeth Scot.

1790. Feb. 10. James Mutton, w. & Ann Oinn, w.

1791. Oct. 20. William Terry, w. & Ann Collard.

1791. Dec. 20. William Goldfinch of Hoath & Sarah Horton by Licence.

1792. Nov 22. Christopher Wood, "minor with consent of his Mother Jane Wood widow & Mary Marsh of the Parish of Stelling Spinster, Minor with consent of Henry Marsh her Father"—by Licence.

1793. July 14. Thomas Finnis & Catherine Hulks of Barham.

1795. Nov. 16. Isaac Bernand & Sarah Scott.

1797. Jan. 21. Thomas Finn & Sarah Pilcher.

1797. Oct 3. William Whaley, w. of St Dunstans in the West, London & Sarah Delahay, by licence.

1797. Oct. 17. Joseph Harris of St Margaret in the City of Canterbury & Elizabeth Wood.

1799. March 30. Robert Featherston & Sarah Goldfinch. w.

1800. Feb. 13. Edward Mutton & Mary Kingsmill, by Licence.

1800. July 12. William Adams & Sarah Finn w.

1800. July 20. Henry Maxted & Winifred Collard.

1800. Oct 19. Ingram Willis of Barham & Elizabeth Pilcher.

1803. Oct 8. Thomas Ellen of Barham & Susanna Finnis.

1804. Ap. 30. William Sawkins & Jane Hart.

1804. Nov. 22. John Garner of Patrixbourne & Mary Steddy, by Licence.

1805. Feb. 14. William Jarman of Barham & Mary Mutton.

K

1805. Feb. 23. John Newport & Ann Paye.
1806. June 5. John Robins & Susannah Hogbin.
1807. Ap. 20. James Culmer & Sarah Elvery, by License.
1808. Feb 27. Valentine Laker of Barham & Ann Hogbin.
1808. Oct 1. Thomas Ford & Rebecca Barton.
1808. Nov. 5. William Cannaby, w. of Nonnington & Hannah Green, by Licence.
1809. May 22. John Willis of Adisham & Francis Rickwood.
1809. June 26. Richard Webb. of Walmer, & Susannah Richards.
1810. Nov. 24. John Dines & Betsy Spain.
1811. Oct. 12. Edmund Files & Mary Pilcher.
1811. Dec 19. Henry Brown & Cælia Jourdan.
1812. Nov 3. Thomas Middleton of Elham & Frances Daniels.

MARRIAGES.

[*1813*—*1837.*]

1813. Aug. 8. Richard Hawkins & Mary Powell.
1813. Sept. 5. William Hyder of Nackington & Mary Brice.
1813. Oct 23. Valentine Laker of Barham & Sarah Baker.
1813. Nov. 25. William Featherstone of Barham & Elizabeth Browning, by License.
1814. July 21. James Dodd of Little Hardres & Ann Maria Baker, by License.
1817. Nov 25. Thomas May of St Laurance in Thanet & Mary Ann Fagg.
1818. Feb. 28. James Dawkins & Elizabeth Brooks.
1818. Sept. 29. John Collard Sankey of Barham & Mary Ann Boys, by License.

* See foot-note, page 103.

1818. Nov. 26. Champion Edward Branfill & Ann Eliza Hammond of St. James Dover, by License.

1819. Ap. 14. George Marshall of Barham & Mary Dines.

1819. Oct 14. William Richards and Sarah Attwood.

1819. Nov. 6. Robert Suters of St James Dover & Elizabeth Benefild.

1822. Ap. 18. Thomas Harrison Clerk & Jemima Elizabeth Branfill of Barham by License.

1824. Feb. 11. John Bevan & Maria Truman.

1824. Oct 13. James Finch Kite of Upper Hardres & Harriet Brooker.

1825. Jan 25. Richard Knock & Elizabeth Wraight of Womens-wold. by License.

1825. Feb. 15. William Rousal & Ann Pilcher.

1825. Feb. 15. Richard Ransley of the Borough of Longport near Canterbury and Charlotte Widgeon, by License.

1825. Ap. 9. John Spratt of Staple & Sarah Benefield.

1825. Sept 1. Thomas Coulter & Mary Rivers, of Holy Cross, Westgate, Canterbury.

1825. Oct 15. William Minter of Hardres & Mary Philpott.

1825. Oct 22. Jesse Pilcher & Hannah Mutton, w.

1826. Oct. 13. Thomas Fagg of Barham & Charlotte Pilcher.

1826. Dec. 23. John Benefield & Elizabeth Foster, of Barham.

1827. Sep. 18. Henry Shrubsole of Denton & Anne Fagg.

1827. Oct 18. Henry Morgan of Bishopsbourne & Charlotte Simmons.

1828. Nov. 17. George Ford & Mary Day.

1830. Oct 24. Thomas Soles & Grace Marsh.

1831. Ap. 30th Edward Ford & Mary Curd.

1831. July 17. Thomas Hollarday & Sarah Smith.

1831. Oct 16. Henry Walters & Esther Howard.

1832. Sept 10 Edward Knocker of St James, Dover & Elizabeth Sarah Martha Bartlett. by Licence.

1832. Oct. 23. James Wilson & Elizabeth Coulthard by Licence.

1833. Jan. 26. John Philpot & Sarah Hall.

1833. Feb 26. John Creed & Elizabeth Beer by Licensc.

1833. Ap. 6. Thomas Ford & Harriett Carey.

1833. Aug 21. Stephen Knott & Sarah Rye.

1834. Ap. 1. Joseph Higgins of Upper Hardres & Susanah Borton.

1834. May 10. William Rye & Mary Dawkins.

1834. May 10. John Deal of Barham & Mary Dawkins.

1834. Sept 1. Stephen Kennett & Maria Measby.

1835. Aug 28. John Sisars & Hester Philpot.

1835. Nov 2. Richard Rose of Barham & Eliza Ann File.

1835. Nov 17. Thomas Rayner & Henrietta Swan.

1837. Ap. 27. Thomas Marsh of Eastry and Eliza Colthup.

REGISTER OF BANNS.*

Thomas Kingsmill, yeoman & Elizabeth Tucker of Woodnesborough. Ap. 7. 1754.

John Goldfinch. Yeoman & Margaret Gibbs of Wingham. Jan 4. 1756.

John Laurence, Labourer & Mary Baker of Barham. Sept. 23 1759.

John Smison Labourer & Ann Eames of St. Mildred's Canterbury. Sept 14 1760.

Richd Belsey Labourer & Mary Sprat of Bridge. Dec 7. 1760.

Willm Knight & Mary Taylor of Lower Hardress Feb. 22. 1761.

Peter Jacob & Mary Bartlett of Northbourne. Feb. 20. 1762.

William Jackson & Elizabeth Sutton of Bishopsbourne. Aug. 14. 1763.

Stephen Finn of Whitstable & Elizabeth Whitehead. Ap. 8. 1764.

Richard Keeler of BishopsBourne & Martha Sutton. Sept. 9 1764.

John Castle & Mary Baker of Upper Hardress. Jan 27 1765.

* To save repetition the Banns of those married at Kingstone are omitted. For abbreviations refer to footnote, page 103. The date here given is always the first time of publication.

William White & Martha Peel of Smeed. Nov. 24. 1765.

John Wood of Barham & Elizabeth Webb. Dec 15 1765.

William Spratt & Mary Belsey of Knowlton. March 30. 1766.

John Finis & Mary Spiser of Bishopsbourne. April 6 1766.

Francis Pilcher of Upper Hardress & Amy White. Sept. 25 1768.

Richard Laurance & Ann Bece of New Romney. Jan. 8. 1769.*

William Newport w. & Elizabeth Friend w. of Barham. Sept. 15 1771.

Richard White & Mary Hulke of Bishopsbourne. Oct 13. 1771.

Joseph Borton & Catharine Alderstone of Deal. Dec 6 1772.

Edward Browning & Mary Collard of Nackington. Sept. 24 1775.

Bartholomew Collard & Mary Laurence of Upper Hardres. Nov. 29. 1778.

Richard Sutton & Mary Bushel of Patrixbourne. Sept. 17, 1780.

John Maple & Ann Stuple of Littlebourne. July 20. 1783.

Richard Cooper of Barham & Sarah Pink. Oct. 19. 1783.

William Wraight & Mary Wootton of St James in Dover. Aug 21 1785.

John Pepper of Barham & Mary Hopkins. Aug 10 1788.

Andrew Morgan of Nonington & Elizabeth Peirce. June 13 1790.

John Horton & Mary Miles of Barham. Sept 5 1790.

Robert Mutton & Alice Bean of Cheriton June 5. 1791.

William Rye of Bishopsbourne & Mary Keeler Dec 30. 1792.

Thomas Holmes & Sarah Daniels of Lower Hardres. June 29. 1794.

William Knott of Lyminge & Mary Holaday. Feb. 7. 1795.

Joseph Dugleys Soldier & Mary Cobling of St. Pauls Canterbury. Aug 30. 1795.

William Williams & Elizabeth Wood of Elmsted. Sept. 18, 1796.

John Horrell, a Private in the Royal Cornwal Militia, now of Barham & Charlotte Holneys. June 25 1797.

William Adams & Mary Rutland of Bishopsbourne. June 16. 1799.

James Yates. a Private in the 9th Regt. of Foot & of this parish & Elizabeth Davis. Aug. 11. 1799.

---

* No entry of 3rd time of publication.

Edward Jones a Private in the 9th Regt. of Foote, in this parish & Martha Jones. Aug 18. 1799.

Thomas Terry & Sarah Lilly of Bridge. Aug 18. 1799.

John Lawton a Private in the Camp & Mary Winter. Sept. 1. 1799.*

William Todd a Private in the Camp & Mary Mutton. Sept. 1. 1799.*

Joseph Tite a private in the Camp & Elizabeth Amis. Sept 1. 1799.*

Richard Standley. a private in the Camp. & Ann Weade. Sept 1. 1799.*

John Baker of Wootton & Ann Leake. June 1. 1800.

William Thiselton & Mary Wood of St Margaret in Canterbury· Sept. 21 1800.

Edward Hannden of Ickham & Mary Brice Sept. 13. 1801.

John Stupple & Sarah Penny. Sept. 20 1801.

George Philpot & Sarah Bushell of Beaksbourn. Sept. 19 1802.

Henry Williams and Mary Wiles of Barham. Sept 19. 1802.

William Higgens & Susannah Marsh of Barham. Sept. 26. 1802.

John Robins & Elizabeth Page of Barham. Jan 29. 1804.

Wiiliam Henry Pritchard & Elizabeth Crow of St. Leonard's, Hythe. Sept. 15 1805.

William May & Sarah Cobb of Harbledown. Nov. 9 1806.

William Osborn & Mary Palmer of Wickhambreux. Jan 4 1807.

Daniel Dawkins & Ann Burvill of Womenswold. July 3. 1808.

Henry Honess & Harriett Ladams of Barham. March 29. 1812.

James Robins & Susanna Spain of Barham. Aug 16. 1812.

John Pilcher w. & Elizabeth Fox of St. Peter's Isle of Thanet 19 Sept 1813.

Launcelot Spain of Deal & Maria Sennock.†

William Atwood & Elizabeth Broadbridge of Upper Hardres.†

William Baker & Sophia Rye of Nonington. May 18. 1817.

Thomas Luke & Sarah Parker of Bishopsbourne. Oct 5. 1817.

John Pilcher w. & Benedicta Wilson of Ash. Sept 13. 1818.

* No entry of 3rd time of publication.
† No dates of publication.

Henry Sutton & Elizabeth Field. Oct 18. 1818.

James Attwood & Sarah Chapman of Barham. March 3. 1822.

Thomas Robins & Margaret Pain of River. Sept. 7 1822.

John Cotton & Mary Belsey of Thanington. Sept 14 1822.

Henry Morris & Mary Morgan. March 2. 1823.

Elizabeth Clayson & William Fillman of Bishopsbourne. March 14 1824.

Thomas Pilcher, St. George Hanover Square & Sarah Ann Shoveller. Oct 3. 1824.

Henry Austin & Ann Knott. of Nonington. Oct 8th 1826.

Thomas Marsh & Susannah Smith of Sheperdswell. July 29 1827.

Thomas Oliver w. & Mary Holman of Charlton. Dec 2nd 1827.

John Robbins & Amelia Daniels of Barham. Sept. 20. 1829.

Thomas Waters & Sarah Higgins of Barham. Sept. 11. 1831.

William Henry Beer & Sarah Nash of Yalden. Sept. 16 : 1831.

Henry Seath & Susannah Higgens of Barham. Sept 23 : 1832.

John Bailey & Mary Hogbin of Elham. Feb 24 : 1833.

William Mount & Fanny Daniels of Barham. Dec 6 : 1835.

Henry Higgins & Susannah Harvey. of Barham. July 31. 1835.

BURIALLES, 1558.

[FIRST REGISTER BOOK.]

September 1558.
1558. 20 daye was buryed John Dennewood *anno* supra.

October.
5 daye wase buryed Annis Sturdaye *anno* sup*ra*.
26 daye wase buryed William Barton *anno* supra.

December.
25 daye wase buryed Egedius Wells *anno* supra.

Maye 1559.
1559. 6 daye wase buryed John Marten *anno* supra.

June.
9 daye was buryed John ffoorde *anno* supra.

ffebruary 1561.
13 daye wase buryed Katherine Cole *anno* sup*ra*.
16 daye was buryed Mildred ffeild *anno* sup*ra*.

Marche.
14 daye wase buryed Jervice Davie anno sup*ra*.

July 1562.
1562. 3 daye wase buryed John Nethersole *anno* sup*ra*.
19 daye wase buryed John Pecker anno sup*ra*.
24 daye wase buryed Annis Hopkine *anno* sup*ra*.

July 1563.
1563. 20 daye[1] was buryed Jone Bradshawe
daughter of Grygorie Bradshawe *anno* sup*ra*.
The same daye[2] also was buryed Thomas Denne *anno* su*pra*.

---

[1] " 16 July," " Jone Bradshute." (*a*)   [2] " 16 July." (*a*)

That daye[1] also was buryed Robert Sheperd anno supra.

November.
10 daye wase buryed Annis Cooke anno supra.

ffebruarye.
4 daye wase buryed Maryan Wilcocke anno supra.

Marche 1564.
1564. 30 daye wase buryed William Gould anno supra.

June.
24 daye wase buryed Thomas Denne anno supra.

June 1565.
1565. 1 daye wase buryed Elizabethe Johnson anno supra.
10 daye wase buryed John Gryme anno supra.

October.
28 daye wase buryed Stephen Blasden anno supra.

ffebruary.
23 daye wase buryed Alice Johnson
daughter of William Johnson anno supra.

December 1566.
1566 * 20 daye was buryed Alice Sturdye[2]
& George Wardrop[3] anno Supra.
(. . . . .)[4]

---

[1] " 21 July." (a)

[2] " 18 Dec. Alicea Sturdi uxor rob. Sturdi." (a)

[3] " 10 March Georgius Wardropp maritus." (a)

[4] " 23 Dec. Gulielmus Pashlei serviens Gulielmo Denn." (a)   (Not in the Register.)

* The following presentment appears in the Transcript (a) for this year.
"These be the Churchwardens Thomas Young & Richard Turner."
"Also we present to you the state of our Church wh. is out of"
"good reparation Rayning in dyvers places thereof."
"And lykewise the persones house out of reparation gretly "
"of the wh. we desire redresse. All other things Is well & in good order."

Marche 1567.

27 daye was buryed Simon Rugley[1] anno supra.

* ROBBE. BASSOCKE ⎫
JOHN HOPKYN ⎰ Churchwardens.

December 1567.

1567. 5 daye[2] was buryed Christofer Packer
sonne of Roger Packer anno supra:

28 daye was buryed John Julyan[3] anno supra.

June 1569.

1569. 14 daye was buryed Thomasine Baylie anno supra.

August.

22 daye was buryed Christian Underdonne widow anno
supra.

January.

5 daye was buryed Thomas Perry sonne
of John Perrye anno supra:

24 daye was buryed Henry Hamerton anno supra.

Marche.

2 daye was buryed the wife of
Thomas Hopkine anno supra:

January 1570.

1570. 2 daye was buryed Danyell Hunt
sonne of William Hunte anno supra.

ffebruary.

14 daye was buryed Isacke Burden
sonne of Thomas Burden anno supra:

Maye 1571.

1571. 7 daye was buryed Davie Sherman
sonne of Robert Sherman anno supra.

---

[1] " 20 March Simon ruglie maritus." (a)   [2] " 5 Nov." (a)
[3] " whoes dwellinge was in the parishe of Sithingborne." (a)
* See footnote on Page 2.

July.

13 daye was buryed Robert Sturdye[1] a*nno* sup*ra*.

ffebruarye.

13 daye was buryed Thomas Milborne[2] a*nno* sup*ra*.

Aprell 1572.

1572. 19 daye was buryed Grygorye Younge
sonne of Thomas Younge anno sup*ra*.

August.

31 daye was buryed John Baker a*nno* sup*ra*.

September.

9 daye was buryed Mildred Cullen
daughter of John Culline a*nno* sup*ra*.

October.

13 daye was buryed Alice gould
wife of Thomas Gould anno: sup*ra*.

21 daye was buried William Denne
sonne of Thomas Denne a*nno* sup*ra*.

Januarye.

27 daye was buryed Martha Bradshawe
daughter of Grigory Bradshawe a*nno* sup*ra*.

ROBB. BASSOCKE }Churchw^rdens.
JOHN HOPKYN

ffebruary 1572.

1572. 20 daye was buryed Alice Haule
danghter of Thomas Hale anno supra.

Maye 1573.

1573. 7 daye was buryed Thomas Gould anno sup*ra*.

November.

20 daye [3] was buryed widow Groome a*nno* sup*ra*.

---

[1] "An olde man." *(a)*   [2] "A pore old man." *(a)*
[3] "4th Dec. Alyce Groome widow." *(a)*

September.

29 daye[1] was buryed Elinor Perrye
wife of John Perrye anno supra:

December.

1 daye was buryed James Denne anno supra.

12 daye was buryed John Bently[2] anno supra.

30 daye was buryed Thomas Gryme *anno* supra.

ffebruarye.

19 daye was buryed Thomas Sylke[3] a*nno* sup*ra*.

Marche.

22 daye was buryed Ellis Stander[4] *anno* supra.

Aprill 1576.

1576.   30 daye was buryed William Nethersole *anno* supra.

September.

13 daye was buryed Vincent Nethersole anno sup*ra*.

November.

2 daye was buryed Jone Nethersole
daughter of John Nethersole a*nno* supra :

Julye 1577.

1577.   27 daye was buryed Sara Pett
daughter of John Pett anno supra :

September.

29 daye was buryed Marye Denne
daughter of Vincent Denne [5] a*nno* sup*ra*.

ffebruary.

18 daye was buryed Jone Denne
daughter of Thomas Denne [6] anno sup*ra*.

---

[1] " 29th Dec." *(a)*   [2] " Servant to Wm. Blackwoode." *(a)*

[3] " Servant to Grigory Bradshawe, gent." *(a)*

[4] " Ellis Standarde widowe." *(a)*   [5] " Gent." *(a)*   [6] " Gent." *(a)*

Marche 1578.

25 daye was buryed Thomas Denne
sonne of James Denne anno sup*ra*,

Maye.

13 daye was buryed Henry Bradshaw
sonne of Grygorie Bradshawe a*nno* sup*ra*
16 daye was buryed ffrancis Boughton
sonne of John Boughton anno sup*ra*.
25 daye was buryed Richard Cooly
sonne of Michaell Coolye anno sup*ra*.

ROBB BASSOCKE
JOHN HOPKYN } Churchwardens.

October 1578.

19 daye was buryed Richard Rugley a*nno* sup*ra*.
27 daye was buryed John Vier[1] anno sup*ra*.

Aprell 1579.

1579.   24 daye was buryed Annis Denne
widowe of James Denne a*nno* sup*ra*.

Julye.

9 daye was buryed Isabell Mughole
wife of James[2] Mughole anno sup*ra*:

August.

9 daye was buryed Jone Peerson
daughter of Vincent Peerson anno sup*ra*.
26 daye was buryed Robert Standard a*nno* sup*ra*.

ffebruarye.

3 daye was buryed Dennis Hopkine
daughter of Thomas Hopkine a*nno* sup*ra*.
28 daye was buryed Jone Hopkine
daughter of John Hopkine anno sup*ra*.

[1] "A souldier an Esixe man." *(a)*
[2] "Thomas." *(a)*

December 1580.

1580. 22 daye was buryed John Rugley
sonne of Robert Rugleye anno sup*ra*.

31 daye was buryed James Rugleye
sonne of Robert Rugley. anno sup*ra*.

January.

1 daye was buryed Christofer Sayer
sonne of James Sayer Anno supra:

20 daye was buryed Jone Kennet[1] a*nno* sup*ra*.

Marche.

5 daye was buryed Elizabethe Sayer
daughter of James Sayer a*nno* sup*ra*.

November 1581.

1581. 29 daye was buryed William Bradshaw
sonne of Grigorye Bradshaw a*nno* sup*ra*.

November 1582.

1582. 2 daye was buryed Thomas Rickard
sonne of John Rickard anno supra:

ffebruarye.

22 daye was buryed Jane Sayer
daughter of James Sayer a*nno* sup*ra*.

Marche.

6 daye was buryed Margarett Boykett
daughter of Elyas Boykett anno sup*ra*.

Maye 1583.

1583. 4 daye was buryed Annis Baldocke
daughter of William Baldocke a*nno* supra.

June.

3 daye was buryed Annis Younge
wife of Thomas Younge anno sup*ra*.

ROBBE. BASSOCKE } Churchwarden.
JOHN HOPKYN }

---

[1] "Wydowe, servante to Symon Casey." *(a)*

October, 1583.

1583. 20 daye was buryed Susan Rushe
daughter of Robert Rushe [1] anno supra :

ffebruary 1584.

1584. 2 daye was buryed Susan Haddine
daughter of Jeffery Haddine anno supra.

Aprell 1585.

1585. 11 daye was buryed Julyan Sturdye anno supra.

June.

15 daye was buryed Thomas Younge anno supra.

July.

6 daye was buryed Dennis Edgar
wife of Thomas Edgare [2] anno supra.

September.

6 daye was buryed Mathew Rayner anno supra.

December.

1 daye was buryed Thomasine Gouldfinche
servante to Robert Denne anno supra :

January.

20 daye was buryed John Sayer
sonne of James Sayer anno supra.

Aprell 1587. [3]

1587. 21 daye was buryed Alice Hastlyne*
wife of John Hastlyn anno supra.

---

[1] "Susanna Rugleye daughter of Robert Rugley." (a)

[2] "Dennis Ergar ye wyfe of George." (a)

[3] The following note occurs in the Transcript (a) for 1586.

"We have none buried, thankes we geve to God for it. John
Hastlyn pr'son. Vincent Young Chwden."

* See "John Hastlyn" in the List of Rectors.

June.

23 daye was buryed Silvester Gouldfinche
servante to Robert Denne anno sup*ra*.

September.

5 daye was buryed Alice Milborne [1] a*nno* sup*ra*.

December.

13 daye was buryed John Bunce anno sup*ra*.

ffebruary.

1 daye was buryed Anne Denne widow [2] a*nno* sup*ra*.

2 daye was buryed Agnis Burton[3] anno sup*ra*.

December, 1588.

1588. 15 daye was buryed John Epps[4] a*nno* sup*ra*.

28 daye was buryed Richard Laban a*nno* su*pra*.

July, 1589.

1589. 20 daye was buryed Silvester Rycard a*nno* su*pra*.

October.

29 daye was buryed Mary Bunce
daughter of John Bunce a*nno* supra :

November.

26 daye was buryed Mary Rugley[5] a*nno* sup*ra*.

ROBBE BASSOCKE } Churchwardens.
JOHN HOPKYN }

December, 1589.

1589. 2 daye was buryed Thomas Mughole [6] a*nno* sup*ra*.

---

[1] " Alice Mylborne widow." (*a*)

[2] " Maisteris Annis Denn widow." (*a*) [3] "Annis Barton widow." (*a*)

[4] " Servante to S^r· Thomas Wilfoorde." (*a*)

[5] " 29 Nov. Marie Rugley widow. She was kept by her sonn
Robart." (*a*)

[6] " He lyved by ye Almes of ye parishe and the help of his sonne." (*a*)

ffebruary.

9 daye was buryed James Rugley
sonne of Robert Rugleye anno supra :

10 daye was buryed Alice Catton[1]
wife of Robert Catton anno supra :

Maye 1590.

26 daye was buryed William Laban
servante to John Hastlyne anno supra.

June.

1 daye was buryed John Gould sonne
of William Gould Anno supra:

August.

9 daye was buryed Thomas Hopkin anno supra.

July 1591.

1591. 16 daye was buryed Job Odleye anno supra.

September.

23 daye was buryed Mr Vincent
Denne[2] Doctor anno supra :

December.

20 daye was buryed John Coorte
sonne of John Coorte anno supra.

25 daye was buryed Jeffery Haddin anno supra.

ffebruary.

7 daye was buryed William Younge
sonne of William Younge anno supra.

13 daye was buryed Elizabethe Coorte
wife of John Coorte anno supra :

August 1592.

1592. 25 daye was buryed Edward Ricard
sonne of John Ricard anno supra :

---

[1] "She and her husband lyved by ye parishe." (a)
[2] "Doctor of ye civil law." (a)

Marche.

23 daye was buryed Robert Catton
of th age of one hundred & two anno sup*ra*.

Aprell 1593.

1593. 4 daye[1] was buryed John Haddine
sonne of Jefferye Haddin a*nno* supra.

6 daye[1] was buryed Jane Boykett
daughter of Elyas Boykett a*nno* supra.

November.

17 daye was buryed Vincent Younge anno supra.

Marche.

7 daye was buryed Edmond Tristram a*nno* s*upra*.

ROBBE. BASSOCKE } Church Wardens.
JOHN HOPKYNS }

Marche 1594.

10 daye was buryed Alexander Browne[2] a*nno* sup*ra*.

1594. 28 daye was buryed Robert Denne[3] anno supra.

Aprell.

22 daye was buryed John Simons[4] anno sup*ra*.

(. . . . .)[5]

July 1595.

1595. 2 daye was buryed Jone Maple
daughter of Henry Maple anno supra:

4 daye was buryed Elizabeth Maple a*nno* supra.

---

[1] "Also 2 children buried Jane boyket 14th April & John Haddyn
4th May." (*a*)

[2] " Servante to John Hastlyn." (*a*)

[3] " Of Denhill." (*a*) Appendix XVI.

[4] " Servant to Sir Thomas Wilfoord." (*a*)

[5] "6 May was buried Jeffery Haddyn the sonn of Jeffery." (*a*) (Not
in the Register.)

August.
3 daye was buryed Margaret Rugley
wife of Robert Rugleye anno supra.

September.
22 daye was buryed Jone Rugley
daughter of Richard Rugley anno supra :

December.
10 daye was buryed Katherine Denne *anno supra.*

September 1596.
1596.   1 daye was buryed Thomas Chamber
sonne of Edward Chamber anno s*u*pra.

ffebruarye.
13 daye was buryed Christofer Winter[1] a*nno* supra.

Aprell 1597.
1597.   10 daye was buryed William Wood
sonne of Abraham Wood anno supra :

Marche.
25 daye was buryed Jone Sayer
wife of James Sayer anno supra :

August.
22 daye was buryed Anne Maple
daughter of Henry Maple. anno supra :

* By me JOHN HASTLYN p'son.

ROBERT BASSOCK Churchwarden.
JOHN HOPKYN Churchwarden.

1598.   15 of Octob*er* Vinsent Younge y° sonne of Vinsent
Younge disseased.
24 was buried George Bassocke the ssonne of Robart Bassocke.

---

[1] " ffarmar to ye parsonage of Kyngstone." (*a*)
* See footnote on Page 22.

1599. The 25. of Marche was buried Rychard Brigge a blynde man.[1]

The 24 of Aprill was buried Thomas Denn ye soonn of Wyll*iam*.

The 17. of June was buried John Denn ye soone of Wyllya*m* also.

The 19. was buryed John Coorte ye sonne of John.

1599. June 17.

June 17 was buried Jhn. Denn the Soone of Wyllyam.

1600. July 27 was buried Elenore Boulton :

August 27 was buried ye sonne of . . . . . .[2] Wrathe of Elam who came to his death by fallinge fro*m* his horse.

August 28 was buried John Hastlinge * late p*ar*son of Kingston.

1601.

August 3. Jane y^e daughter of Richard Gilman buried.

Noveb. 28. was buried Dorythie the wife of Richard Rugley.

Janua : 30. was buried the daughter of Roberte Robinson which died wi*th*out baptisme.

1602.

Marche 26 Was buried John Courte.

July 29 Was buried Lucy the daughter of William Denn.

$$(. \quad . \quad . \quad . \quad .)^{(3)}$$

1603.

May 15 : Was buried Jeremie Rugley.

An : 1604.

Was buried . . . . . the daughter of William Golde.

An : 1605.

Marche 29 Was buried Richarde Rugley.

Septemb : 26 Was buried Abraham Woodd.

---

[1] " That lyved by ye Almes of the Parish." (*a*)

[2] " Henry." (*a*)

[3] "An. 1602. The Lady Wilforde, wife to Sr Thomas Wilforde Knight buried Aug 9." *(a)* (Not in the Register.)

* Appendix xv.

An : 1606.

Marche 27 was buried the wife of Robert Sherman.

Novembr. 14 Was buried Roberte ye sonne of Gregorie Smithson.

An : 1607 May 7 Was buried Daniel the sonne of John Heringe.

January 4. was buried John Cray ye sonne of John Cray.

An : 1608. Januarie 24 was buried John Upton.

March : 1 was buried Mary Woodd the daughter of John Woodd.

March : 7 was buried Anthony Woodd the sonne of John Woodd.

1609. April 5. was buried Silvester Goore.

April 6. was buried Roberte Davis.

June 14. was buried Elsabethe Broomans.

Octobr. 5. was buried Martha ye daughter of Thomas George.

Visitat. Octob. 10.

Noueb : 1. was buried Thomas Ingester the sonne of Timothie Ingester.

An : 1610.   Visitat. April 24.   Visitat : Sep : 25.

Novembr 12 was buried Sr Thomas Wilforde Knight.[1]

December 12. was buried Thomas Page.

An : 1611.   May 4 was buried Mrs Joane Denn Widdowe.

Noveb : 28. was buried Robert Rickwood ye sonne of John Rickwoode.

January. 7. was buried the sonne of Edmunde Uden unchristened.

January 12. was buried Silvester Tayler.

March 3. was buried John Browninge.

Visitat 28. April.

An : 1612.   May 13. was buried Elsabethe Mason ye daughter of Antony Mason.

June 9. was buried Mr Matthewe Nicols clarke.*

July 24. was buried Jane ye daughter of John Simons.

Septemb. 28. was buried ye sonne (not christened) of Richard Prebble.

---

[1] "the elder." (a)

* See " Daniel Nichols" in the List of Rectors.

Octob : 10 was buried y⁰ wife of Richard Preble.

Noveb : 17 was buried Vincent yᵉ sonne of William Denn.

Visitat. April 21.   An : 1613.

July 21 was buried Elsabethe yᵉ wife of Mʳ John Nethersole. [1]

August 30. was buried John Laurence.   Visitat. 28. of September

Octob : 13 was buried Thomasine yᵉ wife of Edwarde Robinson.

An 1614.   Visitat. April 30.   Visitat. Sep. 28.

March. 9. was buried James Sayer.

An. 1615.   January 25. was buried Richarde Hopkin yᵉ sonne of John Hopkin.

Visitat. April 10.   An : 1616.

April 22. was buried Thomas Brabson.

June yᵉ 1 was buried William Golde.

July 22 was buried John Heeringe.   Visitat. Octob. 1. An : 1616.

An : 1617.   April 6 was buried Isabel wife of John Rickwoode. Visitat April 30ᵗʰ·

May 19 was buried Elias Boyket.   Visitat Octob : 3.

Octob : 31 was buried Thomas Trice.

Deceb. 5. was buried Ann yᵉ daughter of Mʳ· John Nethersole.

January 22 was buried James yᵉ sonn of James Question.

March 10 was buried Henry Brabson.

Aprill 18 was buried George Rickwood yᵉ sonn of John Rickwood.

Visitat. Ap : 14.   An : 1618.

Septemb. 20 was buried Joane Browninge widdow.

Visitat. 1. of Sep. an : supra.

Novemb. 23 was buried Edward Robinson.

March 18 was buried Mary yᵉ daughter of John Waginer.

Visitat yᶜ 27 of Sep : An. 1619.

Octob. 19. was buried Ann the wife of William Nookes.

Novemᵇ· 3 was buried John the sonn of John Giles.

---

[1] "the younger" (a)

An. 1620.

May 25. was buried Alis Rickwood.

January. 1. was buried Betterice Boyket widdowe.

March 8 was buried William George. Visitat. 10 April.

An 1621. June 16 was buried Robert Sherman.

June. 24. was buried James ye sonne of James Wrath.

July 14 was buried Marget ye daugh : of William Bridgs.

Sep : 16 was buried Ann ye wife of Nicholas Eaton. Visitat. 28 of
Sep :

Deceb 11 was buried. Abraham Castrell.

The 14 of ye same monethe was buried Roger Golde.

Also ye 15 of ye same monethe was buried Philip Cray.

An : 1622.

Noveb : 26 was buried Mother Brabson.

Decemb : 16 was buried John Cray.[1]

Decemb : 26 was buried Ann ye daughter of S^r· Thomas Wilforde,
knight.

The same day was buried Jaine ye wife of John Boyket.

ffebruary 27. was buried Mother Joane Golde.[2]

An : 1623.

May 19. was buried Joane ye daughter of William Allen.

June 20 was buried Repent Biram.[3] Visitat. ye 23 of Septemb.

January 1 was buried John ye sonne of Matthew Shoveler.

An : 1624.

April ye 8 was buried Thomas Browninge.

May ye 5 was buried the wife of Thomas Hastifere.

May ye 8 was buried Stephen ye sonne of Robert Golde.

May 15 was buried Thomas ye sonne of Thomas Hastifere.

July 13 was buried John Hopkin thelder.

---

[1] "householder" (a)

[2] "Joane Gould" (a) "Mother Gould" (b). In the Register a pen
has been drawn through "Mother" & "Joane" written above.

[3] "householder." (a)

August 11 was buried Katherine the daughter of Thomas
Hopkin. Visitat. Sep. 30.

December 16. was buried Roberte Rugley.

January 25 was buried Samuel Mughole.

January 28 was buried William ye sonne of William Sally.

ffebruary 1. was buried Mary ye wife of Samuel Mughole.
Visitat. April 28.

1625.

August 5 was buried Jone ye daughter of Thomas Hopkin.

January 27. was buried widdow Browninge.

1626.

May 18 was buried Mary ye daughter of Thomas Mershe.

July. 6. was buried widdowe Bassocke.

1627.

July 9 was buried Mr John Nethersole.*

August 23. was buried Widowe Hopkin.

January 28 was buried Jeremie ye sonne of William Sally.

ffebruary 12 was buried Martha ye wife of Daniel Nicols parson.

An : 1628.

July 15 was buried Joane ye base borne daughter of John Hopkin
and Joane Ladd.

November 28. was buried widowe Cray.

December. 7 was buried Anthony Mason.

1629.

Novemb. 3. was buried Elizabethe Marshe.

ffebruary 21. was buried Nicholas ye sonne of James Wrathe.

1630.

May 27. was buried Edmond Kingsmeele.

August 14[1] was buried Ursilla ye wife of John Sterlinge.

---

[1] "Aug 24." (b)

* Appendix X.

Sep : 2 was buried James Question.

Octob. 21. was buried Joane the daughter of John Rickwood.

Noveb. 4 was buried Jane ye daugh^t. of John Rickwood the younger.

Novemb. 18. was buried Thomas Budds

December 28 was buried Marget ye daughter of Thomas Kingsmeele.

1631.

November 8 : was buried Jonas ye sonne William Sally.

1632.

June 6. was buried William Grant.

Novemb^r 29th was buried Mr Daniell Nicols Parson of this parish.

Stephen Barber the sonne of John Barber was buried the 30th of Novemb^r.

Joana Richard was buried the 20 of December 1632.

1633.

Christian Fisher Widdow was buried the 23^d of May.

Katherine the wife of Richard Wood buried ye 13th of June.

Elizabeth the daughter of Henry Peirce buried ye 20 of June.

Richard Bonham the son of Nicholas Bonham was buryed Septemb^r the first, 1633.

Mrs Thamsin Denne Widdowe was buried the 20th of February.

Richard Wood was buried the 23^d. of February.

Paul the sonne of Paul Browning was buried the 9th of March.

1634.

Thomas Hopkin was buried the 23^d of May.

Richard Solly the sonne of William buried the 21 of August.

Thamsin the wife of Nicholas Bonham was buried the 25th of August.

Joane the wife of Robert Browning was buried the 21. of Novemb.

Elizabeth Wilsford the daughter of Mr James Wilsford Esquire buried the last of December.

Mary the daughter of Richard Trapps was buried the 8th of January.

John Rickwood the Elder was buried the 22ᵈ of January.

James Pittocke yᵉ sonne of John was buried the 9th of February.

John White the sonne of Thomas was buried the 10th of February.

1635.

1635. Margaret the daughter of John Rickwood was buried the 12ᵗʰ of May.

Jane Question the Daughter of Joane Question Widdow buried the 23 of Febru:

1636.

1636. Mary Gold daughter of Robert was buried the 11ᵗʰ of June.

Richard Wraight was buryed the 16ᵈ· day of January.

Anne yᵉ wife Nicholas Wraight was buryed the same day.

John yᵉ sonn of John Sterling was buryed yᵉ 25ᵗʰ of January.

William Oakes was buryed the 24ᵗʰ of March:

1637. Thomas Branchly was buryed yᵉ 30ᵗʰ day of May.

Dorathy yᵉ wife of Mʳ Thomas Denn of Canturbury : Counseller, was buryed the 21 day of August.

James yᵉ son of Sʳ Thomas Baker Knyght was buryed 6ᵗʰ of Septemb.[1]

Widdow Kyngsmell buryed yᵉ 8ᵗʰ day of January.

John Pittock buryed the 11ᵗʰ day of January.

John Barbar buryed ye 12ᵗʰ of January.

1638. John Sheppey was buryed June the first.

Elizabeth yᵉ daughter of Richard ad Ann Traps was buryed June yᵉ 11ᵗʰ·

Prudence ye daughter of Abraham and . . . Rye was buryed the 17ᵗʰ day of August.

Mary yᵉ wife of William Allen was buryed yᵉ 21. of August.

Mannering the Sonn of Mʳ James Wilsford and Elizabeth his wife was buryed the 14ᵗʰ of October.

Pleasant Bunce Widdow was buryed Octob : yᵉ 21.

1639. Thomas Taverner Gentl : was buryed July the 10ᵗʰ·

Richard Wynter was buryed the 4ᵗʰ of Septemb.

---

[1] " Sept. 9ᵗʰ." (b)

1640. John y^e son of John Hedgecock & Margret his wife was buryed y^e 20th February.

Sarah. the daughter of Widdow Branchly buryed

Dennis the wife of William Ladd was buryed January y^e 20$^{th.}$

1641. Davie Byshop's servant buryed Apryll the 9$^{th.}$

John the supposed sonn of John Sheppey buryed Apryll y^e 28$^{th.}$

Ann . . . servant buryed Apryll the 23$^{d.}$

Mary the wife of John Stark of Sterry was buryed May the 2$^{d.}$

Nicholas Wraight of Barrham buryed the . . . of November.

the 15th day of March was buryed a way going man, his name as apear*ing* by his Pass, being ffrancis Nethersole.

1642. The wife of Thomas Grey was buryed March the 27$^{th.}$

May the 2^d was buryed Henry Baker a twin-chyld of Sir Thomas Bakers Knt. and ffrancis his Lady.

September the 7th was buryed John the sonn of William Hopkin and Margrett his wife.

1653. March y^e 19 was buried Sam : sonn of Austen Brenchley and Joane his wife.

1656. August y^e 1^s was buried Tho : Denn Esquire who died at his house in ye city of Canterbury but was interred in the parish of Kingston.

february ye 23 1656 was buried Robert Young of this parish.

1658. March ye 31 was buried John Read of this parish.

1661 was buried upon Aprill ye first of the same yeare Ann the daughter of Thomas and Elizabeth Curt.

(. . . . .)[1]

March ye 8.[2] 1662. was buried Elizabeth Addams daughter of Ralph Addams and Margarett his wife.

March ye 10.[3] 1662 was buried Susanna Addams daughter of Ralph & Margarett Addams.

(. . . . .)[4]

---

[1] " April 20 was buried Wilman daughter of Austin Brenchly & Joan his wife." (a) (Not in the Register.)

[2] " March 20." (b)   [3] " March 24." (b)

[4] " May 23 was buried Samuel son of Austin Brenchley & Joane his wife." (a) (Not in the Register.)

(. . . . .)[1]

Septemb. 13 1663 was buried Thomas Brenchley sonn of Augustine Brenchley & Joan his wife.

NIC DINGLEY Rector ibid.
JOHN COCKLINN Churchwarden.

November 20 1663 was buried Katherine Gammon daughter of Elias & Katherine Gammon.

January 15th. 1663 was buried Margarett Grey, daughter of Thomas and Margarett Gray.

January y[e] 24 of the same yeare was buried Susanna Eps of the parish of Barham.

Feb[r.] y[e] 21. of the same yeare was buried William Hopkin, sonn of William Hopkin.

1664.

May 4 of same yeare was buried y[e] widdow Bridges.

August y[e] 18 of the same yeare was buried Charles Questhead.

Septemb[ris] 9 of y[e] same yeare was buried Elizabeth Ford.

November the 2 was buried . . . . Turner.[2]

Novemb[r] the 4 was buried Margarett Grey.

1665.   April y[e] 12 was buried Mary Sturges.

August y[e] 6 was buried Richard Gibbon. Gent.[3]

August y[e] 21 was buried Thomas Young who died at Ash.

1666.   March the 25 was buried the widdow Boykinn.

Aprill 26 was Buried Thomas Simmans.[4]

NIC : DINGLY, Rector.
THO : ATTWOOD, Churchwarden.

Octob. : 15 of y[e] same yeare was buried Richard Tallis y[e] elder.[5]

Octob. 31 of y[e] same yeare was buried John Gold.[6]

---

[1] " Oct 4 was buried Mary daughter of Edward Wood." (a)   (Not in the Register.)

[2] " Richard Turner of Kingston." (a)

[3] " M[r] Richard Gibbon of Kingstone." (a)

[4] " Thomas Symonds, Housekeeper." (a)   [5] " Housekeeper." (a)

[6] " Bachelor." (a)

1667.   July ye 23 was buried Mary Marsh of ye parish of Barham.

Septemb. 3 was buried the widdow Godden.[1]

1668.   August yᵉ 27 of ye same yeare was buried Stephen Maple who died at Adisham.

1668.   John Sonn of John Saxton & Elizabeth his wife was baptised November ye first of ye same yeare.

Henry Sonn of Henry & Dorothea Ford was baptized November ye 8 of yᵉ same yeare 1668.

1669.   Octobr. 6 ye same yeare was buried Robert Question of ye parish of Barham.[2]

1669.   December yᵉ 11 of yᵉ same yeare was buried Joan Bransley.

1670.   May yᵉ 13 of yᵉ same yeare was Buried John Brown.[3]

August yᵉ 12 of yᵉ same yeare was buried John Hedgcock.[4]

1669.   August 14 of yᵉ same yeare was buried William Gibbons who died in Canterbury.

Septemb. 5 of yᵉ same yeare was buried Susanna Denn wid.[5] who died in ye city of Canterbury.

1670.   Octobr. ye 16 of ye same year was buried Judith Wood.

Octobr. ye 17 of ye same yeare was buried Elias Gammon householder.

Novembr. ye 8[6] of ye same yeare was buried Mary Browning daughter of Robert & Mary Browning.

1671.   March yᵉ 28 of yᵉ same yeare was buried the widdow Hedgcock.

May yᵉ 8 of ye same yeare was buried Ann Attwood widdow.

Novemb. yᵉ i of the same yeare was buried Thomas Attwood Houshldr.

febuary yᵉ i of the same yeare was Buried Nicholas Dingley.[7]

1672.   December 19th Jane ye daughter of George and Jane Beech was buried.

---

[1] " Housekeeper." (a)   [2] " Householder." (a)

[3] " Householder." (a)   [4] " Householder." (a)

[5] " Mistress Susanna Denne." (a)   [6] " Nov. 19." (b)

[7] " Rector of Kingstone." (b)

March 3ᵈ Abigall the wife of ffrances Baker was buried.

1673.   Aprill 6 Margarett Read widdow was buried.

1674.   March 25. James Sayer [1] was buried.

July 8. Jane the wife of George Beech was buried.

November 28. Susan the wife of Richard Turner was buried.

January 26. Sarah the daughter of Richard and Anne White was buried.

1675.   Aprill 18. Anne Barber widdow was buried.

May 4ᵗʰ Richard Turner was buried.

October 5. John Muggole was buried.

October 6 Mary Tallis widdow was buried.

1676.   May 9. Jane the daughter of Vincent and Anne Draper was buried.

Octobeʳ 16. Elizabeth the daughter of James and Anne Wood was buried.

January 13. Elizabeth Winter widdow was buried.

March 17. Elizabeth the daughter of Mary Gibbon was buried.

1677.   Aprill 18. Susan the Daughter of Mary Browne [2] was buried.

May 28 Mary the wife of Thomas Browne was buried.

July 8. Thomas the sonne of Gregory and Elizabeth Smithsun was buried.

1678.   October 24. Elizabeth daughter of Richard & Elizabeth Shrubsole was buried.

ffebruary 10. Susan Browne widdow was buried.

1679.   August 29. Mildred yᵉ wife of Richard Mihill was buryed.

September 11. Anne yᵉ wife of James Wood was buried.

September 13. Joane Brensley was buried.

September 14. Robert Jacob was buried.

October 23. Parnell Brenchley widdow was buried.

Nouember 16. Anne yᵉ daughter of Richard & Mary Mihill was buried.

December 1. Elizabeth yᵉ daughter of John & Anne Morris was buried.

[1] "husbandman." (a)   [2] "widow." (b)

March 5. George Beech was buried.

1680. March 25. Anne Atwood widow was buried.

September 10. Thomas Browne was buried.

October 5. Robert Gold was buried.

ROBERT GARRETT Curate.

1680. January 22 Joane Sawyer widow was buried.

february 5. Eve ye wife of Richard Sawyer was buried.

1681. May 11 Elizabeth ffox was buried.

May 23 Edward ffox was buried.

September 4. Edward ye sonne of John Holyday was buried.

September 9. William ye son of Will. Knott was buried.

September 18. Edward ffox [1] was buried.

October. 1.[2] John ye son of John Sole was buried.

December 13. Daniell the son of John Holyday was buried.

ffebruary 28. Elizabeth the wife of William Hopkin was buried.

March 19. Elizabeth the wife of Richard Shrubsole was buried.

1682. Aprill 10 Vincent Draper was buried.

July 17. Edmund Bodkin was buried.

August 17. Alexander Silke was buried.

1683. Septemb. 21th Franciss Cason daughter to Esq. Cason [3] was buried.

168$\frac{3}{4}$. March 13th Edward Hopkins was buried.

1684. Apr. 21th Jones Kingsmill widow was Buried.

May 26 Hewly Bayns was Buried.

Jun 10. Annah wife to Abraham Attwood was Buried.

Jun. 22. John Son to Gregory Smithson was Buried.

1685 Decemb. 18 : Richard son to Thom : Maxted was Buried.

March 30 1685 Martha Hopkins was buried according to ye Act for burying in woollen.

June 28 1686 Mildred Maxted was buried in woollen.

March 26 1687 Anne Hopkins [4] was buried in woollen.

June 6 1687. Peter Graunt was buried in woollen.

---

[1] "jun." (*b*)   [2] " Sept 27." (*a*)   [3] " John Cason, Esqr. " (*b*)
[4] " Ye wife of Edward Hopkins." (*b*)

Septemb 27 1688. Anne Quested was buried in woollen.

Octob 4 1688 Richard White was buried in wollen.

$$(\quad . \quad . \quad . \quad . \quad)^{(1)}$$

Octob. 12 1688 Edward Grant was buried in wollen.

Feb. 9 168⁸⁄₉ Mary yᵉ Daughter of Richard Mihil was buried in woollen.

May 17ᵗʰ 1689 Robert Holyday of this Parish was buried in woollen.

Apr 27 1689 Solomon Bries yᵉ son of Edward & Jane his wife, was baptised buried.*

Aug : 28, 1689 Tho : Betts was buried.

1690.   feb. 20 Richard Moor was buried.

feb 28 Mary Wales was buried.

Septemb : 19ᵗʰ 80. Stephen Brice son of Edw : and Jone his wife was Buried.

Octob : 3ᵈ 80 Will : Pope Sonne of William and Mary his wife was Buried.

$$(\quad . \quad . \quad . \quad . \quad)^{(2)}$$

$$(\quad . \quad . \quad . \quad . \quad)^{(3)}$$

Sptem. 26. 1691.   Rich. Myle was Buried.

feb : 24. 1691.   Anne the wife of Tho. fouell was buried.

March 8, 1691.   Ralph Adams was Buried.

$$(\quad . \quad . \quad . \quad . \quad)^{(4)}$$

$$(\quad . \quad . \quad . \quad . \quad)^{(5)}$$

Dec : 1 The wife of Tho. Wood was Buried in wulen.

---

[1] "Octob 6ᵗʰ Anna Don ye wife of James Don was buried." (b)
(Not in the Register.)

[2] "Oct 27. 1690.   Mary Rye was buried. (a) & (b) (Not in the Register).

[3] "Dec 24.   John Betts was buried." (a) & (b) (Not in the Register).

[4] "April 2.   Ann White was buried." (a) & (b) (Not in the Register).

[5] "July 24 James Wood was buried." (a) & (b) "of Harbledown." (b)
(Not in the Register).

* The pen has been run through this entry, but the burial occurs in both (a) and (b).

$$(\quad . \qquad\qquad)^{(1)}$$
$$(\quad . \quad . \quad . \quad . \quad)^{(2)}$$

Oct : 31. 1693. Mr. Vincent Dean * was buried.

Easter 94.

Decr. 13. 1694. Augustin Brenchly.

Aprile 21. 1695. Mary Holiday.

July 1 1695. Daniel Young was Burried.

Aug. 18th 1695. Rich. Edds was buried. visitat : Octo. 7th, 1695.

feb : 22, 1695. John Betts.

feb. 27th 95. John Holyday. Vis. ap. 21.

Aprile 1. 1696. Abr : Swift.

$$(\quad . \quad . \quad . \quad . \quad)^{(3)}$$

May 12. 96. Rich : Hobdy.

July 28(4) 96. Mary Sanders.

Octobr the 16. 96. Dorothy ffoard was burried.

. . . (5) Elizabeth Mihil : was Buried.

June 2d. 1697. Abr. Atwood was burried.

Oct 12 1697. Ann the daught. of James Burch was buried.

Jan : 25 1697. Tho : Bean.

$$(\quad . \quad . \quad . \quad . \quad)^{(6)}$$

Aug. 9th 1698. Made (7) Turner of Ileden.

Nove. 7 1698. Goodwife (8) Mihil.

March 1st Sara the daughter of John Betts.

March 3d. 169⅞. Mary the daughter of Tho. Mihil & his wife.

May 28 1699. Mary ffowell.

Octr. 4 1699. A poor Child from Barham parish.

---

(1) " 1692. June 19 Rich. Adams." (a) (Not in the Register).

(2) " 1693. Oct 8 Jo. Brenchley" (a) & (b) (Not in the Register).

(3) " April 20 Joan Swift," (b) (Not in the Register.)

(4) " July 8th " (b).   (5) " Nov 10 " (a)

(6) " Jan 27 Mary Andrews " (b) (Not in the Register).

" Madam." (a) Appendix XI.   (8) " Margaret." (b) " Ann " (a).

* Appendix XIII.

N

Jan : 15 1699-1700.   Edw. Brice.[1]

feb : 15 1699-1700.   Hary ffoord from Barham.

Ladyday 25 March 1700.   GILB : BURROUGHS Rector.

May 10 : 1700.   Jean ye wife of John Andrews was Buried.

July 31.[2] 1700.   Mary Atwood was buried.

Octr 24 1700.   Wil : Kennet.

Oct. 30 1700.   Mary Mihil.

Novr 9th 1700.   Henry fford was Buried.

Novr 29 1700.   Richard Mihil was Buried.

March 7th 1700.   Katharine Brice was buried.

March 30 1701.   Ja. Dunn was Burried.

. . . . . [3] Mrs Denn from Canterbury.

feb : 22 1700½.   Eliz. ye daughter of Ja. & Ann Burch.

July 26 1702.   Mary Minies[4] was buried.

Oct. 3 1702.   Martha the daughter of Geo : Sharp.

Oct. 11 1702.   Ann the Daughter of Geo : Sharp.

Novr 7 1702.   Eliz ye daughter of Ja : Browning.

Nov 29. 1702.   An ye daughter of Rich : Andrews.

Dec. 6 1702.   Mary the daughter of Jo : Mihil.

March 9th.   Tho : the son of Wil. Hopkins.

Aprile 25 1703.   James the son of James Burch.

Aprile 30 1703.   Abigail the wife of John Andrews.

Jan 18 1703.   Elizabeth the daughter of Tho. Mile.[5]

Jan 29 170¾.   Elizabeth ye daughter of Abraham Atwood.

Feb [6] 170¾.   John Kingsmell.

June 12[7] 1704.   Tho. Rye.

June 25[8] 1704.   Amy Rye.

Aug 20 1704.   Ed : Sprat.

Septr 17 1704.   Rich : Shroubshole.

---

[1] " Householder " (b).   [2] " July 15 " (a).

[3] " Nov 29 1701." (b)   Appendix XIII.

[4] " Mines." (b)   [5] " Mihil." (a)   [6] " Feb. 20." (a)

[7] " June 15." (a)   " 12." (b)   [8] " June 22nd." (a)   " May 28." (b)

Aprile 4th 1705. Goodman Moor.[1]

Decr 18. Margaret the daughter of Jno. Betts.

Sept. 12 1706. Jno. Mihil.

feb : 5th 1706. Abraham Atwood.

1707 August 17. Susan Holyday.[2]

Septr 2^{d.} Tho : ffowell.[3]

Aprile 21 1708. Tho : ffowell.

June 5th. Rich. ye son of Ed. fford.

1711 July 5th. Jno the son of Isaac Whitnell was Buried.

Aug 27. Richard White.

Septr 23. Stephen Hobday.

1712. August 25. Richard White.

March 8th 17$\frac{12}{13}$ Eliz. the daughter of Ed. Bean.

1713. June 4th. Eliz. Hobdy.

Septr 3^{d.} Mr Jno. Clerk from London.

1714. July 1st 1714. Tho. the son of Dan : Quested.

Septr 26 1714. Wm. Hopkin.*

Septr 26 1714. Mary Saunders.

1714. Novr 21 1714. Sarah Goodwin.

1714. Novr 24. Goodw. Eids. [4]

17$\frac{14}{15}$ Jno. Betts Jan 30.

1715. Aprile 10th. Tho : Turner† of Ileden Esqre.

1715. Sep^{t.} 15. Mrs Jane Turner. [5]

1715. Decr 4th. ffrancis Baker.

Decr 4th. David Holyday.

1715. Jan : 4th. Bennet Holyday.

Jan : 14. Mary Bean.

1716. Sept 26. Tho. Bean.

17$\frac{17}{18}$ *M*ich. [6] Saukins } feb : 27.
ye same day Jno. Sawkins

---

[1] " Richard Moor.' *(a)*   [2] " A child." *(a)*   [3] " A housekeeper." *(a)*

[4] " Eliz. Eeds." *(a)*   " Mary Eids." *(b)*

[5] " The wife of Mr. Jno. Turner." *(b)* Appendix XVII.

[6] " Nicholas." *(b)*   * Appendix XXXV.   † Appendix XI.

May 17 1718.   Sara the wife of Dan : Coller.

June 8th 1718.   Hen : Marsh Esqre.

July 14 1718.   Martha ffoord.[1]

September 3rd 1718.   *Jane* Mooring.

October 1st 1718.   The Reverend Mr. Gilbert Burroughs* Rector of Kingstone.

October 11th 1718.   William Kennet.

Decr. 14th 1718.   Frances Joyner was buried.

February 23^d 1718.   ffeb^{r.} 23.   Dinah Shipwell was buried. Affidavit made ye 28th before ye Revd. Mr. Rigden of Patrixbourne.

March 1^{rst.}   Ann ye Daughter of Thom : Golder was buried. Affidavit made ye 6th before ye Rev^{d.} Mr. Jones Rector of Upper Hard*res.*

March 14^t   Margaret Kingsmell was Buried.   Affidavit made ye 15th before ye Rev^d Mr. Bean, Cur : at Barham.

May 20th 1719.   Elizabeth Brensley was buried.

June 14th 1719.   Thomas Maxsted was buried.

July 20th 1719.   Mildred Sayer was buried.

1719.   Oct 22^d Peter Grant was Buried.†

1719.   Oct 26.   Ann ye Wife of Thos : Golder was buried.

1719.   Octr 30 Edward ye son of William Bridgman was buried

1719.   Decr. 1^{rst} Elizabeth Tofts a Traveller was buried.

ffeb^{r.} 16th 1719.   Richard ye son of Willm Lokar was buried.

Sep^t 4th 1720.   Henry ye son of James Birch was buried.

ffeb^r 1^{rst} 1720.   Mathew Browning was buried.

ffeb^r 3^d 1720.   Ann ye wife of James Birch was buried.

March 19th 1720.   Mary ye Daughter of Daniel & Elizabeth Quested was Buried.

Visitation May ye 5th 1721.   PET: INNES Rector.

May 26th 1721.   Robert the son of John Beer was buried.

July 12 1721.   Ann the wife of Richard Andrews was buried.

July 16 1721.   Mary Moor was buried.

Novr 7th 1721.   Buried John ye Son of Thomas Golder.

---

[1] " Ye Wife of Richard Ford." (a)

* Appendix XIV.   † Appendix XXXIII.

Novr 19 1721. Buried Mary Sabine an Infant.

Jan^{ry} 8th 1721. Buried Mr John Turner* of Chilham.

ffeb^{ry} 11th 1721. Buried Elizabeth Rye. [1]

March 26. 1722. Buried Michael Coller an Infant.

Aprill 30th 1722. Buried Mr Thomas Turner† Son of John Turner of Ileden Esqre.

December 12th 1723. Buried Robert Baker an Infant.

March 21th 1723. Buried Sarah Betts.

October 7th 1724. Buried John Mihils.

Jany 29th 1724. Buried Ann Pilcher an Infant.

Febru^{ry} 12th 1724. Buried Elizabeth Moon.

Feb^{ry} 14th 1724. Buried Elizabeth Rye, daughter of John Rye of Bridge.

May 5th 1725. Buried Mrs Sabine ye wife of Chibborn Sabine Gent.

July 31nd 1726. Buried ye wife of Thomas Atwood.

Augst 11th 1726. Buried Abraham ye son of Tho : Atwood an Infant.

Sep^{tr} 18 1726. Buried William Kingsford.

Octo^{br} 30th 1726. Buried Thomas Brensley.

December 10th 1726. Buried Elizabeth Lishman, a way Faring woman.

Decemb^{r.} 14th 1726. Buried William Rye.

January 26th 1726. Buried Edward Sawkins.

January 29th 1726. Buried Jane Godwin an Infant.

February 2st 1726. Buried Mildred ye wife of Benjamine Pilcher.

February the 17th 1726. Buried Elizabeth Winter.

Aprill ye 9th 1727. Buried Mary Rye.

June ye 18th 1727. Buried Ann Pearson an Infant.

June 25 1727. Buried Elizabeth Pearson an Infant.

August 27 1727. Buried William Homes.

September ye 8th 1727. Buried John Eltonton Senr.

October y^e 19th 1727. Buried Margaret Beer.

Aprill ye 9th 1728. Buried Elizabeth Wraith.

---

[1] " Of Bridge." (a)　　* Appendix XVII.　　† Appendix VII.

Aprill y^e 26th 1728. Buried Richard Sawkins.

July y^e 31^{rst} 1728. Buried Ann y^e wife of Daniel Coller.

Sept$^{r.}$ y^e 16th 1728. Buried Sarah Dennett.

Octob^r y^e 12th 1728. Buried Ann Bean.

Octob^r y^e 16 1728. Buried Stephen Rye.

December 16th 1728. Buried William Lot.

December 22 1728. Buried Elizabeth Mihils Jun$^{r.}$

ffeb^{ry} y^e 23^d 1728-9. Buried Mary Mooring.

May y^e 24th 1729. Buried Thomas Castle an Infant.

ffeb^{ry} y^e 4th 1730/1. Buried Edward Brensley.

August y^e 30th 1731. Buried Thomas Attwood.

Aprill y^e 4th 1732. Buried Stephen Pilcher.

May 18th 1732. Buried Daniel Coller.

Jan^{ry} 27th 1732/3. Buried Elizabeth Mihils Widow.

ffeb^{ry} 17th 1732/3. Buried Mary Kennet. Widow.

ffeb^{ry} 25th 1732/3. Buried David Godwin. An Infant.

March 11th 1732/3. Buried Henry Godwin an Infant.

Decemb 6^h 1733. Buried John Hopkins.

Februay 14th 1733/4. Buried Edward ye son of John Beer.

Decemb^r 11th 1734. A. Traveller was buried.

March ye 12th 1734/5. Buried John Andrews.

Aprill ye 7th 1735. Buried Ann Vitnell [1]

May 25th 1735. Buried Mary Davis.

August 14 1736. Buried Mary Lockar.

September ye 12th 1736. Buried Elizabeth Hopkins.

Jan^{ry} 12th 1736/7. Buried Peter Grant.*

March 24^h 1736/7. Buried James Browning.

April ye 17th 1737. Buried Richard Andrews.

May ye 6th 1737. Buried Samuel Brensley.

May the 24th 1737. Buried Susanna Streeting.

November 1^{rst} 1737. Buried a Travelling Woman.

Jan^{ry} ye 3^d 1737/8. Buried James Tassell.

May the 27 1738. Buried Edward Browning.

---

[1] " Whitnell." (*a*)   * Appendix XXXIV.

Augst the 7th 1738. Buried Jane Beer.

Jan^{ry} the 15th 1738/9. Buried Sr Thomas Lombe * Knight & Alderman of ye City of London.

Jan^{ry} 21^{rst} 1738/9. Buried Francis Baker.

August 3^d 1739. Buried John Beer.

August 15th 1739. Buried William Beer.

Jan^{ry} 9th 1739 : 40. Buried Thomas Mullett.

March 21th 1739 : 40. Buried Widow Shrubshall.

Nov^{br} 4th 1740. Buried Edward Bean.

April 14^h 1741. Buried Thos.⁽¹⁾ Browning.

Aprill 15 1741. Buried John ye son of John Kingsmell.

Augst 11 1741. Buried Jane Whitnail.

Jan 13 1741/2. Buried ye Widow Homes.

ffeb^{ry}25. 1741/2. Buried James Birch Senr.

April 17^h 1742. Buried Henry Lamb.

June 13 1742. Buried ye Widow Coller.

Sep^{tr} 22^d 1742. Buried John Rye ‡ from Bridge.

Jan^{ry} 18 1742/3. Buried Ann Birch.

Ap. 29 1744. Buried Ann Law an Infant.†

May 23 1744. Buried Elizth Browning Widow.

Sept^{br} 23rd 1745. Buried Benjamine Beer.

Jan^{ry} 8th 1745/6. Buried Ellen Hammond.

Jan⁽²⁾ 25^h 1745/6. Buried Thomas Law.†

March ye 19 1745/6. Buried ye Widow Brensley.

---

(1) "James" (a) & (b) so also originally in Register but "James" erased and "Thos." written over.

(2) Dec. (a) & (b).   * Appendix VII.   † Appendix XXXII.   ‡ Appendix XXII.

[End of the Burials in the First Register Book.]

BURIALS.

[*SECOND REGISTER BOOK.*]

Ap^{r.} 26 1746. Buried Mary ye wife of Abraham Baker‡ Senr.

Nov^{b.} 30 1746. Buried Stephen ye son of John Laurence.

Jany. 29 1746-7. Buried John Cullen an Infant.

Feby. 12 : 1746-7. Buried Jane ye wife of Robt. Spratt.

July 21 1747. Buried John Turner Esqr. † late of Ileden.

Jan^{ry.} 28 1747-8. Buried ye Widow Andrews.

Feb^{ry.} 7th 1747-8. Buried Anthony Cullen.

Ap^{r.} 10th 1748. Buried Richard Birch.

June 1st 1748. Buried William Johnson an Infant.

Jan^{ry} 19. 1748.9. Buried Mary ye wife of Peter Innes* Rector.

March ye 25. 1749. Buried Abraham Baker. ‡

1749. March ye 29. Buried Elizerbeth Locker.

June ye 20. Buried Katharine the wife of Benjamine Rye.

Augt. ye 11. Buried Sarah Johnson.

Frances Giles of Preston was Bur^d December 27 1749.

Margaret Bean was bur'd Jan : ye 12th 1749.

Thomas Castleden was bur'd March ye 31 1750.

Sarah Colar Late of Bishops Bourn was bur'd. June ye 15 1750.

Robert Kelk a Stranger buried August 21 1750.

Robert Spratt was buried Novr. ye 23. 1750.

B. FAUSSETT, Curate.

March ye 31st 1751. Thomas Goulder was buried.

May ye 23^d 1751. John Mutton, infant, was buried.

January 26 1752. John Grinstead, infant, was buried.

June 11. 1752. Mary Lott, widow, was buried.

April ye 8th, 1753. Edward Grant was buried.

November ye 2^d 1753. John Kingsmill was buried.

Novmb^r ye 28th 1753. Dame Elizabeth Lombe,† relict of Sir Thomas Lombe Kn^{t.} was buried.

‡ Appendix XXIV.   † Appendix VII.   * Appendix XVIII.

November ye 28th 1753. Thomas ye son[1] of Thomas and Anne Browning was buried.

January ye 2^d 1754. Martha ye daughter of Richard and Elizabeth Casselden.

February ye 14 1754. Jane Kingsmill widow was buried.

BR. FAUSSETT, Curate.

July ye 15th 1754. Buried Mildred ye daughter of Thomas & Wilmot Bewly.

August ye 10th 1754. Buried Elisabeth ye wife of Thomas Kingsmill.

September ye 9th 1754. Buried Ann ye wife of Thomas Browning.

May ye 4th 1755. Buried Elizabeth ye wife of Bartholomew Neame.

November ye 5th 1755. Buried Matthew Browning an infant.

December ye 9th 1755. Buried Elizabeth Sawkins. Widow.

BR. FAUSSETT, Curate.

WILL^{M.} BARRETT, Curate.

April 1th 1756. Michael ye son of Richard and Elizabeth Castleden was buried.

May 24th 1756. Thomas ye son of Thomas & Elizabeth Browning was buried.

September 2th 1756. Margaret Baker widow was buried.

Jan^{ry} 9th 1757. Elizabeth Browning daughter of Thos. & Elizabeth Browning was buried.

March 7th 1757. Martha ye wife of Daniel Quested was buried.

August 14th 1757. Thomas son of Edwd. & Sarah Baker was buried.

Decr. 29th 1757. John Birch was buried.

April 24^t 1758. Elizabeth Mutton was buried.

July 28th 1758. Sarah daughter of Richard & Elizabeth Castleden was buried.

Novr. 19th 1758. Elizabeth Lade was buried.

---

[1] " Ye infant son." (a)

O

Decr. 20th 1758. James Birch was buried.

Decr. 25th 1758. Mary Mihills was buried.

Jan^{ry} 4th 1759. Mary Rye was buried.

April 11th 1759. Mary ye daughter of Ric^d & Elizth Castleden was buried.

April 18th 1759. John Turk was buried.

May 20th 1759. Thos. Browning was buried.

Decr. 25th 1759. Thom^{s.} Kingsmill was buried.

March 9th 1760. Elizabeth Mutton infant was buried.

August 26th 1760. John Brookshaw, Infant was buried.

Novr. 9th 1760. . . . Goulder widow was buried.

Decr. 14th 1760. . . . Beer widow was buried.

Jan^{ry} 26th 1761. Martha daughter of John & Susannah Marsh was buried.

Wm Barrett, Curate.

Feb^{ry} 25th 1761. Jane Kingsmill widow was buried.

May 11th 1761. Ann Gobbs a Stroller was buried.

May 15th 1761. Mary ye wife of Daniel Smith was buried.

June 28th 1761. Joseph Webb buried.

July 19th 1761. Sarah Smith[1] buried.

Sep^t 22th 1761. Ann Sabine ye wife of Chibborn Sabine was buried.

Decr 18th 1761. John Ladd* was buried.

Feb^r 26 1762. Widow Birch was buried.

June 6th 1762. Widow Ladd was buried.

June 14th 1762. William son of Edwd & Margaret Beer was buried.

Octr 9th 1762. Mercy daughter of Ric^d & Elizth Castleden was buried.

Octr 23th 1762. A Stroller was buried.

Jan^{ry} 26^h 1763. Mary wife of Ric^d Belsy was buried.

April 10th 1763. Chibborne Sabine widower was buried.

June 24 1763. Elizabeth wife of John Beer was buried.

---

[1] " An infant." *(a)*   * Appendix XXVII.

H. Fox—Curate.

Octr 26th 1754. Mary Grant was buried.

Decr 30th 1764. Stephen Knight buried.

July 22^d 1765. Mrs Hannah Turner,* grandmother to the Earl of Lauderdale, & Sir Jervis Clifton.

Aug 3^d 1765. Ann Knight buried.

W^M TASWELL, Curate.

1766.

John baseborn son of John Wood and Elizabeth Webb was buried Jan^{ry} 19.

Elizabeth wife of Stephen Sutton was buried Jan^{ry} 29$^{th.}$

Ann Baker was buried June 26th 1766.

Abraham Baker was buried Nov. 10th 1766.

Richard Miles was buried December 27th 1766.

Elizabeth (D^r of John†) Beer was buried March 28$^{th.}$ 1767.

Thos Miles was buried July 12$^{th(1)}$ 1767.

Elizabeth Questead was buried Octr 25th 1767.

Sarah White was buried Sep^{tr} 23^d 1767.

Susan Knight was buried September 29$^{(2)}$ 1767.

W$^{m.}$ Revell was buried March 27th 1768.

Sarah Pilcher the wife of John Pilcher was buried March 22th 1768.

Daniel Quested was buried June y^e 8th 1768.

Thos. Denward‡ was buried June 30th 1768.

The Rev$^{d.}$ Peter Innes Rector of this Parish was buried January 22^d 1769.

Elizabeth Birch was buried March 29th 1769.

Abraham Burton a Traveller was buried April 17th 1769.

Benjamin Rye—Clerk of this Parish, was buried July 21st 1769, antient.

1770. William White was buried March 9th 1770.

1770. July 5th Mary Webb—widow—an antient Woman.

September 21. Thomas Fox, an Infant.

---

(1) " Aug 20." (a)   " July 12." (b)
(2) " Sept. 29." (a)   " Aug. 17$^{th.}$ (b)

* Appendix VII.   † Inserted subsequently.   ‡ Appendix XIX.

1771.   1771.

January 6th. John Fowel—from Bishopsbourn.
January 13. Edward Bean—drowned.
January 23. Ann Miles—Widow—an antient Woman.
March 31. John Church— a youth.
November 12th. Elizabeth Fox—an Infant.

1772.   1772.

March 29. James Jordan—an Infant.
May 13. Edward Castle—an Infant.
December 31. Sarah Finnes—wife of Thos. Finnes.

1773.   1773.

May 18. Elizabeth Waters—an Infant, drown'd.
June 1. Mary White, Spinster.
Septr 5. Joseph Mantle, a Stranger.
July 25. Elizabeth Bartlet, widow.
Decr. 13. William Jacob—Infant.
Dec 20. Elizabeth Mutton—Infant.

JOHN NAIRN Rector,
also Minister of Wingham & Rector of Stourmouth.

1774.

1774. March 2. Mrs Elizabeth Hall,* widow of Doc^{tr} Hall,
late Physician of Greenwich Hospital.
July 22. Stephen Laurence—an Infant.

1775.

January 22. Edward Beer.
September 18. Thomas Ford—from Barham, late of this Parish.
October 21. Thomas Newport—an Infant.
December 17. Ann Newport—an Infant.
December 28. Ann Ford—from Barham.

* Appendix XII.

1776.

1776. January 28. Henry Chandler.
July 14. John Pilcher—an antient Man.
August 1. William Ellen—of the small Pox.
August 9th Sarah Munns—an Infant.
November 3. Thomas Williams—Infant—accident.

1777.

1777. March 12th. Ann Paine*.
July 15th. Mary Morgan—from Feversham.
September 17th. Elizabeth Impett.
December 13. John Jacob—Small Pox.

1778.

1778. May 18. Mary Wood†—an Infant.
September 18. John Wood†—Church Warden.
September 20. James William Pritchard[1]—an Infant.
December 2d. Elizabeth Baker—a widow.
December 6. John Wood.†

1779.

1779. March 25. Richard Pain*—from great Hardres.
Nov. 6. Mary Baker—hang'd her Self.
Nov. 14. John Mutton—an Infant.
Nov. 22. Thos. Baker

1780.

1780. January 13. John Bean—an ancient man.
June 16th. Hannah Pritchard from Newington Butts, Surrey.
June 22. William Beer.
September 7th. Mary wife of Richard Baker.

---

[1] " base born." *(b)*

* Appendix XXIII.   † Appendix XXVIII.

December 28. James Chapman from Canterbury.

JOHN NAIRN, Rector.

1781. Jan 26. Thomas Miles, from Barham.
Feb. 5. Jane, wife of Edward Ford.
March 5. Stephen Sutton.
July 31. William Jacob—Infant.
Dec.r 27. James Beer—Infant.

1782.

1782. Jan 17. Thomas Bewly—ancient Man.
April 6. John Bridges—from Barham.
June 27. John Castle.
Nov.r 26. Wilmot Bewly—from Adisham.

1783.

1783. April 16. John Laurence—ancient. 84.
July 13. Sarah Finnis.
August 17. Mary wife of Peter Jacob.
September 14. Caroline Robins—Infant.
November 9. Robert Ford—Infant.
December 4. John Ford—Infant—from Harbledown.

1784.

May 20. Jemima Margaret Payler.
June 20. Thomas Baker—from Dover.
August 25. Sarah Baker—Widow.
October 24. Benjamin Mutton.

1785.

1785. Jan 26. Sarah Brooks Infant.
March 17th. Judith Fox from Barham.
July 10. Thomas Browning.

1786.

March 1. Peter Jacob.

May 5. Edward Sutton—Infant.

June 4th. Elizabeth, wife of James Mutton.

Aug. 5. John Newport—Infant.

Sep^{t.} 28. Margaret Beer—Widow—from Canterbury.

1787.

1787. Jan. 4th. Amy Mace.

 April 3. Richard Mace.[1]

 April 19. Elizabeth Knight.[2]

 July 9. Stephen Laurence.

 Octr. 12. Sarah wife of John Terry.

1788.

1788. July 24. William Horsepool.   JOHN NAIRN, Rector.

1790.

January 14th. Ann Spain.

January 14. Stephen Spain—Infant.

February 14. Edward Ford, Clerk of this Parish.

May 21st. Elisabeth Nairn* wife of the Reverend John Nairn, Rector.

June 2. William Pilcher.

Nov. 26. Mary wife of James Pritchard.

1791.

1791. March 14. Hannah Pilcher, widow of Wm Pilcher.

 August 23. Elizabeth Bean, Widow.

 October. 16. Edward Browning.

 Decr. 22. Richard Baker.

1792. January 15. Margaret Churchman.

 March 16th. The Reverend William Dejovas Byrchet† A.M. from Canterbury.

 October 7. John Richford—An Infant.

---

[1] "From Bridge." (b) [2] "From Bridge." (b)

 * "Appendix XII." † "Appendix IX."

1793. January 27. Hannah King—Widow.
March 6. Susanna Newman—a Vagrant.
March. 17. Elizabeth Browning.
April 21. Elizabeth Castleden—widow.
May 13. John—base born son of Ann Smithson.
November. 15. Mary, wife of Richard White—jun^{r.}

1794.

Feb^{r.} 16. Anna Mutton, d^{r.} of Robert Mutton.
Sep^{t.} 23. Elizabeth, wife of Richard White Senr.
Sep^{t.} 30. Elizabeth Whitehead.
Octr. 30. Elizabeth Jacob.

1795.

Febr. 24. Elizabeth Laurence—Widow.
April 22. Mary, wife of Thos. Horton—from Herne.
June 16. John Martin—a Soldier.
June 25. . . . . . a Soldier's wife.
August 27. John Lumpton a Soldier.
September 5. John Williams.
September 20. Thomas Jourdan.

1796.

January 31. Henry Atwood—an Infant.
February 4th Richard White.

JOHN NAIRN Rector.

1796. April 22. Sarah Green—an Infant.
August 26. Sarah, wife of Thomas Golder.
August 30. William Curgenwen—a Soldier's Child.
Septr. 12. Ann Mutton—daughter of Robt. Mutton.
Septr. 29. Elizabeth Mutton—daughter of Robt. Mutton.
Octr. 23. James Mutton—son of James Mutton.

1797.

Feb^{r.} 19. Jane Mutton—daughter of Robt. Mutton.
June 11. Thomas Golder, aged 86.
Aug 28. Mary Mutton—daughter of Robt. Mutton.

1798.

Feb. 18. Charlotte, base born daughter of Mary Kingsmill.

June 9. Mrs Charlotte Payler,* wife of Thomas Watkinson Payler Esq$^{r.}$ of Ileden.

July 10. Mrs Elizabeth Byrche,† widow of the Reverend William Dejovas Byrche late of the black Friars in Canterbury.

August 30. Thomas Ford—Clerk of this Parish.

October 29. John Philpot—Infant.

November 12. Christopher Wood.‡

Decr 23. Ann Smitten—Widow

1799.

Feb^r 19. . . . . Spillett, a Traveller.

Feb 28. Vincent Pilcher.

March 7. Elizabeth Brisnall.

July 15. George Philpot, Infant.

August 5. Major Barston—private in 3^d Foot Guards.

August 5. ———————private in 2^d Reg. Foot Guards, no affid^t brought.

Decembr 29. Martha Keeler from Bishopsbourn.

1800. April 2. James Pritchard.

April 27. James Atwood—Infant.

May 3. Richard White.

Octr 30. Charles Pritchard, from Canterbury.

1801.

1801. Aug. 19. William Goldfinch.

1802.

1802. Feb. 2. Thomas Lawrence.

June 20. Thomas Mutton.

June 28. Thomas Castle.

Nov. 14. Thomas Browning.

---

* Appendix v.　　† Appendix ix.　　‡ Appendix xxix.

1804.

1804.   April 6th.   George Rousall—Infant.

JOHN NAIRN, Rector.

1804.

1804.   July 2.   Mary wife of Edward Ford, from Canterbury.
October 30.   George Wood—an Infant.
November 2.   Austin Spain.

1806.

1806.   Feb^{ry} 27th John Nairn,* Rector of Kingston aged about 80^{yrs}.

May . .   Stephen Reynolds.
July 2nd Gibbon Ladd Terry æt. 15.
May 22nd William Williams.

CHARLES HUGHES. Curate.

1806.

John Norris aged 25.   Aug$^{st.}$ 24$^{th.}$
Catharine Lawrance, widow, brought from Dover, was buried Sept 14th Aged 82.
Thomas Terry—aged 31—buried Oct$^{r.}$ 5th 1806.
Alice Pritchard Spinster, aged 55. buried 10th Oct$^{r.}$ 1806.

1807.

Edward Infant son of George & Elizth Newport, Dec$^{r.}$ 15 1807.

1808.

Edward Bean—Batchelor, aged 54 years.—Jan$^{y.}$ 20th 1808.
Thomas Kingsmill.   Aged 87 years.   Jan^{ry} 27. 1808.
Parnel Browning, widow of . . . . Browning. aged 86^{yrs} Feb. 4 : 1808.
Richard Keeler aged 73 years.—Feb. 7 ; 1808.

---

* Appendix XII.

Ann Williams aged 77 years.   Aug 5th. 1808.

John Richardson aged 1 year—buried Aug 21. 1808.

William* son of Thomas & Sarah Ellen (late Sarah Mutton Sp^{r.}) aged 7 years—buried Decr. 14. 1808.

1809.

1809.   Edward base born son of Susannah Codham, aged 2 months, buried Jan^{r.} 1. 1809.

William German aged 2 years, buried Feb. 20. 1809.

John Ford aged 4 months, buried March 13. 1809.

James Williams, aged 74 years, buried March 31. 1809.

Thomas Gosling aged 39 years, buried April 10th 1809.

Sophia Philpot aged 9 months.   Aug^{st.} 16. 1809.

Thomas Beek aged 7 days.   August 30th 1809.

John Fagg. aged 77 years.   Sepr. 29 : 1809.

COOPER WILLYAMS, Rector.

Elizabeth† wife of Thomas Watkinson Payler of Ileden Esqr. aged 50 years, buried March 18. 1810.

Matthew Fagg aged 19. Decr 20th 1810. brought from Hardres. Kill'd by kicks from a horse.

1812.

Henry Pilcher son of W^m & Charlotte, aged 5 months.   Feb. 20. 1812.

Mary, daughter of John & Elizth Dines, aged 9 months.   March 2. 1812.

Mary Ann daug^r of W^m & Charlotte Pilcher aged 2 years.   April 12, 1812.

Sarah Fetherstone aged 36 years.   July 5th 1812.

COOPER WILLYAMS, Rector.

[*End of Burials in the Second Register Book.*]

---

* "Appendix XXV."   † "Appendix VIII."

[The following notes relating to the Church, &c., are entered in this Second Register Book.]

(1.)

Kingston June 2^d 1798.

Be it remembered—that the Reverend John Nairn Rector of this Parish of Kingston hath, at the Request of T. W. Payler Esqre of Ileden in this Parish, given his Consent to his making a burying Vault in the Parish Church of Kingston aforesaid, at the North Entrance thereof, of the Dimensions of 18 feet 4 inches, by 10 feet 4 inches, for the use of his Family*; upon Condition, that the sum of two Guineas shall be paid to himself, and his Successors, the future Rectors of Kingston, for the time being, for every Corpse that shall hereafter, from Time to Time be deposited in the same Vault—

Witness our Hands the Day & Year above mentioned

> JOHN NAIRN, Rector of Kingston.
> THOS. W. PAYLER.

(2.)

In the year 1809 the Rector, by consent of the Churchwarden & principal parishioners, took down the Vane, & in lieu thereof put up a new one with letters N.W.E.S.—the parish having put up a new pole. The alteration with the gilding cost the Rector 2 guineas, besides the letters.

(3.)

In the year 1813, The said Rector the Revd Cooper Willyams having at a parish meeting undertaken to rebuild the Church Porch which was dilapidated for the sum of £20—He completed it as it now stands —at about the expence of £30. The overplus of course he himself supplied.

---

* In course of repaving the Church in 1886, the workmen came upon the entrance to this vault—about 3 feet from the North Door of the Church. From an inspection of the coffin-plates the following members of the Payler family were found to lie interred there:—Jemima Margaret Payler 1784, æt. 2; Charlotte Payler 1798, æt. 50; Elizabeth Payler 1810, æt. 50; Rev. W. Payler 1814, æt. 39; Thos. Watkinson Payler 1816, æt. 68; Maria Payler 1817, æt. 34; Colonel James Payler 1854, æt. 67.

(4.)

In the Autumn of 1846 Kingstone Church was restored.

1.—The Tower & Belfry were repaired, a brick drain laid on the South side, & the Church repewed by the Parishioners, assisted by a contribution of £25 from the Landowners, under the superintendence of Mr. Robert Gardner, Churchwarden.

2.—A new Floor was laid, the Gallery removed & the Church Walls & Ceiling &c. coloured at the expense of the Landowners & others, under the direction of Captain Douglas of Ileden.

3.—The new Oak Doors with their fastenings & the Vestry Door were presented to the Parish by Captain Douglas, who also defrayed the expense of staining the Pews & cleaning the Arches & Stone work.

4.—The Beams were stained & the glass of the East Window enriched by the Honble Daniel Finch.

5. - The East Window was put in & the Chancel was restored by the Reverend Thomas Bartlett, who presented the Font to the Parish, & the carved oak Desk, & opened & renewed the Window near it. The Desk was made in imitation of the Pulpit, from the Old oak-screen which was removed to make way for the new East Window.

March 28. 1847.   THOMAS BARTLETT, Rector.

(5.)

In the Spring of the year 1873 the following repairs were carried out.—The North Porch thoro'ly restored by Voluntary contributions at a cost of £43 10s. 0d.

The Church roof retiled, the cieling removed. Timbers thrown open & thoro'ly cleaned at a cost £125—Voluntary contributions. The Chancel Roof re-tiled the cieling removed—Timbers shewn, thoro'ly cleaned -- Two carved angels placed at the East end of the roof—at a cost of £95. By the Rector, PERCY J. CROFT. The sum also of Fifty six Pounds eleven shillings paid on account in behalf of Parish for Architect's Charge (W. White) for Plans, Specifications, Journey, &c. By the Rector, PERCY J. CROFT.

(6.)

In the Spring of the year 1881—the old Vestry was removed by Faculty, and new one built by Voluntary contributions at a cost of Seventy Pounds. In the year 1882—Oak Door and restoration of Door Way and Window above it leading from Vestry to Chancel, at a cost Sixteen pounds by Voluntary contributions.

158

(7.)

1882.

On Wednesday, July 19th, 1882, the Bishop Suffragan of Dover consecrated twenty one perches of land—the Gift of George Henry Marquis Conyngham, as an additional plot for burial—the land adjoining the present Churchyard to the South West.

(8.)

1886.

The Church was re-opened on Oct 20th, 1886, having been closed for two months during Restoration. The following were the chief portions of the work :—

THE CHANCEL—repaved and furnished with Oak Prayer-desk and Choir Stalls.

THE NAVE—reseated in oak, the floor laid with wooden blocks, passages paved with tiles, windows reglazed and stone (inside) Cills renewed. Heating Stove placed in sunk chamber.

THE TOWER—Roof releaded and new Vane supplied.

THE CHURCHYARD—New Oak Gates. Drain laid to carry off the water from the roof.

The works were carried out by Mr. H. B. Wilson, Builder, of Canterbury, under the direction of Mr. R. Norman Shaw, R.A., Architect.

Total cost of Restoration, £583 19s. 10d., towards which the Canterbury Diocesan Church Building Society granted £100.

C. H. WILKIE, Rector.

APPENDIX.

MONUMENTAL INSCRIPTIONS.

[*IN THE NAVE.*]

I.

THIS TABLET
is erected in Memory of
JAMES PAYLER,
A Colonel in the Army, and sometime
Governor of Zante and Corfu:
Appointed Lieutenant 52nd Foot,
24th March, 1804 ;
Captain in the same Regiment, 18th
August, 1808 ;
Had a silver Medal and four Clasps
for his services at
FUENTES D'ONOR, CIUDAD RODRIGO,
NIVELLE, and NIVE ;

Major 10th Foot, 17th January, 1822,
And Lieutenant Colonel 2nd June,
1825,
Colonel in the Army 28th June, 1838,
Died unmarried 15th April, 1854.

Blessed is he whose end is peace.

This Tablet was erected
At the joint expence of various
Charitable Institutions,
To which Colonel James Payler was
a munificent contributor.

II.

Sacred to the Memory of
MARY LUCY,
The beloved wife of Robert Deane
Parker, Esqre.
Of the Honble. the East India
Company's Civil Service,
And Daughter of the Revd. T. Bart-
lett, M.A.,
Rector of this Parish.
Who died at Mercara in the Coorg
Country in the East Indies,
On the 10th day of March, A.D. 1846,

Aged 23 years.
This tablet is erected by her bereaved
husband, in
Affectionate testimony of her great
worth as a wife
And a mother, and with an humble
trust, that, "Justified
By faith, in the righteousness of the
Saviour, she has
Found peace with God through our
Lord Jesus Christ."

ARMS.—On a Lozenge, gules a chevron
between three leopards' faces or,
impaling sable, three dexter gloves
pendent argent tasselled or.

III.

Sacred to the memory of a sincere
Christian,
Endeared to his family by the most
affectionate kindness,
As a son, a brother, a husband, and
a father,
And to a large circle of friends,
By social and engaging manners,
goodness of heart,
And a variety of talents.

This tablet is erected by his widow,
Elizabeth,
Daughter of Peter Snell *of Whitley
Court, in the County of Gloucester, Esqr.*
Deeply afflicted,
Yet not mourning like those without
hope,
To
The Revd. COOPER WILLYAMS, M.A.
Rector of this Parish and of Stourmouth,
Whose remains are deposited
With those of his beloved sister,
Beata,

At Fulham in Middlesex.
He was born June 22d, 1762, and died
July 17th, 1816.

ARMS *⁎*—Quarterly 1 and 4 Argent a fesse
chequy gules and argent, between three
otters' heads erased gules ; each gorged
with a ducal coronet or ; a crescent
for difference. 2 gules a fesse between
two chevrons vaire ; (Goodere) 3 argent
a fesse sable, in chief a mullet of the
last between two pellets ; (Dineley)
Impaling, quarterly gules and azure
over all a cross moline or.

IV.

Sacred
To the Memory of
The Rev. WILLIAM PAYLER, M.A.
Late Vicar of
Patrixbourne and Bridge,
And Second son of
T. W. Payler, *Esqre.* of Ileden ;
Who died the 19th day of June, 1814,
Ætat 38.
In the discharge of his Ministerial
duties,
He was most zealous and exemplary,
As a husband most amiable
And affectionate.
As a just tribute to his merits
This Tablet is erected
By his afflicted widow,
Who died the 19th day of November,
1817,
Ætat 34.
Deeply and deservedly lamented.

SARAH MARIA, their youngest
daughter,
Died at *Kensington*
The 15th day of December, 1827,
Ætat 15.

V.

To the memory
of
CHARLOTTE PAYLER, wife of
THOMAS WATKINSON PAYLER,
of Ileden, Esquire.

She was Daughter of WILLIAM
HAMMOND, Esqre,
of *St. Alban's,* and CHARLOTTE his wife
Daughter of WILLIAM EGERTON,
LL.D.,

⁎ According to Burke the correct
Arms of Willyams are, Argent a fesse
chequy gules and vert, between three
griffins' heads erased of the third ; each
gorged with a ducal coronet or.

Grandson of JOHN Earl of Bridg-
water.
She excelled where it was real honor
to excell
In the character of *Wife, Mother, Sister,
Friend.*
Her eminent virtues were confirmed
and improved
By a regular attendance on her
religious duties.
Tho' endued with exquisite sensibility
And awaked to all the charities of life
She possesd her soul in that calmness
and fortitude
Which true religion only can inspire.
Having lived a blessing to her family
And an animating example to all who
knew her
She was parted from them for a little
while
On the second day of June, 1798,
In the fiftieth year of her age.
Heaven gives us friends
To bless the present scene,
Resumes them
To prepare us for the next.

CREST.—Over a blank shield a dove, wings
extended, holding an olive branch
between the beak.

VI.

In a VAULT near this Church
Lie the mortal remains of ELIZABETH
SARAH MARTHA,
The beloved wife of EDWARD
KNOCKER, Esqr., of Dovor,
And the eldest daughter of the
Reverend THOMAS BARTLETT, A.M.,
Rector of this Parish, and of
CATHARINE SARAH his wife ;
She departed this life on the 6th day
of March, 1835,
Aged 21 years ; leaving one infant
daughter, EMILY ELIZABETH.

A bright example of filial duty and
sisterly affection from her
Earliest years, her brief career proved
that the piety which adorned her
Youthful course, and peculiarly endeared her to her parents, could shed
A lustre equally edifying and lovely
over her character as a wife and
mother.
Alive to the duty of redeeming the
time, she was "*fervent in spirit
Serving the Lord :*" and submissive to
the divine will, she was "*patient
In tribulation, continuing instant in
prayer.*"

They who witnessed her *"Life"* traced the grace of God working in her The fruit of *"Love without dissimulation,"* and leading her to *"abhor that which Is evil and to cleave to that which is good."* They who witnessed her *"Death"* Traced the same divine grace spiritualizing her affections, elevating her hope, Confirming her faith, and enabling her to rely in calmness and peace upon the Merits and mercy of her Saviour! *"Blessed are the dead which die in the Lord."*

Also in the same vault lie the remains of EDWARD TOTTENHAM KNOCKER, the son of the aforementioned EDWARD and ELIZABETH SARAH MARTHA KNOCKER, who died on the 10th day of February, 1835, aged three days.

ARMS.—On a lozenge, sable a fesse or fretty of the field between three fleurs-de-lis of the second impaling sable three dexter gloves pendent argent tasselled or.

VII.

To the Precious Memory of THOMAS TURNER Son of JOHN TURNER of Ileden Esqre. & HANNAH his Wife Daughter of THO : LOWFEILD of Surrey Esq. Whose Duty to God, his Parents, Relations & Friends, Express'd in a course of early Piety & strict Probity, Made him sooner than ordinary ripe for Heaven. *Immodicis brevis est Ætas, et rara Senectus.* ·He was expert in Business, And of such sweet & affable Deportment, As made him much beloved in his life And more lamented at his Death, being but 23 years old. He died at DRAPER'S HALL, LONDON, 21st April 1722. And lies buried here in a New Vault. *Hic si Casta Fides, Juvenumq Exempla Piorum Quid poterant, nondum debuit ille mori : Sed voluit Deus hæc: et Dignum vivere Terris Præripuit, Cælo quod magè Dignus erat.* The said JOHN TURNER had 3 other children

ELIZABETH since married to SR THO : LOMBE of Londo : Mercht And JOHN, & SUSANNA, who died Infants.

Here also lieth the said JOHN TURNER who Departed this life the 13th day of July 1747 In the 73rd year of his age.

The above SR THOMAS LOMBE * departed this life The 3d of January 1738 Aged 53, & left Issue Two Daughters, HANNAH the Eldest married To SR ROBERT CLIFTON Baronet & Knight of the BATH, the youngest MARY TURNER married to the Right Honble JAMES Earl of LAUDERDALE.

DAME ELIZABETH LOMBE Relict of SR THOMAS LOMBE & Daughter of the above JOHN & HANNAH TURNER departed this life the 18th of November 1753 Aged 52 & both are Interred in this Vault.

Here also lieth the said HANNAH TURNER Who departed this Life the 11th day of July 1765 in the 91st year of her age.

ARMS.—Quarterly 1 and 4. Per fesse sable and ermine a pale, counterchanged and three fers-de-moline or, two and one (Turner). 2 and 3. Gules six crosses crosslet fitchée or, three two and one. (Theobald) Impaling; per fesse vert and or, a pale, counterchanged, in chief a bull's head couped sable; in base two garbs gules. (Lowfield) Crest a lion sejant ermine, holding in the dexter paw a fer-de-moline or. (The fer-de-Moline has disappeared.) Beneath the above are two angels each supporting a shield, one bearing the arms of Turner & Theobald quarterly as above—the other shield the arms of Turner.

On the north wall a short distance from the Tablet is suspended a Surcoat bearing the Arms of Lombe—Azure two Combs in fesse between a broken lance barwise, one piece in chief with the head respecting the dexter point of the shield, the broken part of the other half towards the dexter base point or. Beneath the Surcoat is a shield bearing the same arms. Above is a funeral helmet supporting the crest Two lances in saltire or, each with a small pendant gules. Of the crest only the lower portions of the lances remain. On either side of the Surcoat hang the gauntlets and beneath, the Spurs and funeral sword.

---

* One of three brothers, merchants (sons of Henry Lombe of Norwich), through whom the manufacture of silk was introduced into England. The youngest brother,

VIII.

Sacred to the memory of
Elizabeth Payler, second wife of
Thomas Watkinson Payler *Esqre* of
Ileden:
She was daughter of Edmund Winn,
*Esqre, of Ackton Hall in the County of
York.*

She departed this life March the
10th 1810.
Aged 50 years.
Her husband hath erected this tablet,
As a monument of her virtues,
And of his affection.

[*IN THE CHANCEL.*]

IX.

Viro reverendo,
probo, erudito, bono,
Gulielmo DEJOVAS BYRCHE,
A.M. *
juxta hanc parietem condito,
hujusmodi marmor erigi voletat
Uxor ejus ELIZABETHA
THOMÆ BARRETT de Lee armigeri
filia :
Quæ cum interim
post diuturnos dolores
tam corporis quam animi,
pie et patienter toleratos
vita functa est :
et hic prope maritum sepulta :
Hoc qualecunque
virtutum utriusque ΜΝΗΜΟΣΥΝΟΝ
desiderii sui ΤΕΚΜΗΡΙΟΝ
fieri curavit
Frater ejus ex patre
THOMAS BARRETT.
Obiit Ille, liberis duobus susceptus
THOMA PETERS ET ELIZABETHA
die 7 Martii 1792 æt. 63.
Illa vero
die 1mo Julii 1798 æt. 70.

Hasted states that the Rev. W. D. Byrche
obtained (1758) a grant of the Arms
as blazoned in the second and third
quarterings of the Byrche Hatchment,
now in the Tower of the Church.
These are—Quarterly 1 and 4 Azure,

a lion rampant argent armed gules
(Byrche) 2 and 3. Azure, on a chevron argent, between three fleurs-de-
lis or, a cross clichée gules, on a chief
of the last a portcullis chained of the
second (Byrche) Impaling quarterly 1
and 4 Or, on a chevron between three
mullets sable, as many lions passant
guardant or. (Barrett) 2 and 3 Or,
three roses gules (Peters).

X.

Johannes Nethersole de Nethersole,
Vincenti filius; Thomæ, Johannis,
Wilsfordi,
Francisci, Gulielmi, Annæ, Saræ,
Rebeccæ, ex Peregrina Francis-
ci Wilsfordi filia Pater optumus,
Natus A.D°. 1546, Denatus 1627.
Hic in
Illo quiescens expectat diem ultimum.
Tantum est. Cætera in vtrivs-
qve parentis honorem adscribenda,
si isti tacerent, lapides hi loqve-
rentur. Abi, lector, bene itidem
merere de tuis, epitaphio ad en-
conium, vel non habeas, non carebis.

(A Mural Alabaster Monument between
two black marble columns, consisting
of two kneeling figures, representing
man and wife, face to face on either
side of a desk. The inscription on a
black marble slab beneath. There has
been a shield of arms—now lost—
under the inscription).

John, at the great risk of his life brought over the secret from Savoy, having under
disguise obtained employment in one of the mills of that country, and thus gained
a knowledge of the machinery (*Old England*, Bk. VII. Cap II) The Lombes set
up the famous silk mill at Derby, and obtained a Royal Patent in 1718, which
was renewed in 1732 for another 14 years on the Petition of Sir T. Lombe, Parliament at the same time giving him a grant of £14,000. Thomas Lombe was an Alderman of the Ward of Bassishaw. and was knighted when Sheriff of London in 1727.
He died at his house in the parish of St. Olave, Old Jewry, leaving a fortune of
£120,000 (*Gent's Mag. 1739*).

* Son of the Rev. W. Byrche (by Jane d. of Mr. W. Dejovas) curate of St. Mary's
Dover & Rector of Gt. Monegham, deceased 1756. Through his wife Elizabeth d. of
Thomas Barrett he became entitled to the Manor and Advowson of Kingstone. Their
only son Thomas Peters, Lt. in the Marines, dying unmarried (1784) the manor, &c.
passed to Sir S. E. Brydges, Bart., of Denton, on his marriage with Elizabeth the surviving daughter.

XI.

M. S.

The remaines of Margaret ye wife of
Thomas
Turner of Ileden Esqre. By whom
he had yssue :
John, Thomas, William, Charles &
Henry, Mary, Martha,
And Susanna, All liveing at the
tyme of her decease.
Also 2 sons & 3 daughters more
that dyed young.
She was humble vertuous and
Religious
A benefactor and Physitian to the
poor
An excellent wife, a true friend, &
indulgent Parent.
She dyed at Lincoln's Inn, Augt the
4th, 1698,
In ye 47th year of her age and 26th
of her Marryage
Her body vnderneath doth rest
Her soul (no doubt) in heaven is blest.
GLORIA IN EXCELSIS DEO.

Also ye said Thomas Turner
Died Apl: 1th, 1715, in ye 68th
Year of his Age, & lyes
In ye same Vault.

ARMS.—Per fesse, Sable and ermine a pale
counterchanged, and three fers-de-
moline or, two and one (Turner). On
an escutcheon of pretence, Gules, six
crosses crosslet fitchée or, three, two,
and one. Impaling, Gules, six crosses
crosslet fitchée or, three two and one.
Crests : 1. a Lion sejant ermine.
2. a Phœnix rising out of flames proper.

XII.

To the Memory of
The Revd JOHN NAIRN
37 years Rector of this Parish.
He died on the 19th February 1806.
Much regretted by all
Who had the happiness of knowing
him.
His constant and uniform attention
to every duty, gained him the
gratitude and respect of his
parishioners,
And his benevolent and friendly
disposition secured to him universal
esteem.

In the same vault
Lieth the remains of
MRS NAIRN
1st wife of the Revd. John Nairn.
She was daughter of DR. HALL, M.D.

Also MRS HALL
Mother to the above-mentioned
Mrs Nairn.
ANN Second Wife of the
above-named John Nairn
Died the 12th January 1818.

XIII.

Near this Place lyes interr'd the
Bodyes of
VINCENT DENNE Esqr : Serjeant at
law,
and MARY his Wife
Daughter of THOMAS DENNE Esqr.
Deceased :
By which said Mary He had Issue
four Daughters viz.
DOROTHY, MARY, BRIDGETT, &
HONYWOOD ;
Which three last are all dead :
And the said DOROTHY, the Surviving
Sister, who
is the Widow & Relict of THOMAS
GINDER gent. deceased
Caused this Monument to be set up
in Memory of Her
said Father and Mother.
He departed this Life the 28th of
October 1693
Aged 65,
She departed this Life the 19th of
November 1701
Aged 78.
ARMS.—Azure, three leopards faces or.

XIV.

Hic sitœ sunt reliquiæ
GILBERTI BURROUGHS Scoto-
Britanni.
Hujus Ecclesiœ per annos viginti
sex rectoris,
Necnon regiæ Scholæ Cantuariensis,
Hypodidascali perdiligentis ;
Quâ de Provinciâ, quinque post
Lustra,
Sex centos vèro labores ibidem haustos
Demigravit, ut sibi viveret,
Accedente senecta ;
Cujus ipso in limine,
Quinto quinquagesimo Anno,
In febrim delapsus,
Quod mortale fuit, morti concessit,
Summo cum dolore, ac desiderio
Omnium, quibus perspecta fuerat
Mirifica illius adversus superiores
libertas

Erga æquales comitas, in alumnos
lenitas,
Qui illi secundùm liberos suos ita
fuerunt
Ut pœnè pares essent.
Uxorem habuit, Margaretam filiam
unicam
Thomæ Seyliard Rectoris de Deal.
Morum suavitatis, prudentiæ, atq
Οικονομιας
egregium exemplar
dein Jaaam filiam Tristrami Stevens
Dubrensis,
ex hac nullam prolem, ex illâ tres
filios,
Totidem filias suscepit, quorum tres
superstites
Gilbertus, Gulielmus, atq Anna,
hoc saxum pietatis ergo statuerunt,
Diem Obiit v Kalen. Octob :
A.D. MDCCXVIII.

XV.

(*Brass*)

Here lyeth John Hastlyn that was
P'son of Kingston 28 yeares, He had
to wife Margaret Hogbenn and had
children by
her Mary, John, Joane and Affry.
Hee Dyed
Anno Dni. 1600, Die August 24.

XVI.

(*Brass*)

Robertus Denn Charus pauperibus
Cœteris dilectus, exiguo Vitæ
Curriculo recte et laudate con-
fecto, ardente febri imaturam
mortem Obiit, Ex vnica uxore Tho-
masinæ filios quinque duasque
filias superstites relinqvens
Vicesimo septimo die mensis Martii
Anno Domini Millesimo quinqen-
tesimo nonagesimo quarto, annum
ætatis suæ agens quadragesimum
quintum *

[*IN THE CHURCHYARD.*]

XVII.

(*A flat stone East of Chancel*)

Here Lyeth *buried* . . . of JANE wife
of JOHN TURNER . . . . . departed
this life
Sept. . . . . . .
Here Lyeth ye body of JOHN
TURNER . . . . . . Husband of Jane
Turner . . . . . . ry 11
1721 Aged 84 years.

XVIII.

(*An altar tomb*)

Here lieth Interred the Body of
MARY Wife of the Revd Mr Peter
Innes Rector of this Parish. She
was the only surviving Daughtr
of Stepn & Catharine Nethersole
late of Wimingswold. She died
Jan. 11th 1748. Aged 60 years.

ARMS.—A fess engrailed between three
stars impaling per pale three Griffins
segreant. No tinctures recorded.

XIX.

(*A flat stone*)

*Here lieth
interred*
The body of
THOMAS DENWARD,
Who departed this Life
June 25th 1768, Aged
75 years.

XX.

In pious memory of
MARY ELLEN
The beloved wife of
PERCY JAMES CROFT, M.A.
Rector of this parish.
She departed this life
September 13th 1869. Aged 37.
" Those that seek Me early shall find
Me "

---

* The above 2 Brasses are only plain inscriptions. On another stone in the
Chancel the matrix shows the figures of a man & wife with son and daughters &
legend beneath. At the corners were 4 shields, two of which still remain. One
has the figure of a bull, the other of a goat, with the letters *Agraciar* on a scroll
in each shield. The Brass has been assigned by competent authority to the end of
the 15th century. *Hasted* is in error in stating that it is to the memory of Tho.
Boteler, who was Rector here in 1414. See his name in the List of Rectors.

Also
In Loving memory of the above
PERCY JAMES CROFT, M.A.
23 years Rector of this parish,
Who departed this life
April 11th 1884,
Aged 64 years.
"Ye are My friends if ye do
Whatsoever I command you."

XXI.

(*A Marble Cross*)
In affectionate memory of
Amelia Anna Croft *
Died January 24th 1886
Aged 42 years.

XXII.

Here lieth interred ye
Body of Mr. John Rye
Late of Bridge, who
Departed this life ye
17th of Sept 1742, in
Ye 61st year of his age.

XXIII.

Here lieth the body of
Ann Pain, wife of
RICHARD PAIN,
She departed this life
March ye 7th, 1777,
Aged 76 years.

Also the above Rich. Pain,
He died ye 20th of March
1779. Aged 73 years.

XXIV.

Here lieth the Body of
Abraham Baker & Mary
His wife. He died Mar: 21
1749. Aged 87 years. She
Died April 21 1746
Aged 72 years and left
Issue 4 children, viz., Ann,
Mary, Abr: & Thos.

XXV.

William
Only Son of
THOMAS & SARAH
ELLEN
Died Decr 6th, 1808,
Aged 7 years.

XXVI.

Here lie Interred the remains
of JOHN APOSTLE
Who departed this life
Suddenly Dec. 13th, 1824,
Aged 62 years.
"Boast not thyself of to-morrow
For thou knowest not what a day may
bring forth."– Prov. xxvii.,
"There is but a step between me and
death."—1 Sam. xx., 3.

XXVII.

Here lieth Interred ye Body of
JOHN LADE of this Parish
Who departed this life Dec. 15th, 1761,
In the 70th year of his Age.
Leaving *Mary* the Wife of
William Coates his surviving Issue.
He maried *Jane Atwood* of Upper
Hardres
Deceased who left issue by the said
John Lade, 4 children
ANN who died in ye 18th year of her
Age.
JOHN who died in ye 13 year of his Age.
ELIZ. who died in ye 34 year of her
Age.
The said *Mary Coates* who in obedience
to so Good a Parent, Erected this
stone.

XXVIII.

IN MEMORY
of JOHN WOOD, late of this Parish, He
died 13th Sept, 1778, aged 60 years.
Also two children by Jane his Wife
Mary } died { May 12th 1778 }
John } died { Dec. 1st 1778 }
Aged { 10 weeks
      { 9 yrs. 7 months.
Tho in Dust we lay our Heads,
Yett Gracious God, Thou wilt not leave
Our Souls for ever, with the Dead,
Nor Lose thy Children in the Grave ;
Our Flesh, shall thy first call Obey,
Shake off the Dust, and rise on High
Then shalt Thou lead, the wondrous way
Up to thy Throne above the Sky.

XXIX.

To the Memory of
CHRISTOPHER WOOD
Late of this Parish
Who departed this life
Nov. the 6th 1798
Aged 26 years,
He left to survive him
MARY his Wife and One Son
JOHN MARSH.

---

* Widow of the Rev. P. J. Croft.

XXX.

In Memory of
JOHN MARSH WOOD
Late of Westwood Farm in this Parish
Who departed this life the 18th day of
December 1875
Aged 80 years.

In memory of
MARY ANN wife of JOHN MARSH
WOOD
Late of Westwood Farm in this Parish
Who departed this life the 10th day
of April 1866
Aged 71 years.

XXXI.

In affectionate Remembrance of
JOHN WOOD
Of Westwood in this Parish
Who died Jan 20th 1870
Aged 45 years
" Thy Will be done."
"To die is Gain."

XXXII.

Here lieth ye Body of
Thomas Law he died
Jan 23rd. 1745, in the
34th year of his Age.
Also here lieth Ann
his Daughtr Aged 2 months.

XXXIII.

Here lieth the Body
of Peter Grant of
this Parish who died
Oct. 18th. 1719 Aged
44 years.

XXXIV.

Here lieth ye Body of
PETER GRANT son of
Peter Grant of this
Parish, who departed this
life Jan 9th 1737
Aged 25 years.

XXXV.

Here lyes ye body of
William Hopkins of
this Parish who Dyed
the 20 day of Sept,
1714. Aged 68 years.

XXXVI.

BENEATH this Tablet
Are deposited the
Mortal remains of
ELIZABETH BARTLETT
Who departed this life
November 20th 1829
Aged 43 years.
Lowly contrite patient
And resigned to Him
Whose mercy chastened
And whose Spirit guided her
She lived.
Lowly, contrite, patient
And resigned to Him
Whose blood redeemed,
And grace supported her
She died.
" *Thanks be to* GOD,
Which giveth us the victory
Through our LORD JESUS CHRIST."
1 Corinthns., XV Ch , 57 v.

XXXVII.

(*An altar tomb enclosed with iron railings*)
Sacred
To the memory of
Sarah Gardner
Wife of Robert Gardner
Who died August, 7. 1828
Aged 43 years.

And also
The following children
Of Robert and Sarah Gardner

Austen Gardner
Who died May 4th 1813
Aged 5 months.

Sarah Gardner
Who died March, 29. 1824
Aged 13 years.

Henry Gardner
Who died May 22nd 1824
Aged 7 years.

Austen Gardner
Who died June 28th 1824
Aged 13 months.

Martha Gardner
Who died April 11th ; 1825
Aged 6 years.

William Gardner
Who died June 25th 1829
Aged 20 years.

Robert Gardner
Who died Decr. 15th 1829
Aged 23 years.

Richard Gardner
Who died May 21st 1831
Aged 23 years.

Helen Gardner
Who died June 3rd 1831
Aged 13 years.

Harry Gardner
Who died March 25th 1835
Aged 10 years.

Also the above
Robert Gardner, Senr
Who died on the 25th June 1856
Aged 75.

XXXVIII.

John Ballard Johnstone
Born June 15th. Died August 4th 1831.

XXXIX.

This Stone is erected to
The Memory of
GEORGE BENEFIELD
Of this Parish
Who died June 19th 1854
Aged 89 years
Leaving a widow
(To whom he had been
United 64 years)
And a numerous family
of Children and
Great grandchildren
To lament their loss.

Jesus said

"*I am the* WAY *and the* TRUTH
And the LIFE. *No man cometh
Unto the* FATHER *but by* ME."

XIV. St. John 6.

"*And him that cometh unto* ME
I will in no wise cast out."

VI. St. John, 37.

Also ELIZABETH

The widow of the above who
Died the 21st day of May 1857
Aged 93 years.

XL.

Sacred to the Memory of
JAMES BROOKS
who departed this life
April 19 1829
Aged 62 years.
He had lived much respected for his
exemplary conduct 37 years in the
service of
JAMES HALLETT *Esqre of Higham*
and on his master's death retired
for the
remainder of his days to his own
freehold in this parish,
contentedly but not ostentatiously
showing the good effects here below of
Industry, Sobriety and Honesty, and
looking
with steady Faith in his Redeemer
JESUS CHRIST for the fulfilment
of that time at which Just Men
will be made perfect.
This Stone was placed near his remains
by his affectionate Sister Elizabeth
the wife of GEORGE MORGAN.

XLI.

Sacred
To the Memory of
GEORGE MORGAN
Late of this Parish
Who died Feb. 3rd 1830
Aged 68 years

Also ELIZABETH his wife
Who died Jany. 9th 1843
Aged 79 years
A good servant
and a faithful friend.

*This stone was erected
By their affectionate niece*
ANGELIA RICHARDSON
1845

XLII.

To the memory of
JOSEPH BROOKS
*Late of Marley Farm
in this Parish*
Who departed this life
on the 8th of February
1839. Aged 61 years.

*This Stone was erected
by his beloved Wife*
CHARLOTTE BROOKS

XLIII.

Here lyeth the Body of Rosellen Eliza,
relict of Colonel Torré
of Sugdale
In the County of York.
She departed this life January XIXth
MD.CCCLXII aged LXXXI years.
"To be with Christ is far better."

XLIV.

In memory of
Julius Benson Collard
Who died May 7th 1868
Aged 3 months.

XLV.

In Loving Memory of
JAMES COLTHAM
Born 14th August 1812
Died 22nd Oct 1877.
" Blessed are the dead that die in the
Lord."

XLVI.

In memory of
RICHARD ALBERT
BENEFIELD
Who fell asleep
at Headcorn
January 17th 1876
Aged 24 years.
" Thy will be done."

XLVII.

MARY A. BENEFIELD
1855 . 1859
SUSANNA L. BENEFIELD
1860 . 1861
Ere sin could blight or sorrow fade
Death came with friendly care
The opening buds to heaven convey'd
And bade them blossom there.

XLVIII.

In memory of
JAMES ROBBINS
Who departed this life
November 23rd 1862
Aged 73 years.
" Blessed are the dead which die in
the Lord."
Also of
SUSANNAH
The beloved wife of the above,
Who died 15th December 1874
Aged 84 years.

XLIX.

In affectionate Remembrance of
THOMAS WHITE
Late of this Parish
Who departed this life
December 14th 1870
Aged 42 years.
" Not my will but Thine be done."

L.

In loving remembrance of
WALTER CHARLES BROOKS
Who fell asleep at Ashford
April 4th 1880 aged 24 years.
"What I do thou knowest not now
"but thou shalt know hereafter."

LI.

In Memory of
SARAH
Wife of JOHN HORTON
Who died Febry 5th 1818
Aged 78 years.
"Afflictions sore "—&c., &c.

LII.

In Memory of
JOHN PILCHER
of this Parish
Who departed this life
24th of July 1831, aged 70 years.

Also of
ELIZABETH
Second Wife of the above
Who departed this life
18th of June 1817, aged 53 years.

The following Inscriptions are from
Monuments to former Rectors
of Kingstone who were interred
elsewhere :—

LIII.

(*In Chirke Church, Denbighshire.*)

M.S.

" Hic situs est vir eximius Gualterus
Balcanquallus S. S. Theol., Professor,
qui ex Scotia oriundus, ob singu-
larem eruditionem aulæ Pembrochi-
anæ in acad. Cantabr. socius factus

est, et inter theologos Britannos Synodo Dordracensi interfuit (1618), mox regiæ majestati a sacris, Xenodochii Sabaudiensis Londini præpositus, et decanus primo Roffensis (12 May 1624) dein Dunelmensis (14 May 1639) omnia hæc officia sive dignitates magnis virtutibus ornavit. Tum vero in Scotianæ Rebellionis arcanis motibus observandis atque detegendis solentissime versatus est, in rebellione Anglicana regi maxime fidus ; obsidione Eboraci liberatus, et in has oras se contulit, ubi perhumaniter exceptus, sed ab hostibus cupidissime quæsitus, et exturbatus hiemali tempestate mire sœviente tutelam castelli in proximo confugit, et morbo ex infesti itineris tædio corruptus, ipso die Nativitatis Christi ad Dominum migravit. An. Œræ Christianœ 1645.

Hœc in memoriam defuncti scripsit Johannes Cestriensis rogatu viri nobilissimi Thomœ Middleton, baronetti, qui ex pio animi proposito sua cura atque sumptu hoc monumentum posuit." (*Wood's "Athenœ Oxon.,"* & *" Durham Cathedral," Willis.*)

LIV.

(In the Chancel of Barham Church, Kent).

M.S.

Gulielmi Barne Generosi
Filii Reverendi Milesii Barne
Ecclesiœ Anglicanœ Presbuteri et
Janæ illius
Uxoris quæ illi peperit sex filios
Filiasque Duas.
Avum habuit Dom. Gulielmum Barne
De Woolwich Militem Auratum,
Erat dum vixit Pater optimus
Conjux Amantissimus
Subditus fidelis Pauperum Amicus
At jam Bonis omnibus flebilis occidit
Mensis Jun. Die 16 : A.D. 1706.
Ætatis suæ 64.
Pater extremum diem clausit
Mens. Sep. Die 1 An. D. 1670
Ætat. suæ 70.
Mater obiit
Apr die 6
1680.

LV.

(In the North Transept of Chartham Church. Kent.)

Hic situs est
JOHANNES MAXIMILIANUS De
L'ANGLE
Ecclesiœ Metropoliticœ Cantuarensis
Canonicus,
Et Hujus Ecclesiœ Parochialis Rector;
Ortu quidem Gallus,
Sed et Affectu et Disciplina Noster.
Cujus Pater, Ecclesiâ Reformatâ
Rothomagi Minister
Anglicanam quam magni fecerit
Ecclesiam
Testimoniis satis apertis indicavit,
Cum aliâs, tum maxime, quod hunc
suum Filium
Ejusdem Ecclesiœ Ordinibus insigniri
voluit :
Alterum vero Samuelem ita instituit,
Ut Carentonii celeberrimam Protestantium Ecclesiam
Pastor Acciperet
Eiq. multa cum laude prœesset,
Donec An : Ch : 1682 flagrante Persecutionis Furore
Religionis Reformatœ cultoribus
Nihil restaret, præter carceres et
Exilia ;
Tum demum, cæteris rebus relictis
Cum uxore et liberis in Angliam
migravit,
Ubi pro meritis suis benigne acceptus
est,
Et Præbendâ Ecc : Westmonasteriensis Honestatus
Ita apud nos uterq. Frater
Ut Riveti, Molinæij et Bocharti
cognatus decuit,
Et dignitatem, et Emolumenta satis
ampla consecuti
Ingentem, quam Exteri sœpe conflant, Invidiam
Morum facilitate,
Animi Candore,
Largitione in pauperes,
Et cœteris, quæ Christianum ornant,
dotibus
Fœliciter extinxerunt.
Obiit JOHANNES Nov. 14, 1724, Æt. 83.
Juxta dormit uxor ejus Genevova
Quœ senio confecta obiit Oct: 30,
1729 Æt. 99.
Utrisque Monumentum hoc ponendum curavit
Nepos omnibus nodis devinctus
THEOPH : De L'ANGLE.

R

LVI.

(In Fulham Churchyard, Middlesex.,

Here lieth the Remains of Beata
Willyams
youngest Daughter of John Willyams
Esqr
of Plaistow House, Essex, by Annie
his wife, sister of John Dineley Bart.
of Burghope in Herefordshire.
She was born Sept. 29 1766 & died
Oct 3 1791.
In the same Vault are deposited
the Remains of the Rev. Cooper
Willyams, Late
Rector of Kingstone & of Stour-
mouth in
the County of Kent, son of the above-
named John & Annie Willyams.
He was born June 22th 1762
Died July 17th 1816.

LVII.

*(In Burton Latimer Churchyard,
Northampton.)*

In Memory of
Thomas Bartlett A.M.

For 15 years
Rector of this Parish.
He entered into rest
May 28th 1872. Aged 82 years.
" Them also which sleep in JESUS will
GOD bring with Him."
I Thess. iv. 14.

In Memory of Catherine Sarah the
beloved
Wife of Thomas Bartlett M.A,
Rector of this
Parish. She departed Sept. 9th 1863,
aged 74 years
In humble but firm Reliance upon
the Merits of her
Redeemer, almost her last words
were—" How
beautiful it is to fall asleep in Jesus."

LVIII.

*(In Carleton Forehoe Churchyard,
Norfolk.)*

Philip George Bartlett, Rector of
Kirton, Suffolk.
Died March 19th 1876. 56 years.
" Through Jesus Christ our Lord."

INDEX OF BAPTISMS, (pp. 1—85.)

(When a name is printed in Italics it denotes that the entry occurs in the Transcript only, and will be found in the footnotes of the page of the Registers for the year quoted.)

Adam,
  Susanna, 1662.
  Catherine, 1666.
{ Affield,
{ Haffield,
{ Harfield,
  Alice, 1562.
  Elinor, 1569.
{ Allen,
{ Alleine,
  Mary, 1590.
  Margaret, 1619.
  Joane, 1622.
  John, 1625.
  Mildred, 1628
  Mary, 1630.
  Elizabeth, 1632.
  Griffin, 1641.
Andrews,
  Ann, 1692.
  John, 1692.
  Ric., 1695.
  Thomasin, 1697.
Anselme,
  Ja., 1709.
{ Arger,
{ Argor,
{ Argill,
  Richard, 1558.
  Joanne, 1563.
  Margery, 1563.
  Anna, 1565.
Ashby,
  John, 1739.
Atwood,
  Elizabeth, 1659.
  Ann, 1662.
  Abraham, 1666.
  Abigal, 1670.
  Ann, 1675.
  Mary, 1683.
  Tho., 1699.
  Eliz., 1702.
  John, 1704.
  Abraham, 1726.
  William, 1788.
  Henry, 1795.
  Edward, 1797.
  James, 1799.
  James, 1801.
  Elizabeth, 1804.

Atwo xl *(cont.)*
  Sarah, 1804
  Mary, 1805.
Auger,
  Jane, 1624.
Austen,
  Elizabeth, 1575.
  Anna, 1577.
Backer,
  Richard, 1701.
  Edward, 1701.
Bailey,
  Ann, 1779.
Baits,
  (See Betts).
Baker,
  Alice, 1561.
  Jane, 1597.
  ffrancis, 1630.
  Thomas, 1633.
  Margaret, 1634.
  James, 1635.
  Richard, 1638.
  Henry, 1641.
  Elizabeth, 1641.
  Charles, 1642
  Edward, 1699.
  Abigal, 1699.
  John, 1702.
  Ann, 1704.
  Hen., 1712.
  Rich., 1713.
  Thomas, 1715.
  Thomas, 1716.
  Edward, 1716.
  ffrancis, 1718.
  Robert, 1721.
  Margaret, 1730
  Henry, 1736.
  Sarah, 1739.
  Ann, 1741.
  Sarah, 1743.
  Mary, 1748.
  Margaret, 1753.
  Thomas, 1758.
  Edward, 1759.
  Elizabeth, 1759.
Baldock,
  Elizabeth, 1582.
  Matthew, 1584.

Baldock *(cont.)*
  Margaret, 1601.
Barber,
  Nicholas, 1629.
  Ruth, 1638.
Barron,
  William, 1782.
Bassock,
  George, 1596.
  Mary, 1597.
  Jane, 1600.
Bates,
  (See Betts).
Baynes,
  Hewly, 1684.
Beak,
  Mary, 1635.
  Thomas, 1637.
  William, 1640.
  Margaret, 1642.
Bean,
  Elizabeth, 1692.
  Mary, 1693.
  Tho., 1696.
  John, 1698.
  Sarah, 1703.
  Amy, 1706.
  Carolina, 1752.
  Edward, 1755.
Beek,
  Elizabeth, 1807.
  Thomas, 1809.
Beer,
  Barbara, 1633.
  William, 1636.
  Leah, 1638.
  Jno., 1709.
  Dav., 1715.
  Rob., 1717.
  Edward, 1722.
  Mary, 1724.
  Jane, 1728.
  Margaret, 1731.
  Mary, 1731.
  Edward, 1734.
  Benjamin, 1737.
  William, 1739.
  Edward, 1749.
  Margaret, 1752.
  Richard, 1754.
  James, 1756.

Beer *(cont.)*
  Mary, 1759.
  William, 1762.
  Elizabeth, 1766.
  Elizabeth, 1769.
  John, 1774.
  Ann, 1778.
  Francis, 1780.
  Sarah, 1800.
  Maria, 1803.
  William H. 1806.
  Elizabeth, 1807.
  Amelia, 1809.
Belsey.
  John, 1762.
Benefield,
  William, 1806.
Best,
  John, 1775.
  Joseph, 1778.
  Catherine, 1779.
{ Betts,
{ Baits,
{ Bates,
  Thos., 1692.
  Will., 1693.
  John, 1695.
  Matthew, 1697.
  Sarah, 1699.
  Margaret, 1700.
Bewley,
  Mildred, 1733.
  Thomas, 1735.
  Wilmot, 1738.
  Stephen, 1741.
{ Birch,
{ Burch,
  An, 1607.
  Ann, 1699.
  Eliz., 1701.
  James 1703.
  Jno., 1705.
  Jno., 1708.
  Tho., 1710.
  Rich., 1713.
  Mary, 1716.
  Henry, 1718.
  Ann, 1730.
  Mary, 1732.
  Sarah, 1735.
  Elizabeth, 1737.

INDEX OF BAPTISMS, (pp. 1—85.)

Birch (cont.)
Esther, 1740.
Hannah, 1742.
James, 1745.
James, 1746.
Martha, 1747.
Mary, 1751.
John, 1752.
Blackewood,
Thos., 1568.
Bonham,
Vincent, 1633.
Richard, 1633.
Boughton,
Jone, 1575.
Ann, 1778.
{ Boultane,
{ Boulton,
Matthew, 1559.
Luke, 1565.
John, 1566.
Bowes,
George, 1801.
Susanna, 1801.
Bownes,
John, 1569.
{ Boyce,
{ Boyes,
{ Boys,
Thomas, 1656.
Robert, 1658.
Mary, 1660.
Elizabeth, 1661.
Jane, 1663.
John, 1666.
Ann, 1668.
William, 1671.
Edward, 1674.
{ Boykett,
{ Boykins,
Joane. 1572.
Elizabeth, 1579.
Arthur, 1580.
John, 1582.
Margaret, 1582.
Robert, 1585.
Nicholas, 1588.
John, 1590
Jane, 1593.
Mathie, 1605.
Elias, 1614.
Marget, 1617.
Mary, 1620.
John, 1625.
Ann, 1628.
Bradbury,
William, 1799.
Bradshaw,
Edward, 1566.
Henry, 1568.
William, 1570.
Martha, 1572.
Jane, 1573
Charles, 1575.

{ Branslet,
{ Bransley,
{ Branchly,
{ Brenchley,
Thomas, 1624.
Vincent, 1627.
Benet, 1629.
Augustine, 1629.
Samuel, 1631.
Sarah, 1631.
Joane, 1634.
John, 1636.
Mary, 1639.
William 1642.
Samuel, 1653.
Willman, 1653.
Mary, 1655.
Augustine, 1656.
Thomas, 1659.
Sam., 1660.
Sam., 1661.
Edward, 1661.
Samuel, 1663.
Affery, 1665.
Henrietta 1669.
* Ann, 1681.
Brett,
Stephen, 1739.
{ Brice,
{ Brise,
Susanna, 1662.
John † 1669.
Catharine. 1665.
Jane, 1677.
John, 1687.
Stephen, 1689.
Solomon, 1689.
Cathrain 1696.
{ Bridge,
{ Bridges,
William, 1615.
John, 1617.
Marget, 1620.
Mary, 1622.
Brigge,
William, 1594.
Brisley,
William, 1761.
Edward, 1764.
Brooks,
Elizabeth, 1763.
Thomas, 1765.
Ann, 1768.
John, 1770.
Richard, 1773.
Michael, 1775.
Joseph, 1778.
Charlotte, 1780.
Sarah, 1782.
Isaac, 1784.
William, 1787.
Thomas, 1801.
Browne,
Ann, 1635.

Browne (cont.)
Elizabeth, 1638.
Thomas, 1641.
Bennet, 1656.
Browning,
Richard, 1558.
Mathew, 1566.
Nicholas, 1568.
Christyan, 1570.
Jane. 1573.
John, 1577.
Paul, 1580.
Edward, 1581.
John, 1583.
Mary. 1588.
Margaret, 1593.
Jane, 1594.
Katherine, 1595.
John, 1596.
Robert, 1601.
James, 1603.
Joane, 1611.
Sara, 1613.
Richard, 1614.
Anne, 1615.
Marget, 1616.
Mary, 1616.
Paul, 1618.
Edward, 1619.
Ann, 1620.
Mary, 1623.
Elizabeth, 1624.
Homfray, 1627.
Mary, 1670.
John, 1678.
Mathew, 1702.
John, 1707.
Jane, 1710.
Tho, 1716.
Edward, 1718.
John, 1752.
Thomas, 1753.
Thomas, 1754.
Matthew, 1755.
Elizabeth, 1756.
Thos., 1759.
Edward, 1764.
Elizabeth, 1764.
Edward, 1777.
Ann, 1782.
Thomas, 1785.
Martha, 1799.
John, 1803.
Edward, 1807.
Buddell,
Thomas, 1719.
Francis, 1722
Budds,
Sarah, 1648.
Bunce,
Jone, 1573.
Vincent, 1575.
Mary, 1577.
Margaret, 1580.

Bunce (cont.)
Susan, 1582.
Jane, 1584.
Alice, 1586.
Burch,
(See Birch).
Burton,
Richard, 1642.
Bushell,
Christian, 1644.
Thomas, 1667.
John, 1751.
Thomas, 1753.
Butler,
Thomas, 1591.
Robert, 1744.
Valentine, 1746.
Mary, 1749.
Camborne,
Thos., 1697.
Sarah, 1697.
Carden,
Catharine, 1738.
Cason,
Susanna, 1678.
Frances, 1683.
Henry, 1684.
Ann, 1688.
{ Casselden,
{ Castleden,
Ann, 1748.
Thomas, 1750.
Eliz., 1750.
Mary, 1751.
Mary, 1752
Martha, 1753.
Martha, 1753.
Henry, 1754.
Michael, 1754.
Sarah, 1757.
John, 1760.
Marcey, 1762.
Richard, 1765.
Castle,
Jane, 1764.
Edward, 1773.
Ann, 1776.
Henry, 1779.
Sarah, 1787.
Sarah, 1794.
Catchpole,
Jane, 1687.
Sarah, 1689
Tho., 1692.
Chambers,
Mary, 1589.
Thomas, 1595.
Elizabeth, 1597.
Richard, 1600.
Martha, 1604.
Chandler,
Mercy, 1581.

INDEX OF BAPTISMS, (pp. 1—85.)

Church,
  Jane, 1768.
Churchman,
  John, 1589.
Claringbold,
  Mary, 1631
  Thomas, 1632.
  John, 1737.
  Nicholson, 1739.
  Thomas B. 1741.
  Joanna, 1743.
  Jane, 1746.
  Richard Da-
    vison, 1748
Cocklin,
  George, 1660.
  Martha. 1662.
  Elizabeth, 1665.
Codham,
  Edward, 1808.
  Maria, 1809.
  Eliza, 1811.
Cole,
  Katherine, 1559.
Collard,
  Bartholo-
    mew 1779.
  Winifred, 1781.
  Ann, 1794.
Collens,
  Thomasine, 1577.
{ Collar,
{ Coller,
  Mary, 1714.
  Edward, 1719.
  Michael, 1721.
  Mary, 1723.
  Richard, 1725.
  Henry, 1727.
  Mary, 1744.
  Sarah, 1746.
  Elizabeth, 1783.
  Rich, C. 1785.
  John, 1786.
  Ann, 1792.
  Mary, 1795.
  William, 1798.
  Catherine, 1801.
Collison,
  William, 1780.
Cook,
  Ann, 1732.
Cooley,
  John, 1578.
Cooman,
  Mary, 1726.
  Elizabeth, 1729.
{ Coorte,
{ Court,
  John, 1589.
  Jone, 1594.
  Thomasin, 1643.
  Clement, 1659.
  Ann, 1661.

Coppin, *
  Mary, 1597.
Cosbye,
  Alice, 1575.
  Martha, 1577.
Couchman,
  Mary, 1784.
  Grace, 1786.
  Alice, 1797.
  Gregory, 1790.
Coulson,
  Mary, 1582.
Covenny,
  James, 1792.
Cox,
  Nicholas, 1654.
Craye,
  John, 1577.
  Elizabeth, 1580.
  Jane,† 1583.
  Mary, 1587.
  Vincent, 1589.
  Thomas, 1621.
  Mary, 1625.
Crome,‡
  Nic, 1579.
{ Culline,
{ Cullen,
  Gylion, 1580.
  Thomas,|| 1587.
  Robert, 1609.
  William, 1631.
  Gregory, 1641.
  John, 1746.
  John, 1751.
Dale,
  Sibell, 1596.
  Jane, 1600.
  Edward, 1602.
Davie,
  Mary, 1560.
Davis,
  Elizabeth, 1597.
  Mary, 1727.
  John, 1782.
Dawkins,
  Ann, 1771.
Denne,
  Jane, 1573.
  Thomas, 1574.
  Thomas, 1577.
  Mary, 1577.
  Henry, 1579.
  Vincent, 1579.
  Vincent, 1581.
  Nicholas, 1581.
  Silvester, 1582.
  Ann, 1584.
  John, 1584.
  Mary, 1587.
  Catharine, 1587.
  Edward, 1589.
  Robert, 1591.

Denne (cont.)
  John, 1597.
  Anna, 1600.
  Lucy, 1602.
  Vincent, 1603.
  Vincent, 1612.
  Catherine, 1613.
  Edward, 1616.
Dewell,
  Edwin, 1626.
Dilnot,
  Elizabeth, 1734.
  Thomas, 1739.
  John, 1760.
Dine,
  William, 1780.
  John, 1786.
  Charlotte, 1788.
  James, 1791.
  William, 1793.
  Mary, 1796.
Dines,
  Mary, 1811.
Dingley,
  Paull, 1648.
  Nicholas, 1649.
  Christian, 1658.
Dixon,
  Thomas, 1642.
Donne,
  John, 1665.
  James, 1668.
Dorne,
  Margaret, 1573.
  William, 1575.
Draper,
  Mary, 1665.
  William, 1670.
  Ann, 1673.
  Jane, 1676.
  Alice, 1677.
Eareth,
  William, 1809.
  Sarah, 1811.
Eaton,
  Marget, 1610.
  William, 1612.
  Elizabeth, 1613.
  Robert, 1617.
Ellen,
  Halke, 1771.
  Elizabeth, 1774.
  Elizabeth, 1793.
  Valentine, 1797.
  William, 1801.
  Sarah, 1803.
{ Eltington,
{ Eltonton,
  John, 1722.
  Edward, 1724.
  Thomas, 1726.
Eridge,
  John, 1696.

Everden,
  Robert, 1620.
  Mary, 1622.
Ewell,
  Anna, 1659.
Fagg,
  James, 1795.
  Stephen, 1810.
  Charlotte, 1811.
Faunce,
  Mary, 1669.
  Elizabeth, 1671.
  Margaret, 1673.
  Robert, 1675.
Faussett,
  Bryan, 1753.
Fetherston,
  Thomas, 1790.
File,
  Eliza, A. 1812.
Finch,
  Susanna, 1771.
Finnis,
  Thomas, 1760.
  Sarah, 1764.
  Elizabeth, 1765.
  Elizabeth, 1766.
  Thomas, 1771.
  Maria, 1774.
  Thomasine 1776.
Fisher,
  John, 1806.
Fittell,
  (See Vittell).
Fogg,
  Hezechias, 1632.
  Elizabeth, 1633.
  Thomas, 1634.
  William, 1635.
{ Foord,
{ Forde,
  Stephen, 1596.
  Henry, 1663.
  James, 1663.
  Jane, 1664.
  Sarah, 1665.
  Mary, 1667.
  Henry,§ 1668.
  Jane, 1671.
  Richard, 1672.
  William, 1675.
  Margrit, 1684.
  Thomas, 1687.
  ———, 1689.
  Richard, 1691.
  Robert, 1711.
  Edward, 1711.
  Tho., 1714.
  Eliz., 1715.
  Ann, 1716.
  Elizabeth, 1718.
  Thomas, 1747.
  Robert, 1749.

---

* Toppin (?)   † John Cray, Transcript.   ‡ Trome (?).
|| Tomsen Cullen, Transcript.   § Inserted in Burials Register, Page 133.

S

INDEX OF BAPTISMS, (pp. 1—85.)

Foord, }
Forde, } (cont.)
Edward, 1751.
Thomas, 1781.
Edward, 1782.
Robert, 1783.
Thomas, 1783.
Robert, 1785.
Sarah, 1788.
Mary, 1792.
George, 1798.
Edward, 1807.
Thomas, 1809.
John, 1809.
Mary, 1811.
Robert, 1811.
Fowell, }
Vowell, }
Elizabeth, 1650.
Thomas, 1653.
Elizabeth, 1689.
Tho., 1692.
An., 1694.
Mary, 1698.
John, 1700.
Mary, 1703.
Friend,
John, 1630.
Thomas, 1633.
John, 1746.
Robert, 1750.
Frierson,
Mary, 1654.
Fuller,
William, 1740.
Gammon,
Katherine, 1665.
Elizabeth, 1666.
Gansine,
Alice, 1564.
Gardner,
Robert, 1806.
Richard, 1807.
William, 1809.
Gasking,
Mary, 1739
George,
Martha, 1609.
German,
Elizabeth, 1810.
Sarah, 1811.
Mary, 1812.
Gibbon,
William, 1649.
Elizabeth, 1650.
Dameris, 1655.
Giles,
Mary, 1617.
John, 1619.
Margery, 1620.
John, 1625.
Gloover,
Richard, 1602.

Godden, }
Godding, }
(See Goodwin).
Godfray,
Joane, 1625.
Gold, }
Gould, }
Elizabeth, 1563.:
Thomas, 1575.
Robert, 1577.
Phillip, 1580.
Elnor, 1582.
John, 1585
John, 1589
Margarett, 1591.
William, 1613.
Mary, 1615.
John, 1617.
Roger, 1620.
George 1622.
Stephen, 1622.
Robert, 1626.
Ann, 1637.
Marie, 1643.
Golder, }
Goulder, }
Mary, 1681.
Elizabeth, 1683.
Ann, 1687.
Catharine, 1691.
Tho : 1699.
Mary, 1708.
Tho : 1710.
Ann 1715.
Steph., 1717.
John, 1752.
Sarah, 1756.
Ann, 1761.
Goodwin, }
Godwyn, }
Godden. }
Godding, }
Margaret, 1594.
Elizabeth, 1597.
Mary, 1637.
Margaret, 1642.
Griffin, 1644.
John, 1645.
Sarah, 1648.
Susanna, 1717.
Thomas, 1722.
Mary, 1726.
Jane, 1726.
Margaret, 1729.
Henry, 1731.
David, 1731.
Sarah, 1756.
William, 1760.
James, 1764.
Gookine,
Mary, 1569.
Grant,
Edmund, 1673.
Peter, 1675.

Grant (cont.)
Henry, 1677.
Elizabeth, 1680.
John, 1682.
Jane, 1685.
Mary, 1689.
Gray,
(See Grey).
Green,
Ann, 1710.
Thomas, 1791.
Mary, 1793.
Sarah, 1795.
Greenstreet,
John, 1786.
Gregorie,
Elene, 1608.
Grew,
Abigail, 1732.
Grey, }
Gray, }
John, 1649.
Sara, 1652.
Thomas, 1656.
Margaret, 1663.
Margaret, 1666.
Tho., 1667.
Judith, 1670.
Jane, 1746.
Grigg,
Joane, 1615.
Grime, }
Gryme, }
Agnis, 1558.
Mercie, 1558.
Simon, 1562.
Groome,
John, 1565.
William, 1566.
Haddine. }
Hadden, }
Haddinge, }
Haddyne, }
Isabell, 1572.
Thomas, 1577.
Susan, 1579.
Dennis, 1582.
Jeffery, 1585.
John, 1589.
Haffield,
(See Affield).
Hallaiday,
(See Holliday).
Hambrook,
James, 1682.
Richard, 1685.
Elizabeth, 1688.
Mary, 1691.
Harffield,
(See Affield).
Harnett,
Sarah, 1765.

Hastifer, }
Hasley, }
Edward, 1620.
Thomas, 1624.
Hastlyn,
Mary, 1588.
John, 1590.
Joane, 1593.
Affra, 1597.
Hatcher,
Edward, 1613.
Haule,
Alice, 1572.
Hayward,
*Elizabeth,1655.
* Arthur, 1657.
Ann, 1662.
Hedgecock,
John, 1639.
John, 1640.
Henrie, 1643.
John, 1660.
Richard, 1664.
Heringe,
Daniel, 1607.
Hersefield,
John, 1804.
Hobday,
Elizabeth, 1636.
Richard, 1639.
John, 1643.
Mildred, 1695.
Willmot, 1697.
Thomas, 1701.
Hogben,
Clemente, 1608.
Stephen 1633.
Elizabeth, 1677.
Parnell, 1746.
William, 1747.
Richard, 1749.
Hogbone,
Anne, 1614.
Hoge,
Walter, 1720.
Holliday, }
Holyday, }
Halliday. }
Thomas, 1663.
William, 1665.
Daniel, 1669.
Thomas, 1672.
Edward, 1674.
David, 1676.
John, 1696.
Tho., 1698.
An, 1700.
John, 1704.
Susanna, 1706.
Thomas, 1708.
Hollams,
Elizabeth, 1782.
Holloway,
Peter, 1563.

* Entered among Marriage Registers, pp. 96-97.

INDEX OF BAPTISMS, (*pp. 1—85.*)

Holman,
Thomasine,1794.
Holmes,
JohnHanley,1795.
Thomas, 1796.
{ Hopkin,
{ Hopkins,
Thomas, 1572.
Jone, 1579.
Dennis, 1579.
Mildred, 1582.
Susan, 1582.
Thomasine,1585.
Dionys, 1611.
Mary, 1616.
William, 1617.
Sarah, 1619.
Edmonde, 1620.
Martha, 1623.
Jane, 1624.
Catherine, 1624.
Thomas, 1635.
Thomas, 1642.
Mary, 1662.
John, 1664.
Elizabeth, 1677.
Thomas, 1680.
Will, 1681.
Sarah, 1717.
Susanna, 1720.
Michael, 1772.
Horton,.
Peter, 1559.
John, 1563.
Sarah, 1703.
William, 1761.
John, 1765.
Thos., 1768.
Sarah, 1775.
Hudson,
John, 1760.
Huffam,
Steven, 1639.
Michael, 1640.
Thos., 1642.
Huse,
Annie, 1605.
Ingester,
Thos., 1608.
Inkepitt,
John, 1679.
Thos., 1680.
Jacob,
John, 1767.
Sam., 1769.
William, 1771.
Eliz. A., 1774.
William, 1776.
Jemmett,
Sarah A., 1790.
Johnson,
Thomas, 1565.
George, 1607.
Eliz., 1608.
William, 1746.

Jones.
Eliz., 1635.
Myhill, 1637.
Jordan,
Thos. T., 1795.
Juce,
Thos., 1680.
Jull,
Robert, 1661.
Eles, 1659.
Eliz., 1662.
Jure,
(*See* Juce).
Keeler,
Elizabeth, 1766.
Mary, 1772.
Thomas, 1776.
John, 1804.
Kelsey,
Mary, 1712.
Kennett,
Mary, 1697.
Wm., 1700.
Catharine, 1735
Charlotte, 1794.
Kidham,
Wm., 1711.
Kingsmell,
Mary, 1621.
Thomas, 1625.
Margery, 1626.
Anne, 1635.
Dorothy, 1638.
Elizabeth, 1643.
Anne, 1652.
Thomas, 1671.
John, 1674.
Elizabeth, 1681.
Thomas, 1721.
Jane, 1728.
Mary, 1761.
Charlotte, 1794.
Knight,
Wm., 1739.
John, 1740
Mary, 1742.
Susanna, 1744.
Elizabeth, 1764.
John, 1767.
Knott,
William, 1681.
{ Laban,
{ Laborne,
Thomasine,1585.
John, 1588.
Ladd,
Joanne, 1627.
Gibbon, 1763.
Thomas, 1765.
Susanna, 1767.
Law,
Ann, 1744.
Elizabeth, 1746.
Lawrence,
Elizabeth, 1577.
Mary, 1725.
Elizabeth, 1727.

Lawrence (*cont.*)
John, 1729
William, 1737.
Stephen, 1739.
Thomas, 1740.
Ann, 1743.
Richard, 1745.
William, 1772.
George, 1789.
{ Lockar,
{ Lokar,
Tho., 1717.
Richard. 1719.
Elizabeth, 1721.
Margaret, 1749.
Loude,
Ann, 1605.
Daniel, 1606.
John, 1608.
Jane, 1618.
Thomasine,1618.
{ Lucas,
{ Luckas,
Ann, 1607.
Elizabeth, 1758.
Maine,
Elizabeth, 1741.
Makey,
Mary, 1754.
Sarah, 1757.
Maple,
Henry, 1591.
Jone, 1595.
Henry, 1649.
Ann, 1653.
Elizabeth, 1654.
Elizabeth, 1655.
Damaris, 1660.
Steven, 1662.
Mary, 1664.
Thomas, 1666.
{ Marshe,
{ Mershe,
Katherine, 1589.
John, 1614.
Elizabeth, 1623.
Mary, 1626.
Mary, 1639.
Henry, 1680.
Susanna, 1751.
Henry, 1754.
John, 1756.
Jane, 1758.
Martha, 1760
Mason,
Jone, 1582.
Elizabeth, 1586.
Matson,
John, 1575.
Robert, 1577.
Alice, 1580.
Benjamin, 1730.
Ann, 1732.
Maxted,
Elizabeth, 1674.
Richard, 1679.
James, 1800.

Maxted (*cont.*)
Henry, 1801.
May,
Hannah, 1794.
George, 1796.
James, 1797.
Edward, 1799.
Charlotte, 1800.
Maytam,
George. 1799.
Mershe,
(*See* Marshe).
{ Mihil,
{ Mihils,
{ Mihles,
{ Myhil,
{ Myle,
Ann, 1635.
William, 1637.
John, 1638.
Elizabeth, 1642.
Francis, 1643.
Richard, 1650.
Ann, 1667.
Elizabeth, 1669.
John, 1672.
Thomas, 1675.
Ann, 1678.
Ann, 1679.
Ann, 1681.
Rich., 1684.
Mary, 1687.
Augustine, 1689.
Mary, 1691.
Afferay, 1696.
Elizabeth, 1696.
Tho., 1697.
Mary, 1699.
Eliz., 1699.
John, 1701.
Mary, 1702.
Mary, 1702.
Jno., 1706.
Jno., 1708.
Wm., 1710.
——, 1716.
John, 1727.
Thomas, 1729.
Elizabeth, 1732.
Ann, 1735.
Henry, 1750.
Richard, 1752.
William, 1753.
Sarah, 1754.
Thomas, 1756.
John, 1759.
Minter,
Sarah, 1809.
Mitchison,
Catherine, 1776.
{ Moore,
{ Mooring,
Ruth, 1688.
Richard, 1689.
William, 1691.
Morley,
James, 1595.

{ Morris,
{ Morrice,
Elizabeth, 1675.
Mary, 1678.
Catherine, 1805.
Moyse,
John, 1561.
Mughole,
John, 1596.
Dennis, 1599.
Robert, 1604.
Marget, 1620.
Thomas, 1632.
John, 1670.
Munns,
John, 1749.
Sarah, 1776.
Murrell,
John, 1760.
Mutton,
John, 1751.
John, 1752.
Sophia, 1754.
Sarah, 1755.
Eleanor, 1758.
Elizabeth, 1760.
William, 1761.
John, 1764.
Henry, 1765.
Robert, 1766.
Thomas, 1766.
Thos., 1768.
Mary, 1770.
Smith, 1771.
Ralph, 1772.
Mary. 1773.
Elizabeth, 1773.
Ann, 1774.
John, 1774.
Pleasant, 1775.
James, 1777.
John, 1779.
John, 1780.
Mary, 1785.
Elizabeth, 1792.
John, 1790.
Thomas, 1800.
Henry, 1801.
John, 1803.
Edward, 1805.
James, 1807.
Sarah, 1811.
{ Myhil,
{ Myle,
(See Mihil).
Nash,
Danyell, 1638.
Nethersole,
William, 1565.
Jone, 1576.
Marye, 1577.
Anne, 1579.
Josias, 1580.
John, 1583.
Wilsford, 1585.
John, 1586.

Nethersole (cont.)
Francis, 1586.
William, 1589.
Anne, 1591.
Sarah, 1596.
Rebekah, 1598.
Ann, 1616.
Newport,
Edward, 1774.
Thomas, 1775.
Eliz. S. 1777.
John, 1780.
George, 1782.
William, 1794.
William, 1805.
John, 1807.
Edward, 1807.
John, 1808.
Newstreet,
John, 1586.
Nicholson,*
Thos. B., 1741.
Nicols,
John, 1604.
Richard, 1607.
Jane, 1609.
Daniel, 1611.
Elizabeth, 1614.
Matthew, 1616.
William, 1617.
Thomas, 1620.
Norington.
Marget, 1612.
Stephen, 1614.
Norman,
James, 1804.
Norton,
John, 1790.
Not,
William, 1706.
Odley,
William, 1859.
John, 1591.
Oldfield,
Thomas, 1643.
William, 1645.
Oyns,
William, 1781.
Robert, 1786.
{ Packer,
{ Peckar,
Katherine, 1558.
Anthony, 1563.
Marye, 1565.
Christofer, 1567.
Page,
Thomas, 1756.
William, 1760.
Harrison, 1769.
Palmer,
John, 1583.
Pantry,
Elizabeth, 1576.
Pay,
Rich., 1708.

Payler, †
Thomas, 1772.
CharlotteC. 1773.
William 1776
Henry W., 1777.
Francis R., 1779.
Jemima M., 1781.
John A. ‡ 1785.
{ Pearce,
{ Pearse,
{ Pierce,
Henry, 1580.
Joue. 1580.
Jane, 1608.
Jane, 1723.
Mary, 1773.
Ann, 1773.
Sarah, 1774.
William, 1777.
James, 1781.
Pearson,
Jone, 1579.
Vincent, 1582.
Matthew, 1582.
Mary, 1584.
Edward, 1725.
Elizabeth, 1726.
Ann, 1726.
Matthew 1728.
{ Perry,
{ Perye,
Thomas, 1569.
Jone, 1573.
Pettit,
Elizabeth, 1748.
Philpott,
Steven, 1642.
Mary, 1794.
Elizabeth, 1794.
Charlotte, 1794.
George, 1795.
Edward, 1796.
John, 1798.
Mary, 1799.
Harriet, 1800.
Michael, 1802.
Stephen, 1804.
Thomas, 1807.
Hester, 1807.
William, 1808.
Sophia, 1809.
Elizabeth, 1810.
Caroline, 1811.
Phinees,
Susanna, 1758.
Pierce,
(See Pearce).
Pilcher,
Nicholas, 1687.
Ann, 1723.
Stephen, 1725.
Jesse, 1774.
John, 1778.
William, 1792.
John, 1793.
Sarah, 1804.

Pilcher (cont.)
John, 1806.
Charlotte, 1808.
Mary Ann, 1810.
Henry, 1811.
Pingle,
Sarah, 1741.
Pittock,
James, 1634.
James, 1636.
Sarah, 1638.
Pope,
William, 1690.
William, 1691.
Preble,
Richard, 1610.
Prickett,
Alice, 1686.
Sarah, 1 86.
Pritchard,
George, 1772.
James W., 1778.
Henry, 1806.
Question,
Thomas, 1643.
Quested,
Jno., 1713.
Tho., 1714.
Mary, 1715.
Elizabeth, 1720.
Daniel, 1733.
Rafe,
William, 1718.
Elizth., 1741.
Ratley,
James, 1752.
William, 1764.
Rayner,
Alice, 1585.
Ann, 1615.
Ann, 1725.
Mary, 1727.
Mary, 1729.
Read,
Mary, 1658.
Reading,
Edw., 1692.
Reynolds,
Belinda, 1809.
{ Richard,
{ Rycarde,
{ Richwood,
{ Rickwood,
Thomas, 1582.
Margaret, 1583.
John, 1585.
George, 1592.
William, 1595.
Daniel, 1598.
John, 1611.
Robert, 1611.
Mary, 1614.
Catherine, 1617.
Thomas, 1620.
Vincent, 1620.
Marget, 1623.

INDEX OF BAPTISMS, (*pp. 1—85.*)

Richard *(cont.)*
Lucke,	1627.
Jane,	1629.
Joane,	1030.
Anne,	1636.
Danyell,	1638.
William.	1642.
John,	1648.
Henry,	1755.

Richford,
Ann,	1788.
John,	1792.

Rigden,
Margaret,	1600.
Jane,	1687.
David,	1096.
Sarah,	1700.
Susanna,	1704.
Benjamin,	1758.

Robars,
Mary,	1677.

Robins,
John,	1569.
Affra,	1571.
Thomas,	1573.
Caroline.	1782.
Carolina,	1784.
William,	1787.
James,	1789.
Sarah,	1791.
Thomas,	1795.
John,	1807.

Robinson,
Ann,	1599.
Mary,	1603.
Thomasine,	1606.

Rogers,
Margaret,	1799.

Rose,
Richard,	1773.
Mary,	1802.

Rowland,
Michael,	1798.

Rugley,
Mary,	1562.
Richard,	1564.
Robert,	1566.
Annis,	1569.
Isacke,	1571.
Jeramey,	1576.
Simon,	1578.
Mary,	1578.
John,	1580.
Abraham,	1580.
Danyell,	1581.
James,	1582.
Jane,	1584.
Jone,	1586.
Annis,	1588.
James,	1589.
Margaret,	1590.
William,	1593.
Jone,	1595.
Jane,	1599.
Richard,	1603.
John,	1604.

Rngley *(cont.)*
Robert,	1611.

Rutherford
Elizabeth,	1811.

Rye, / Wry,
Thomas,	1677.
Elizabeth,	1680.
Ann,	1082.
John,	1682.
Aime,	1684.
Stephen,	1686.
William,	1688.
Mary,	1689.
Benjamin,	1690.
Sarah,	1693.
Ben.,	1695.
Mary,	1690.
Sam.,	1700.
William,	1701.
Mary,	1709.
Eliz.,	1716.
Tho.,	1717.
Mary,	1720.
Sarah,	1720.
Ann,	1722.
Elizabeth,	1725.
Catherine,	1728.
Charlotte,	1797.
William,	1809.
John,	1811.

Sabin, / Sabine, / Savin,
John,	1607.
ffrances,	1627.
Susan,	1029.
John,	1723.
Ann,	1727.
Alfred,	1730.
Catherine,	1730.
Phillis,	1736.
Joseph,	1736.
Mary,	1738.
Anne,	1740.
Chibborne,	1754.
Ann,	1758.

Saddleton,
Thomas,	1677.
Nicholas,	1681.
Annah,	1684.
Mary,	1689
Jos.,	1602.
Mary,	1719.

Sally, / Solly,
John,	1621.
William,	1623.
Elisabethe,	1626.
Jeremy,	1627.
Paul,	1631.
Jonas,	1631.
Richard,	1633.
Hellen,	1654.

Sanchey,
Robert,	1662.

Sanchey *(cont.)*
Edward.	1663.

Sanders. / Saunders,
Mary,	1696.
Rich.,	1698.
Thomas,	1701.
Susanna,	1715.
Susanna,	1753.

Savin,
(*See* Sabin).

Sandys,
Sarah,	1797.
John,	1799.

Savage,
John,	1798.

Sawkins,
Ed.,	1708.
Ja.,	1709.
Mary,	1712.
Eliz.,	1713.
Sarah,	1715.
Jno.,	1717.
Ann,	1804

Sawyer, / Sayer,
William	1568.
Christofer,	1570.
Richard,	1573.
Mary,	1576.
Edward,	1578.
Elizabeth,	1580.
Jane,	1582.
John,	1585.
James,	1610.
Thomas,	1643.
————	1648.
Elizabeth,	1675.
John,	1677.
Thomas,	1680.

Saxton,
John, *	1668.
Elizabeth,	1672.

Scriben, †
Grace,	1592.

Sharpe,
Thomas,	1684.
William,	1687.
Elizabeth,	1689.
Sarah, ‡	1692.
Martha,	1693.
An,	1696.
Mary,	1699.
Geo.,	1702.

Sherman,
Thomas,	1569.
James,	1571.

Shipton,
Elizabeth,	1635.

Shirley,
Mary,	1806.

Shoveler,
John,	1623.
Thomas,	1624.

Shrubsole,
Elizabeth,	1676.

Shrubsole *(cont.)*
Elizabeth,	1679.
Mary,	1681.
Susanna,	1684.
Rich.,	1696.
Mary,	1808.
Charlotte,	1810.
Thomas,	1812.

Silke,
Vincent,	1564.
Alice,	1627.
Alexander,	1630.
Elizabeth,	1731.
Mary,	1734.
Sarah,	1736.

Simons,
Thomas,	1581.
Jane,	1611.
John,	1613.

Simpson,
Mary,	1770.

Sladden,
William,	1783.
George,	1785.

Smith,
Richard,	1578.
Matthew,	1620.
James,	1629.
Elizabeth,	1751.
John,	1752.
Richard,	1754.
Mary,	1758.
Sarah,	1761.
Elizabeth,	1784.

Smithet,
Luke,	1617.

Smithson,
Robert,	1604.
Jone,	1606.
Gregory,	1609.
Judith,	1611.
Jane,	1614.
Thomas,	1675.
Sarah,	1676.
John,	1684.
John,	1793.

Snapes,
Richard,	1636.

Soale,
Ann,	1670.
Dorothy,	1672.
Sarah,	1672.
John,	1675.
Nicholas,	1676.
Edward,	1678.
Ann,	1679.
Edward,	1680.

Solly,
(*See* Sally.)

Spaine,
William,	1763.
Augustin,	1778.
Hannah,	1781.
Charlotte,	1783.
Stephen,	1790.

* Inserted in Burial Register, see p. 133.   † or Scriven.   ‡ *Susan* (?)

T

INDEX OF BAPTISMS, (pp. 1—85.)

Sprat,
Edward, 1701.
Ann, 1706.
Steed,
Isaacke, 1678.
Sterling,
John, 1636.
Stokes,
Mary, 1581.
Stone,
Ann, 1785.
Stonedaers,
Katherine, 1558.
Stringer,
John 1678.
Elizabeth, 1670.
Strowd,
Richard 1659.
Stupple,
Michael, 1794.
Sturdye,
William, 1562.
Sutton,
John, 1747.
Dau., 1749.
Anne, 1751.
Elizabeth, 1771.
Mary, 1781.
Richard, 1783.
Edward, 1786.
Elizabeth, 1788.
Sarah, 1791.
Swain,
John, 1765.
Swift,
John, 1692.
Swiney,
John, 1799.
Tallis,
George, 1623.
William, 1626.
Thomas, 1629.
Annah, 1634.
Richard, 1630.
Anne, 1660.
Richard, 1672.
Mary, 1675.
Taylor,
Margery, 1618.
Terry,
Gibbon Ladd 1792.
Mary Ladd, 1793.
Thanet,
Isac, 1693.
{ Thraps,
{ Traps,
Elizabeth, 1637.
Elizabeth, 1640.
Toppin, *
Mary, 1597.
Trewe,
Thomas, 1558.

Trome, †
Nicholas, 1579.
Tumber,
William, 1810.
Turner,
Katherine, 1558.
Elizabeth, 1561.
Robert, 1635.
Susan, 1639.
Henry, 1688.
Thos. Wat-
kinson ‡ 1748.
Sara Eliza, 1804.
Twig,
Sarah, 1804.
Uden,
William, 1615.
Usmor,
Sarah, 1593.
Ventiman,
Ann, 1619.
{ Vittell,
{ Fittell,
John, 1570.
Silvester, 1572.
John, 1575.
Jone, 1581.
William, 1654.
Vowell,
(See Fowell.)
Waginer,
Mary, 1618.
{ Wallys,
{ Wealls,
Egidius, 1558.
1560.
Wanstall,
Ann, 1659.
Warburton,
George, 1801.
Thomas, 1803.
Sarah, 1805.
Wayte,
Elizabeth, 1589.
Webb,
John, 1766.
West,
Susan, 1691.
Parnell, 1722.
William, 1724.
Richard, 1727.
Richard, 1730.
Susanna, 1733.
Whitaker,
Catherine, 1709.
William, 1791.
White,
John, 1634.
John, 1649.
Mildred, 1666.
Richard, 1674.
Thomas, 1676.

White (cont.)
Wm., 1740.
Mary, 1743.
Richard, 1745.
Ann, 1748.
Richard, 1766.
Sarah, 1769.
Mary, 1770.
Elizabeth, 1772.
Ann, 1772.
Harriet, 1774.
Richard, 1774.
Jane, 1776.
Edward, 1777.
John, 1780.
John, 1794.
Whitehead,
Daniel, 1754.
Elizabeth, 1763.
Whitnell,
Ann, 1705.
Jno., 1710.
Jno, 1713.
James, 1715.
Mary, 1754.
Wild,
Mary Ann, 1809.
{ Wilford,
{ Wilsford,
James, 1608.
Katherine, 1609.
Edwarde, 1613.
Elizabeth, 1615.
Anne, 1622.
Water, 1626.
ffrancis, 1640.
Thomas, 1658.
Wilkes,
Abraham, 1779.
Willis,
John, 1809.
Williams,
Willm., 1762.
Sarah, 1763.
Mary, 1763.
James, 1765.
Thos., 1767.
Alexander, 1760.
John, 1771.
Henry, 1773.
Catherine, 1799.
Ann, 1800.
John, 1803.
Willyams,
Thos. Eger-
ton, 1806.
John Vyner, 1809.
Wilsford,
(See Wilford.)
Winter,
John, 1628.
Isaac, 1633.

Winter (cont.)
Mary, 1635.
Wonstan,
William, 1710.
Stephen, 1722.
Wood,
Anthony, 1608.
Mary, 1608.
Joane, 1610.
Elisabeth, 1613.
Susan, 1629.
Abraham, 1639.
Thomas, 1640.
Richard, 1642.
Richard, 1642.
James, 1643.
Elizabeth, 1647.
Richard, 1746.
John, 1760.
Christopher, 1772.
Mary, 1773.
John, 1791.
Elizabeth, 1791.
Thomas, 1793.
Thomas, 1794.
John Marsh 1795.
George, 1804.
Sarah, 1806.
James, 1807.
Woodland,
Steven, 1663.
Woodle,
Margaret, 1641.
Woollett,
Esther, 1739.
Wrathe,
Martha, 1622.
Nicholas, 1628.
Richard, 1628.
Ann, 1609.
Tho., 1700.
Elizabeth, 1703.
Wright,
John, 1760.
Wry,
(See Rye.)
Young,
Vincent, 1560.
Annes, 1564.
William, 1567.
Annis, 1589.
William, 1591.
Vincent, 1594.
Ann, 1616.
Elisabethe, 1618.
Marget, 1623.
Thomas, 1625.
Daniel, 1628.

* Coppin (?)   † Crome (?)   ‡ Took the name of Payler. See p. 71, footnote.

INDEX OF MARRIAGES (pp. 86—108).

Adams and Pettit, 1732.
Adams and Finn, 1800.
Ady and Marsh, 1605.
Alleyn and Maurice, 1633.
Alleyn and Starling, 1635.
Amies and Morton, 1613.
Andrews and Jull, 1701.
Apricharde and Soome, 1629.
Argar and Fordred, 1781.
Arnold and Marsh, 1749.
Arnold and Saffery, 1760.
Atwood and Tallies, 1665.
Atwood and Simpson, 1703.
Atwood and Pilcher, 1768.
Atwood and Richards, 1819.
Audley and Brigge, 1593.
Auger and Gibbon, 1611.
Austen and Quilter, 1587.

Baker and Keyse, 1561.
Baker and Pittock, 1638.
Baker and Foord, 1678.
Baker and Clement, 1711.
Baker and Lot, 1733.
Baker and Streeting, 1739.
Baker and Fox, 1741.
Baker and Quested, 1745.
Baker and Rose, 1773.
Baker and Dine, 1779.
Baker and Laker, 1813.
Baker and Dodd, 1814.
Baldrie and Question, 1632.
Balderstone and Nairn, 1779.
Barbar and Young, 1619.
Barrett and Browning, 1770.
Bartlett and Knoeker, 1832.
Barton and Rugley, 1563.
Barton and Gould, 1574.
Barton and Ford, 1808.
Bassock and Young, 1595.
Bassock and Boyce, 1621.
Beagent and Boykett, 1577.
Beal and Holness, 1786.
Bean and Chaekfield, 1821.
Bean and Bogben, 1744.
Beer and Homes, 1745.
Beer and Swain, 1769.
Beer and Bottler, 1779.
Beer and Collison, 1779.
Beer and Creed, 1833.
Belsey and Ford, 1719.
Benchkin and Osborne, 1624.
Benefield and Suters, 1819.
Benefield and Sprat, 1825.
Benefield and Foster, 1826.
Bernand and Scott, 1795.
Bevan and Truman, 1824.
Bewley and Hobday, 1732.
Binge and Danton, 1619.
Birch and Mihill, 1696.
Birch and Dadson, 1741.

Birch and Williams, 1762.
Birde and Dale, 1613.
Blasht and Rugley, 1588.
Borton and Higgins, 1834.
Bottler and Beer, 1779.
Boughton and Furnley, 1623.
Boulton and ——, 1561.
Boyce and Bassocke, 1621.
Boys and Sankey, 1818.
Boykett and Beagent, 1577.
Boykett and Scarlett, 1578.
Boykett and Smithe, 1624.
Branfill'and Hammond, 1818.
Branfill and Harrison, 1822.
Brenchley and Laker, 1666.
Brensley and Mihill, 1678.
Brensley and Hobday, 1722.
Brett and Craye, 1613.
Brice and Turner, 1703.
Brice and Hyder, 1813.
Brigge and Audley, 1593.
Brockman and Collar, 1746.
Brooker and Kite, 1824.
Brooks and Lawes, 1763.
Brooks and Dawkins, 1818.
Brown and Mihill, 1634.
Brown and Early, 1833.
Brown and Cheeseman, 1676.
Brown and Jourdan, 1811.
Browning and Rugleye, 1565.
Browning and Kember, 1593.
Browning and Knott, 1597.
Browning and Young, 1610.
Browning & Chackson, 1613.
Browning & Rickwood, 1626.
Browning & Crickman, 1632.
Browning and Murrey, 1636.
Browning and Fox, 1701.
Browning and Pilcher, 1745.
Browning and West, 1746.
Browning and Palmer, 1750.
Browning and Hogbin, 1752.
Browning and Mihill, 1756.
Browning and Rutley, 1764.
Browning and Barrett, 1770.
Browning & Newport, 1774.
Browning & Fetherston, 1813.
Brumhead and Kelson, 1786.
Buck and Marsh, 1667.
Buckhurst and Gibbon, 1618.
Buddell and White, 1739.
Budds and Mihell, 1636.
Bunce and Chourthop, 1577.
Bunce and Tristram, 1591.
Burche (see Birche).
Bush and Russell, 1737.
Butcher and Hopkin, 1634.
Butler (see Bottler).

Cannaby and Green, 1808.
Carey and Ford, 1833.

Carpenter and Hogbean, 1592.
Castle and Sprat, 1761.
Castle & Worringham, 1785.
Castle and Dine, 1786.
Castle and Sutton, 1789.
Castleden and Law, 1747.
Chackfield and Beane, 1621.
Chackson & Browning, 1613.
Chambers and Dale, 1588.
Champkin and Wrakes, 1740.
Chandler and Thomas, 1772.
Chapman & Nethersole, 1575.
Chapman and Gold, 1700.
Chapman and Stewart, 1766.
Cheeseman and Brown, 1676.
Cheyton and Homesby, 1641.
Chourthope and Bunce, 1577.
Christian and Sweeting, 1579.
Church and Hopkins, 1741.
Church and Lawrence, 1705.
Churchman & Swinford, 1588.
Claringbull and Nicholson, 1736.
Clarke and Johnson, 1611.
Clarke and Watson, 1746.
Clement and Baker, 1711.
Cobb and Sutton, 1773.
Collard and Terry, 1791.
Collard and Maxted, 1800.
Coller and Hogben, 1729.
Collar and Brockman, 1746.
Collison and Beer, 1779.
Colthup and Marsh, 1837.
Cooke and Curlinge, 1597.
Cooling and Pette, 1568.
Cooman and Sayer, 1609.
Cooper and Elgar, 1626.
Cooper and Turner, 1658.
Coorte and ——, 1593.
Courte and Sterling, 1602.
Courte and Sayer, 1622.
Court and Sabine, 1759.
Coulter and Rivers, 1825.
Coulthard and Wilson, 1832.
Cranbrooke and Maple, 1648.
Craye and Wrathe, 1608.
Craye and Lawrence, 1612.
Craye and Brett, 1613.
Creed and Beer, 1833.
Crickman and Marsh, 1609.
Crickman & Browning, 1635.
Cullen and Rugley, 1608.
Cullen and Herset or
    Hastifer, 1624.
Culmer and Elvery, 1807.
Curd and Ford, 1831.
Curlinge and Cook, 1597.
Cuelern and Keeler, 1700.
    or
(Curloine and Kidder),

INDEX OF MARRIAGES, (pp. 86—108.)

Dadd and Driland, 1606.
Dadd and Rickwood, 1648.
Dadson and Sprat, 1739.
Dadson and Birch, 1741.
Dale and Chambers, 1588.
Dale and Fells, 1608.
Dale and Birde, 1613.
Danell and Rugley, 1587.
Daniels and Middleton, 1812.
Danton and Binge, 1619.
Danton and Milnell, 1634.
Davis and Shelley, 1730.
Dawkins and Brooks, 1818.
Dawkins and Rye, 1834.
Dawkins and Deal 1834.
Day and Ford, 1828.
Deal and Friend, 1734.
Deal and Dawkins, 1834.
Delahay and Whaley, 1797.
Denne and Nethersole, 1588.
Denne and Sabin, 1606.
Denne and Kingsmeel, 1627.
Denne and Proud, 1632.
Dilnot and Mutton, 1764.
Dine and Baker, 1779.
Dine and Castle, 1786.
Dines and Spain, 1810.
Dines and Marshall, 1819.
Ditton and Rugley, 1576.
Dixon and Rye, 1640.
Dixon and Wood, 1653.
Dodd and Baker, 1814.
Duning and Nookes, 1600.
Douninge and Rugley, 1602.
Draper and Gold. 1665.
Draper and Richfoot, 1702.
Driland and Dadd, 1606.
Dunguy and Webb, 1783.

Early and Brown, 1638.
Elgar and Cooper, 1620.
Elgar and Mummery, 1783.
Ellen and Finnis, 1803.
Ellenden & Kingsford, 1750.
Ellet and Terry, 1770.
Elvery and Culmer, 1807.
Epps and Serjante, 1588.
Everden and Rugley, 1619.

Fagg and Osborne, 1629.
Fagg and Stokes, 1757.
Fagg and May, 1817.
Fagg and Pilcher, 1826.
Fagg and Shrubsole, 1827.
Featherstone and Gold-
finch, 1799.
Featherstone & Brown-
ing, 1813.
Fells and Dale, 1608.
Feux and Rickwood, · 1668.
Files and Pilcher, 1811.
File and Rose, 1835.
Finn and Pilcher, 1797.
Finn and Adams, 1800.
Finnis and West, 1734.

Finnis and Hogben, 1744.
Finnis and Hulks, 1793.
Finnis and Ellen, 1803.
Ford and Baker, 1678.
Ford and White, 1684.
Ford and Taylior, 1691.
Ford and Pingle, 1741.
Ford and Sprat, 1745.
Ford and Shaw, 1775.
Ford and Belsey, 1779.
Ford and Green, 1782.
Ford and Barton, 1808.
Ford and Day, 1828.
Ford and Curd, 1831.
Ford and Carey, 1833.
Fordred and Argar, 1781.
Foreman and Ruck, 1668.
Foster and Benefield, 1826.
Fowell and Weeks, 1707.
Fox and Browning, 1701.
Fox and Golder, 1722.
Fox and Baker, 1741.
Fox and Sutton, 1768.
Frank and Stuple, 1709.
Free and Yeomans, 1636.
Friend and Deal, 1734.
Furnley and Boughton, 1623.

Garner and Steddy, 1804.
George and Hopkin, 1605.
Gibbon and Auger, 1611.
Gibbon and Buckhurst, 1618.
Giles and Hopkin, 1580.
Giles and Shoveler, 1620.
Godden and Ladd, 1762.
Gould and Milborne, 1565.
Gould and Hall, 1571.
Gould and Barton, 1574.
Golde and Harries, 1614.
Gould and Read, 1637.
Gold and Draper, 1665.
Gold and Chapman, 1700.
Goulder and Wellbank, 1714.
Goulder and Fox, 1722
Golder and Wellard, 1737.
Goldfinch and Horton, 1791.
Goldfinch and Feather-
stone, 1799.
Green and Vyle, 1701.
Green and Ford, 1782.
Green and Cannaby, 1808.
* Grome and Rugley, 1565.
Gundy and Hoge, 1720.
Gyles (see Giles)

Hall and Gould, 1571.
Hall and Smith, 1753.
Hall and Philpott, 1833.
Halladay and Nash, 1776.
Hammond & Branfill, 1818.
Harfield and Hopkine, 1571.
Harnett and Hogben, 1632.
Harries and Golde, 1614.
Harris and Wood, 1797.
Harrison and Branfill, 1822.

Hart and Sawkins, 1804.
Hastifer and Cullen, 1624.
Hatcher and Morris, 1583.
Hawkins and Powell, 1813.
Herset (see Hastifer)
Higgins and Toms, 1775.
Higgins and Borton, 1834.
Hilles and Newstreate, 1586.
Hills and Wood, 1657.
Hills and Tyrrill 1734.
Hills and Kingsford, 1749.
Hobday and Slowman, 1560.
Hobday and Sayer, 1694.
Hobday and Brensley, 1722.
Hobday and Bewley, 1732.
Hobday and Stonham, 1776.
Hogbean & Carpenter, 1592.
Hogben and Stace, 1593.
Hogben and Sturges, 1597.*
Hogben and Harnett, 1632.
Hogben and Coller, 1729.
Hogben and Wraith, 1732.
Hogben and Bean, 1744.
Hogben and Finns, 1744.
Hogbin and Browning, 1752.
Hogbin and Robins, 1806.
Hogbin and Luker, 1808.
Hoge and Gundy, 1720.
Hollaiday and Smith, 1831.
Holness and Beal, 1786.
Homesby and Cheyton, 1641.
Homes and Weeks, 1714.
Homes and Beer, 1745.
Hounifold and Swann, 1666.
Hopkin and Marche, 1564.
Hopkin and Harffield, 1571.
Hopkine and Gyles, 1580.
Hopkin and George, 1605.
Hopkin and Rigden, 1611.
Hopkin and Butcher, 1634.
Hopkin and Rofe, 1640.
Hopkin and Pay, 1707.
Hopkins and Oldfield, 1734.
Hopkins and Church, 1741.
Horton and Morris, 1738.
Horton and Goldfinch, 1791.
Howard and Walters, 1831.
Hulks and Finnis, 1793.
Hunt and Medmer, 1630.
Hyder and Brice, 1813.

Iniester and Rugley, 1606.
Inues and Stringer, 1733.

Jarman and Mutton, 1805.
Johnson and Younge, 1577.
Johnson and Rickard, 1581.
Johnson and Wayte, 1588.
Johnson and Clarke, 1611.
Jourdan and Brown, 1811.
Jull and Andrews, 1701.

Keeler and Cuelern,† 1700.
Keeler and Kemp, 1769.
Kelson and Brumhead, 1786.

* Or Moone.   † Or Curloin.

INDEX OF MARRIAGES, (pp. 86—108.)

Kember and Browning, 1593.
Kemp and Keeler, 1769.
Kemp and Tyrrell, 1788.
Kennett and Measby, 1834.
Keyse and Baker, 1561.
Kiddam and Low, 1710.
Kiddar (*see* Keeler),
Kingsford and Hills, 1749.
Kingsford & Ellenden, 1750.
Kingsmell and Young, 1619.
Kingsmell and Denn, 1627.
Kingsmell and Power, 1670.
Kingsmill and Neam, 1760.
Kingsmill and Mutton, 1800.
Kite and Brooker, 1824.
Knock and Wraight, 1825.
Knocker and Bartlett, 1832.
Knott and Browning, 1597.
Knott and Rye, 1833.

Labanne and Seryven, 1592.
Ladd and Godden, 1762.
Laker and Brenchley, 1666.
Laker and Hogben, 1808.
Laker and Baker, 1813.
Law and Castleden, 1747.
Lawes and Sabine, 1743.
Lawes and Brooks, 1763.
Laurence and Woode, 1599.
Laurence and Craye, 1612.
Laurence and Pettit, 1748.
Laurence and Church, 1765.
Laurence and Spain, 1776.
Lemon and Minter, 1746.
Lewes and Rickwood, 1610.
Lockewood & Wilcocke, 1565.
Lot and Baker, 1733.
Low and Kiddam, 1710.
Lucke and Sturdye, 1567.

Makey and Rigden, 1779.
Maple and Cranbrooke, 1648.
Maple and Whitnell, 1728.
Marche and Hopkine, 1564.
Mare and Moore, 1558.
Marsh and Odleye, 1597.
Marsh and Crickman, 1609.
Marsh and Paramore, 1624.
Marsh and Masterson, 1664.
Marsh and Ady, 1665.
Marsh and Buck, 1667.
Marsh and Arnold, 1749.
Marsh and Wood, 1792.
Marsh and Soles, 1830.
Marsh and Colthup, 1837.
Marshall and Scot, 1789.
Marshall and Dines, 1819.
Mason and Prestod, 1581.
Mason and Pierse, 1607.
Masterson and Marsh, 1664.
Maurice and Alleyne, 1633.
Maxted and Mihill, 1674.
Maxted and Collard, 1800.
Maye and Sayer, 1603.
May and Fagg, 1817.

Measby and Kennett, 1834.
Medmer and Hunt, 1630.
Mersh (*see* Marsh).
Middleton and Daniels, 1812.
Mihill and Danton, 1634.
Mihill and Brown, 1634.
Mihell and Budds, 1636.
Mihill and —— 1661.
Mihill and White, 1665.
Mihill and Maxtead, 1674.
Mihill and Brensley, 1678.
Mihill and Burche, 1695.
Mihill and Taylior, 1695.
Mihi l and —— 1698.
Mihils and Browning, 1756.
Milborne and Gould, 1565.
* Milles and Wilsford, 1589.
Mills and Turner, 1738.
Minter and Lemon, 1746.
Minter and Philpott, 1825.
Monro and Tunbridge, 1746.
† Moon and Rugley, 1565.
Moore and Mare, 1558.
Moore and Reed, 1683.
Morgan and Simmons, 1827.
Morris and Hatche, 1583.
Morris and Horton, 1738.
Morton and Amies, 1613.
Mughole and Nicholas, 1579.
Mughole and Sally, 1620.
Mummery and Elgar, 1783.
Murrey and Browning, 1636.
Murton and White, 1606.
Mutton and Spaine, 1763.
Mutton and Dilnot, 1764.
Mutton and Smith, 1765.
Mutton and Wood, 1769.
Mutton and Smith, 1770.
Mutton and Oinn, 1790.
Mutton and Kingsmill, 1800.
Mutton and Jarman, 1805.
Mutton and Pilcher, 1825.

Nairn and Balderston, 1779.
Nash and Halladay, 1776.
Neame and Ovell, 1642.
Neams and Safary, 1732.
Neam and Kingsmill, 1760.
Nethersole and Turner, 1558.
Nethersole & Chapman, 1575.
Nethersole and Stokes, 1583.
Nethersole and Denne, 1584.
Newman and Partridge, 1660.
Newport and Browning, 1774.
Newport and Paye, 1805.
Newstreate and Hilles, 1586.
Nicholas and Mughole, 1579.
Nicholson and Claring-
bull, 1736.
Nookes and Duninge, 1600.

Odley and Marshe, 1597.
Oinn and Mutton, 1790.
Oldfield and Hopkins, 1734.
Osborne and Benchkin, 1624.

Osborne and Fagg, 1629.
Ovell and Neame, 1642.

Palmer and Browning, 1750.
Paramore and Rugley, 1610.
Paramore and Mershe, 1624.
Partriche and Pierse, 1608.
Partridge and Newman, 1660.
Pay and Hopkin, 1707.
Pay and Newport, 1805.
Peerce and Rayner, 1575.
Pierce and Mason, 1607.
Peirse and Partriche, 1608.
Peirse and Trappam, 1617.
Pearse and Rogers, 1774.
Pette and Coolinge, 1568.
Pettit and Adams, 1732.
Pettit and Laurence, 1748.
Philpott and Swift, 1592.
Philpott and Wrathe, 1627.
Philpott and Minter, 1825.
Philpott and Hall, 1833.
Philpott and Sisars, 1835.
Pierce (*see* Pearse).
Pilcher and Talis, 1683.
Pilcher and Sharp, 1710.
Pilcher and Browning, 1745.
Pilcher and Attwood, 1768.
Pilcher and Finn, 1797.
Pilcher and Willis, 1800.
Pilcher and Files, 1811.
Pilcher and Housal, 1825.
Pilcher and Mutton, 1825.
Pilcher and Fagg, 1826.
Pingle and Ford, 1741.
Pittock and Bakar, 1638.
Pout and White, 1775.
Powell and Hawkins, 1813.
Power and Kingsmell, 1670.
Prestod and Mason, 1581.
Proud and Denn, 1632.

Question and Baldrie, 1632.
‡ Question and Sayer, 1670.
Quested and Baker, 1745.
Quested and Tatnall, 1755.
Quilter and Austen, 1587.

Ransley and Widgeon, 1825.
Ratclif and Sabine, 1763.
Rayner and Peerce, 1575.
Rayner and Swan, 1835.
Read and Gould, 1637.
Reed and Moore, 1688.
Readwood and Verrier, 1662.
Renolds and West, 1748.
Richards and Webb, 1809.
Richards and Attwood, 1819.
Richford and Draper, 1702.
Rickard and Johnson, 1581.
Rickwood and Simous, 1607.
Rickwoode and Lewes, 1610.
Rickwood & Browning, 1626.
Rickwood and Dadd, 1648.
Rickwood and Feux, 1668.

---

* or *Willes.*   † or *Grome.*   ‡ or *Questhead.*

U

INDEX OF MARRIAGES, (pp. 86—108.)

Rickwood and Willis, 1809.
Rigden and Hopkin, 1611.
Rigden and Toddys, 1621.
Rigden and Makey, 1779.
Rivers and Coulter, 1825.
Robins and Hogben, 1806.
Robinson and Talpot, 1724.
Rofe and Hopkin, 1640.
Rofe and Saddleton, 1739.
Rogers and Pearse, 1774.
Rose and Baker, 1773.
Rose and File, 1835.
Rousal and Pilcher, 1825.
Ruck and Foreman, 1668.
Rugley and Bartun, 1563.
Rugley and Moone (or
Grome) 1565.
Rugley and Browning, 1565.
Rugley and Sayer, 1567.
Rugley and Wyer, 1574.
Rugley and Ditton, 1576.
Rugley and Danyell, 1587.
Rugley and Blasht, 1588.
Ragley and Weevell, 1600.
Rugley and Douning, 1602.
Rugley and Smithsonne, 1603.
Rugley and Iniester, 1606.
Rugley and Cullen, 1608.
Rugley and Paramour, 1610.
Rugley and Everden, 1619.
Russell and Bush, 1737.
Ruttley and Browning, 1764.
Rye and Dixen, 1640.
Rye and Wedlard, 1769.
Rye and Knott, 1833.
Rye and Dawkins, 1834.

Sabin and Denne, 1606.
Sabine and Stokes, 1739.
Sabine and Laws, 1743.
Sabine and Court, 1759.
Sabine and Ratclif, 1763.
Saddleton and Rofe, 1739.
Safary and Neame, 1732.
Safary and Arnold, 1769.
Sally and Mughole, 1620.
Sampson and Wood, 1565.
Sanchy and Watson, 1614.
Sankey and Boys, 1818.
Sawkins and Hart, 1804.
Sayer and Rugly, 1567.
Sayer and Maye, 1603.
Sayer and Cooman, 1609.
Sayer and Courte, 1622.
Sayer and Question, 1670.
Sayer and Hobday, 1694.
Scarlett and Boykett, 1578.
Scot and Marshall, 1789.
Scott and Bernand, 1795
Serieant and Epps, 1588.
Sergeant and Winter, 1597.
* Seryven and Labanne, 1592.
Sharpe and Thanet, 1693.
Sharpe and Sharpe,† 1710.

Sharpe and Whitnall, 1760.
Shaw and Ford, 1775.
Shelley and Davis, 1730.
Shoveler and Giles, 1620.
Shrubsole and Fagg, 1827.
Simons and Rickwood, 1607.
Simmons and Morgan, 1827.
Simpson and Attwood, 1763.
Sisars and Philpot, 1835.
Slowman and Hobdaye, 1560.
Smith and Boykett, 1624.
Smith and Walker, 1733.
Smith and Hall, 1753.
Smith and Mutton, 1765.
Smith and Mutton, 1770.
Smith and Wraight, 1779.
Sm th and Hollaiday, 1831.
Smithson and Rugley, 1603.
Soale and Turner, 1669.
Soles and Marsh, 1830.
Soome and Apricharde, 1620.
Spayne and Spayne, 1646.
Spaine and Mutton, 1763.
Spain and Lawrence, 1776.
Spain and Dines, 1810.
Sprat and Dadson, 1739.
Sprat and Ford, 1745.
Sprat and Castle, 1761.
Spratt and Benefield, 1825.
Stace and Hogben, 1593.
Starling (see Sterling)
Steddy and Garner, 1804.
Sterling and Courte, 1602.
Sterling and Alleyn, 1635.
Stewart and Chapman, 1706.
Stokes and Nethersole, 1583.
Stokes and Sabine, 1739.
Stokes and Fagge, 1757.
Stonham and Hobday, 1776.
Stoubridge and Sucket, 1628.
Streeting and Baker, 1739.
Stringer and Innes, 1733.
Stuple and Frank, 1709.
Sturdy and Lucke, 1567.
Sturges and Hogben, 1597.
Sucket and Stoubridge, 1628.
Suters and Benefield, 1819
Sutton and Fox, 1768.
Sutton and Cobb, 1773.
Sutton and Castle, 1789.
Swann and Honnifold, 1666.
Swan and Rayner, 1835.
Swain and Beer, 1769.
Sweeting and Christian, 1579.
Swift and Philpott, 1592.
Swinford & Churchman, 1588.

Tallis and Attwood, 1665.
Talis and Pilcher, 1683.
Talpot and Robinson, 1724.
Tanton and Wood, 1600.
Tatnall and Quested, 1755.
Taylior and Ford, 1691.
Taylior and Mihill, 1695.

Terry and Ellet, 1770.
Terry and Collard, 1791.
Thanet and Sharp, 1693.
Thomas and Chandler, 1772.
Thompson & Whiting, 1592.
Toddys and Rigden, 1621.
Toms and Higgens, 1775.
Trappam and Peirse 1617.
Trapps and Wanstall, 1659.
Tristram and Bunce, 1591.
Truman and Bevan, 1824.
Tunbridge and Monro, 1746.
Turner and Nethersole, 1558.
Turner and Cooper, 1658.
Turner and Soale, 1669.
Turner and Brice, 1703.
Turner and Mills, 1738.
Tyrrill and Hills, - 1734.
Tyrrell and Kemp, 1788.

Verrier and Readwood, 1662.
Vyle and Green, 1701.

Waddall and Yongue, 1640.
Walker and Smith, 1733.
Wanstall and Trapps, 1659.
Walters and Howard, 1831.
Watson and Sauchy, 1614.
Watson and Clarke, 1746.
Wayte and Johnson, 1588.
Webb and White, 1729.
Webb and Dunguy, 1783.
Webb and Richards, 1809.
Weeks and Fowell, 1707.
Weeks and Homes, 1714.
Weevell and Rugley, 1600.
Welbank and Goulder, 1714.
Wellard and Golder, 1737.
Wellard and Rye, 1769.
West and Finnis, 1734.
West and Browning, 1746.
West and Renolds, 1748.
Whaley and Delahay, 1797.
White and Murton, 1606.
White and Mihill, 1665.
White and Ford, 1684.
White and Webb, 1729.
White and Buddell, 1739.
White and Pout, 1775.
Whiting & Thompson, 1593.
Whitnel and Maple, 1728.
Whitnall and Sharpe, 1760.
Widgeon and Ransley, 1825.
Wilcocke & Lockwood, 1565.
Willes and Wilsford,‡ 1589.
Williams and Birch, 1762.
Willis and Pilcher, 1800.
Willis and Rickwood, 1809.
‡ Wilsford and Willes, 1589.
Wilson and Coulthard, 1832.
Winter and Sergeant, 1597.
Wood and Sampson, 1565.
Wood and Lawrence, 1509.
Wood and Tanton, 1600.

* Probably " Scriven." See " Scriven " in Index of Baptisms.
† or *Pilcher.* ‡ or Milles.

INDEX OF MARRIAGES, (pp. 86—108.)

Wood and Dixon, 1653.
Wood and Hills, 1657.
Wood and Mutton, 1769.
Wood and Marsh, 1792.
Wood and Harris, 1797.
Worriugham & Castle, 1785.
Wrathe and Craye, 1608.

Wreathe and Philpott, 1627.
Wraith and Hogben, 1732.
Wraight and Smith, 1779
Wraight and Knock, 1825.
Wrakes and Champkin 1740.
Wyer and Rugley, 1574.
Yeomans and Free, 1636.

Younge and Johnson, 1577.
Younge and Bassocke, 1595.
Young and Browning, 1610.
Young and Kingsmeel, 1619.
Young and Barbar, 1619.
Yongue and Waddall, 1640.

INDEX OF BANNS (pp. 108—111.)

Adams and Rutland, 1799.
Alderstone and Borton, 1772.
Amis and Tite, 1799.
Atwood & Broadbridge, 1816.
Attwood and Chapman, 1822.
Austin and Knott, 1826.

Bailey and Hogbin 1833.
Baker and Laurence, 1759.
Baker and Castle. 1765.
Baker and Leake, 1800.
Baker and Rye, 1817
Bartlett and Jacob, 1762.
Bean and Mutton, 1791.
Bece and Laurence, 1769.
Beer and Nash, 1831.
Belsey and Spratt, 1760.
Belsey and Spratt, 1766.
Belsey and Cotton, 1822.
Borton and Alderstone, 1772.
Brice and Hannden, 1801.
Broadbridge & Atwood, 1816.
Browning and Collard, 1775.
Burvill and Dawkins, 1808.
Bushell and Sutton, 1780.
Bushell and Philpott, 1802.

Castle and Baker, 1765.
Chapman and Attwood, 1822.
Clayson and Fillman, 1824.
Cobb and May, 1806.
Cobling and Dugleys, 1795.
Collard and Browning, 1775.
Collard and Laurence, 1778.
Cooper and Pink, 1783.
Cotton and Belsey, 1822.
Crow and Pritchard, 1805.

Daniels and Holmes, 1794.
Daniels and Robbins, 1829.
Daniels and Mount, 1835.
Davis and Yates, 1799.
Dawkins and Burvill, 1808.
Dugleys and Cobling, 1795.

Eames and Smison, 1760.

Field and Sutton, 1818.
Fillman and Clayson, 1824.
Finis and Spiser, 1766.

Finn and Whitehead, 1764.
Fox and Pilcher, 1813.
Friend and Newport, 1771.

Gibbs and Goldfinch, 1756.
Goldfinch and Gibbs, 1756.

Hannden and Brice, 1801.
Harvey and Higgins, 1835.
Higgins and Marsh, 1802.
Higgins and Waters, 1831.
Higgins and Seath, 1832.
Higgins and Harvey, 1835.
Hogbin and Bailey, 1833.
Holaday and Knott, 1795.
Holman and Oliver, 1827.
Holmes and Daniels, 1794.
Holneys and Horrell, 1797.
Honess and Ladams 1812.
Hopkins and Pepper, 1788.
Horrell and Holneys, 1797.
Horton and Miles, 1790.
Hulke and White, 1771.

Jackson and Sutton, 1763.
Jacob and Bartlett, 1762.
Jones and Jones, 1799.

Keeler and Sutton, 1764.
Keeler and Rye, 1792.
Kingsmill and Tucker, 1754
Knight and Taylor, 1761.
Knott and Holaday, 1795.
Knott and Austin, 1826.

Ladams and Honess, 1812.
Lawrence and Baker, 1759.
Lawrence and Bece, 1769.
Lawrence and Collard, 1778.
Lawton and Winter, 1799.
Leake and Baker, 1800.
Lilly and Terry, 1799.
Luke and Parker, 1817.

Maple and Stuple, 1783.
Marsh and Higgins, 1802.
Marsh and Smith, 1827.
May and Cobb, 1806.
Miles and Horton, 1790.
Morgan and Peirce 1790.

Morgan and Morris, 1823.
Morris and Morgan, 1823.
Mount and Daniels, 1835.
Mutton and Bean, 1791.
Mutton and Todd, 1799.

Nash and Beer. 1831.
Newport and Friend, 1771.

Oliver and Holman, 1827.
Osborn and Palmer, 1807.

Page and Robins, 1804.
Pain and Robins, 1822.
Palmer and Osborn, 1807.
Parker and Luke, 1817.
Peel and White, 1765.
Peirce and Morgan, 1790.
Penny and Stupple, 1801.
Pepper and Hopkins, 1783.
Philpot and Bushell, 1802.
Pilcher and White, 1768.
Pilcher and Fox, 1813.
Pilcher and Wilson, 1818.
Pilcher and Shoveler, 1824.
Pink and Cooper, 1783.
Pritchard and Crow, 1805.

Robins and Page, 1804.
Robins and Spain, 1812.
Robins and Pain, 1822.
Robins and Daniels, 1829.
Rutland and Adams, 1799.
Rye and Keeler, 1792.
Rye and Baker, 1817.

Seath and Higgens, 1832.
Sennock and Spain, 1816.
Shoveller and Pilcher, 1824.
Smison and Eames, 1760.
Smith and Marsh, 1827.
Spain and Robins, 1812.
Spain and Sennock, 1816.
Spiser and Finis, 1766.
Sprat and Belsey, 1760.
Sprat and Belsey, 1766.
Standley and Weade, 1799.
Stuple and Maple, 1783.
Stupple and Penny, 1801.
Sutton and Jackson, 1763.

INDEX OF BANNS (*pp. 108—111*).

Sutton and Keeler, 1764.
Sutton and Bushel, 1780.
Sutton and Field, 1818.

Taylor and Knight, 1761.
Terry and Lilly, 1799.
Thiselton and Wood, 1800.
Tite and Amis, 1799.
Todd and Mutton, 1799.
Tucker and Kingsmill, 1764.

Waters and Higgins, 1831.
Weade and Standley, 1799.
Webb and Wood, 1765.
White and Peel, 1765.
White and Pilcher. 1768.
White and Hulke, 1771.
Whitehead and Finn, 1764.
Wiles and Williams, 1802.
Williams and Wood, 1796.
Williams and Wiles, 1802.

Wilson and Pilcher, 1818.
Winter and Lawton, 1799.
Wood and Webb, 1765.
Wood and Williams, 1796.
Wood and Thiselton, 1800.
Wooton and Wraight, 1785.
Wraight and Wooton, 1785.

Yates and Davis, 1799.

INDEX OF BURIALS (pp. 112—155.)

{ Adams,
{ Addams,
Elizabeth, 1662.
Susanna, 1662.
Ralph, 1691.
Rich. 1692.
Allen,
Joane, 1623.
Mary, 1638.
Andrews,
Mary, 1697.
. Jean, 1700.
. An, 1702.
Abigail, 1703.
Ann, 1721.
John, 1735.
Richard, 1737.
Widow, 1748.
{ Attwood,
{ Atwood,
Ann, 1671.
Thomas, 1671.
Anne, 1680.
Aunah, 1684.
Abr. 1697.
Mary, 1700.
Elizabeth, 1704.
Abraham, 1706.
(wife of Thos.) 1726.
Abraham, 1726.
Thomas, 1731.
Henry, 1796.
James, 1800.

Baker,
John, 1572.
James, 1637.
Henry, 1642.
Abigail, 1672.
ffrancis, 1715.
Robert, 1723.
Francis, 1739.
Mary, 1746.
Abraham, 1749.
Margaret, 1756.
Thomas, 1757.
Ann, 1766.
Abraham, 1766.
Elizabeth, 1778.
Mary, 1779.
Thomas, 1779.
Mary, 1780.
Thomas, 1784.
Sarah, 1784.
Richard, 1791.
Baldock,
Annis, 1583.
Barber,
Stephen, 1632.
John, 1637.
Ann, 1675.

Barston,
Major, 1799.
Bartlet,
Elizabeth, 1773.
Barton,
William, 1558.
(See also Burton.)
Bassocke,
George, 1598.
Widdowe, 1626.
Baylie,
Thomasine,1569.
Bayns,
Hewly, 1684.
Bean,
Tho., 1697.
Eliz., 1713.
Mary, 1715.
Tho., 1716.
Ann, 1728.
Edward, 1740.
Margaret, 1749.
Edward, 1771.
John, 1780.
Elizabeth, 1791.
Edward, 1808.
Beech,
Jane, 1672.
Jane, 1674.
George, 1679.
Beek,
Thomas, 1809.
Beer,
Robert, 1721.
Margaret, 1727.
Edward, 1734.
Jane, 1738.
John, 1739.
William, 1739.
Benjamin, 1745.
Widow, 1760.
William, 1762.
Elizabeth, 1763.
Elizabeth, 1767.
Edward, 1775.
William, 1780.
James, 1781.
Margaret, 1786.
Belsy,
Mary, 1763.
Bently,
John, 1573.
Betts,
Tho., 1689.
John, 1690.
John, 1695.
Sara, 1698.
Margaret, 1705.
Jno., 1715.
Sarah, 1723.

Bewly,
Mildred, 1754.
Thomas, 1782.
Wilmot, 1782.
Biram,
Repent, 1623.
{ Birch,
{ Burch,
Ann, 1697.
Eliza, 1702.
James, 1703.
Henry, 1720.
Ann, 1720.
James, 1742.
Ann, 1743.
Richard, 1748.
John, 1767.
James, 1758.
Widow, 1762.
Elizabeth, 1769.
Blasden,
Stephen, 1565.
Bodkin,
Edmund, 1682.
Bonham,
Richard, 1633.
Thamsin, 1634.
Boughton,
ffrancis, 1578.
Boulton,
Elenore, 1600.
Boykett,
Margarett, 1582.
Jane, 1593.
Elias, 1617.
Betterice, 1620.
Jaine, 1622.
Boykinn,
Widow, 1666.
Brabson,
Thomas, 1616.
Henry, 1617.
Mother, 1622.
Bradshaw,
Jone, 1563.
Martha, 1572.
Henry, 1578.
William, 1581.
{ Branchley,
{ Brenchley,
{ Bransley,
{ Breusley,
Thomas, 1637.
Sarah, 1640.
Sam, 1653.
Wilman, 1661.
Samuel, 1662.
Thomas, 1663.
Joan, 1669.
Joane, 1679.
Parnell, 1679.

Brensley (cont.)
Jo, 1693.
Augustin, 1694.
Elizabeth, 1719.
Thomas, 1726.
Edward, 1731.
Samuel, 1737.
Widow, 1746.
{ Brice,
{ Bries,
Solomon, 1689.
Stephen, 1690.
Edward, 1700.
Katherine, 1700.
Bridgman,
Edward, 1719.
Bridges,
Marget, 1621.
Widow, 1664.
John, 1782.
Brigge,
Richard, 1599.
Brisnall,
Elizabeth, 1799.
Brooks,
Sarah, 1785.
Brookshaw,
John, 1760.
Broomans,
Elizabeth, 1609.
Brown,
Alexander, 1593.
John, 1670.
Susan, 1677.
Mary, 1677.
Susan, 1678.
Thomas, 1680.
Browning,
John, 1611.
Joane, 1618.
Thomas, 1624.
Widow, 1625.
Paul, 1633.
Joane, 1634.
Mary, 1670.
Eliz., 1702.
Matthew, 1720.
James, 1737.
Edward, 1738.
Thos. (or
Jas.), 1741.
Eliz., 1744.
Thomas, 1753.
Ann, 1754.
Matthew, 1755.
Thomas, 1756.
Elizabeth, 1757.
Thos., 1759.
Thomas, 1785.
Edward, 1791.
Elizabeth, 1793.

INDEX OF BURIALS, (*pp. 112—155.*)

Browning (*cont,*)
  Thomas, 1802.
  Parnell, 1808.
Budds,
  Thomas, 1630.
Bunce
  John, 1587.
  Mary, 1589.
  Pleasant, 1633.
Burch,
  (*See* Birch.)
Burden,
  Isaac, 1570.
Burroughs,
  Gilbert, 1718.
Burton,
  Agnis, * 1587.
  Abraham, 1769.
Byrche,
  William De-
    jovas, 1792.
  Elizabeth, 1798.

Cason,
  Franciss, 1683.
Castle,
  Thomas, 1729.
  Edward, 1772.
  John, 1782.
  Thomas, 1802.
{ Casselden,
{ Castleden,
  Thomas, 1750.
  Martha, 1754.
  Michael, 1756.
  Sarah, 1758.
  Mary, 1759.
  Mercy, 1762.
  Elizabeth, 1793.
Castrell,
  Abraham, 1621.
Catton,
  Alice, 1589.
  Robert, 1592.
Chamber,
  Thomas, 1596.
Chandler,
  Henry, 1776.
Chapman,
  James, 1780.
Church,
  John, 1771.
Churchman,
  Margaret, 1792.
Clerk,
  Jno., 1713.
Codham,
  Edward, 1609
Cole,
  Katherine, 1561.
{ Collar,
{ Coller,
  Sarah, 1718.
  Michael, 1722.
  Ann, 1728.

Coller (*cont.*)
  Daniel, 1732.
  Widow, 1742.
  Sarah, 1750.
Cooke,
  Annis, 1563.
Cooly,
  Richard, 1578.
{ Coorte,
{ Courte,
{ Curte,
  John, 1591.
  Elizabethe, 1591.
  John, 1599.
  John, 1602.
  Ann, 1661.
Cray,
  John, 1607.
  Philip, 1621.
  John, 1622.
  Widow, 1628.
Cu'len.
  Mildred, 1572.
  John, 1747.
  Anthony, 1748.
Curgenwen,
  William, 1796.
Davie.
  Jervice, 1561.
Davis,
  Robert, 1609.
  Mary, 1735.
Denne,
  Thomas, 1563.
  Thomas, 1564.
  William, 1572.
  James, 1573.
  Marye, 1577.
  Jone, 1577.
  Thomas, 1578.
  Annis, 1579.
  Anne, 1587.
  Vincent, 1591.
  Robert, 1594.
  Katherine, 1595.
  Thomas, 1599.
  John, 1599.
  Jhn, 1599.
  Lucy, 1602.
  Joane, 1611.
  Vincent, 1612.
  Thamsin, 1633.
  Dorothy, 1637.
  Tho: 1656.
  Susanna, 1669.
  Vincent, 1693.
  Mrs., 1701.
Dennett.
  Sarah, 1728.
Dennewood,
  John, 1558.
Denward,
  Thomas, 1768.

Dines,
  Mary, 1812.
Dingley,
  Nicholas, 1671.
Don,
  Anna, 1687.
Draper,
  Jane, 1676.
  Vincent, 1682.
Dunn,
  Jas., 1701.

Eaton,
  Ann, 1621.
{ Edgar,
{ Erxar,
  Dennis, 1585.
{ Edds,
{ Eids,
  Richard, 1695.
  Goodw., 1714.
Ellen,
  William, 1776.
  William, 1808.
Eltonton,
  John, 1727.
Epps,
  John, 1588.
  Susanna, 1663.
Ergar,
  (*see* Edgar.)
Fagg,
  John, 1809.
  Matthew, 1810.
Feild.
  Mildred, 1561.
Fetherston,
  Sarah, 1812.
{ Finnes,
{ Finnis,
  Sarah, 1772.
  Sarah, 1783.
Fisher,
  Christian, 1633.
{ Foord,
{ Ford,
  John, 1559.
  Elizabeth, 1664·
  Dorothy, 1696.
  Hary, 1700.
  Henry, 1700.
  Rich., 1708.
  Martha, 1718.
  Thomas, 1775.
  Ann, 1775.
  Jane, 1781.
  Robert, 1783.
  John, 1783.
  Edward, 1790.
  Thomas, 1798.
  Mary, 1804.
  John, 1800.
Fowell,
  Anne, 1691.

Fowell (*cont.*)
  Mary, 1699.
  Thos., 1707.
  Thos., 1703.
  John, 1771.
Fox,
  Elizabeth, 1681.
  Edward, 1681.
  Edward, 1681.
  Thomas, 1770.
  Elizabeth, 1771.
  Judith, 1785.

Gammon,
  Katherine, 1663.
  Elias, 1670.
George,
  Martha, 1609.
  William, 1620.
German,
  William, 1809.
{ Gibbon,
{ Gibbons,
  Richard, 1665.
  William, 1669.
  Elizabeth, 1676.
Giles,
  John, 1619.
  Francis, 1749.
Gilman,
  Richard, 1601.
Gobbs,
  Ann, 1761.
{ Godden,
{ Godwin,
{ Goodwin,
  Widow, 1667.
  Sarah, 1714.
  Jane, 1726.
  David, 1733.
  Henry, 1733.
{ Golde,
{ Gould,
  William, 1584.
  Alice, 1572.
  Thomas, 1573.
  John, 1590.
  ————, 1604.
  William, 1616.
  Joanne, 1622.
  Stephen, 1624.
  Mary, 1636.
  John, 1666.
  Robert, 1680.
{ Golder,
{ Goulder,
  Ann, 1718.
  Ann, 1719.
  John, 1721.
  Thomas, 1751.
  Widow, 1760.
  Sarah, 1796.
  Thomas, 1797.

* or Barton,

Goldfinch,
{ Gouldfinch,
Thomasine,1585.
Silvester, 1587.
William, 1801.
Goodwyn,
(See Godden.)
Goore,
Silvester, 1609.
Gosling,
Thomas, 1809.
Grant,
William, 1632.
Peter, 1687.
Edward, 1688.
Peter, 1719.
Peter, 1737.
Edward, 1753.
Mary, 1764.
Green,
Sarah, 1796.
Grey,
————, 1642.
Margarett, 1663.
Margarett, 1664.
Grinstead,
John, 1752.
Groome,
Widow, 1573.
Gryme,
John, 1565.
Thomas, 1573.

Haddin,
Susan, 1584.
Jeffery, 1591.
John, 1593.
Jeffery, 1594.
{ Hale,
{ Haile,
Alice, 1572.
Hall,
Elizabeth, 1774.
Hamertou,
Henry, 1569.
Hammond,
Ellen, 1746.
Hastifer,
————, 1624.
Thomas, 1624.
Hastlyn,
Alice, 1587.
John, 1600.
Hering,
Daniel, 1607.
John, 1616.
Hedgecock,
John, 1610.
John, 1670.
Widow, 1671.
Hobday,
Rich., 1696.
Stephen, 1711.
Eliz., 1713.
Holyday,
Edward, 1681.
Daniel, 1681.

Holyday (cont.)
Robert, 1689.
Mary, 1695.
John, 1695.
Susau, 1707.
David, 1715.
Bennet, 1715.
Homes,
William, 1727.
Widow, 1742.
{ Hopkin,
{ Hopkins,
Annis, 1562.
(wife of Thos.) 1569.
Dennis, 1579.
Jone, 1579.
Thomas, 1590.
Richard, 1615.
John, 1624.
Katherine, 1624.
Jone, 1625.
Widow, 1627.
Thomas, 1634.
John, 1642.
William, 1663.
Elizabeth, 1681.
Edward, 1684.
Martha, 1685.
Ann, 1687.
Tho., 1702.
Wm., 1714.
John, 1733.
Elizabeth, 1736.
Horsepool,
William, 1788.
Horton,
Mary, 1795.
Hunt,
Danyell, 1570.

Impett,
Elizabeth, 1777.
Ingester,
Thomas, 1609.
Innes,
Mary, 1749.
Peter, 1769.

Jacob,
Robert, 1679.
William, 1773.
John, 1777.
William, 1781.
Mary, 1783.
Peter, 1786.
Elizabeth, 1794.
Johnson,
Elizabeth, 1565.
Alice, 1565.
William, 1748.
Sarah, 1749.
Jordan,
James, 1772.
Jourdan,
Thomas, 1795.
Joyner,
Francis, 1718.

Julyau,
John, 1567.
Keeler,
Martha, 1799
Richard. 1808.
Kelk,
Robert, 1750.
Kennet,
Jone, 1580.
Will., 1700.
Will., 1718.
Mary, 1733.
King, -
Hannah, 1793.
Kingsford,
William, 1726.
{ Kingsmeel,
{ Kingsmill,
Edmond, 1630.
Marget, 1630.
Widow, 1637.
Jone, 1684.
John, 1703.
Margaret, 1718.
John, 1741.
John, 1753.
Jane, 1754.
Elizabeth, 1754.
Thomas, 1759.
Jane, 1761.
Charlotte, 1798.
Thomas, 1808.
Knight,
Stephen, 1764.
Ann, 1765.
Susan, 1767.
Elizabeth, 1787.
Knott,
William, 1681.
Laban,
Richard. 1588.
William, 1590.
{ Ladd,
{ Lade,
Joane, 1628.
Dennis, 1640.
Elizabeth, 1758.
John, 1761.
Widow, 1762.
Lamb,
Henry, 1742.
{ Laurence,
{ Lawrence,
John, 1613.
Stephen, 1746.
Stephen, 1774.
John, 1783.
Stephen, 1787.
Elizabeth, 1795.
Thomas, 1802.
Catharine, 1806.
Law,
Ann, 1744.
Thomas, 1746.

Lishman,
Elizabeth, 1726.
{ Locker,
{ Lokar,
Richard, 1719.
Mary, 1736.
Elizabeth, 1749.
Lombe,
Thos., 1739.
Elizabeth, 1753.
Lott,
William, 1728.
Mary, 1752.
Lumpton,
John, 1795.

Mace,
Amy, 1787.
Richard, 1787.
Mantle,
Joseph, 1773.
Maple,
Jone, 1505.
Elizabeth, 1595.
Ann, 1597.
Stephen, 1608.
{ Marsh,
{ Mersh,
Mary, 1626.
Elizabeth, 1629.
Mary, 1667.
Hen., 1718.
Martha, 1761.
Martin,
John, 1559.
John, 1795.
Mason,
Elizabeth, 1612.
Authony, 1628.
Maxted,
Rich., 1685.
Mildred, 1686.
Thomas, 1719.
{ Mihill,
{ Mihils,
{ Miles,
{ Myle,
Mildred, 1679.
Anne, 1679.
Mary, 1689.
Rich., 1691.
Elizabeth, 1696.
Goodwife, 1698.
Mary, 1699.
Mary, 1700.
Richard, 1700.
Mary, 1702.
Elizabeth, 1703.
Jno., 1706.
John, 1724.
Elizabeth, 1728.
Elizabeth, 1733.
Mary, 1758.
Richard, 1766.
Thos., 1767.
Anne, 1771.
Thomas, 1781.

INDEX OF BURIALS (*pp. 112—155*).

Milbourne,
  Thomas, 1571.
  Alice, 1587.
Minles,
  Mary, 1702.
Moon,
  Elizabeth, 1724.
Moor,
  Richard, 1690.
  Richard, 1705.
  Mary, 1721.
Mooring,
  Jane, 1718.
  Mary, 1729.
Morgan,
  Mary, 1777.
Morris,
  Elizabeth, 1679.
Mughole,
  Isabell, 1579.
  Thomas, 1589.
  Samuel, 1624.
  Mary, 1624.
  John, 1675.
Mullett,
  Thomas, 1740.
Munns,
  Sarah, 1776.
Mutton,
  John, 1751.
  Elizabeth, 1758.
  Elizabeth, 1760.
  Elizabeth, 1773.
  John, 1779.
  Benjamin, 1784.
  Elizabeth, 1786.
  Anna, 1794.
  Ann, 1796.
  Elizabeth, 1796.
  James, 1796.
  Jane, 1797.
  Mary, 1797.
  Thomas, 1802.

Nairn,
  Elizabeth, 1790.
  John, 1800.
Neame,
  Elizabeth, 1755.
Nethersole,
  John, 1562.
  William, 1576.
  Vincent, 1576.
  Jone, 1576.
  Elsabethe, 1613.
  Ann, 1617.
  John, 1627.
  Francis, 1641.
Newman,
  Susanna, 1793.
Newport,
  Thomas, 1775.
  Ann, 1775.
  John, 1786.
  Edward, 1807.

Nicols,
  Matthew, 1612.
  Martha, 1627.
  Daniel, 1632.
Nooks,
  Ann, 1619.
Norris,
  John, 1806.
Oakes,
  William, 1636.
Odleye,
  Job, 1591.
{ Packer,
{ Pecker,
  John, 1562.
  Christofer, 1567.
Page,
  Thomas, 1610.
Paine,
  Anne, 1777.
  Richard, 1779.
Pashlei,
  Gulielmus, 1566.
† Payler,
  Jem. Marg., 1784.
  Charlotte, 1798.
  Elizabeth, 1810.
{ Pearson,
{ Peerson,
  Jone, 1579.
  Ann, 1727.
  Elizabeth, 1727.
Peirce,
  Elizabeth, 1633.
Perry,
  Thomas, 1569.
  Elinor, 1573.
Pett,
  Sara, 1577.
Philpott,
  Mary, * 1794.
  John, 1798.
  George, 1799.
  Sophia, 1809.
Pilcher,
  Ann, 1724.
  Mildred, 1726.
  Stephen, 1732.
  Sarah, 1768.
  John, 1776.
  William, 1790.
  Hannah, 1791.
  Vincent, 1799.
  Henry, 1812.
  Mary Ann, 1812.
Pittock,
  James, 1634.
  John, 1637.
Pope,
  Will, 1690.
Prebble,
  ———, 1612.

Prebble (*cont.*)
  (Wife of
   Richard), 1612.
Pritchard,
  James Will., 1778.
  Hannah, 1780.
  Mary, 1790.
  James, 1800.
  Charles, 1800.
  Alice, 1806.
Quested,
  Charles, 1664.
  Anne, 1688.
  Thos., 1714.
  Mary, 1720.
  Martha, 1757.
  Elizabeth, 1767.
  Daniel, 1768.
Question,
  James, 1617.
  James, 1630.
  Jane, 1635.
  Robert, 1669.
Rayner,
  Matthew, 1585.
Read,
  John, 1658.
  Margaret, 1673.
Revell,
  William, 1768.
Reynolds,
  Stephen, 1806.
{ Richard,
{ Ricard,
{ Rickard,
{ Rycard,
  Thomas, 1582.
  Silvester, 1589.
  Edward, 1592.
  Joana, 1632.
Richardson,
  John, 1808.
Richford,
  John, 1792.
Rickwood,
  Robert, 1611.
  Isabel, 1617.
  George, 1618.
  Alis, 1620.
  Joane, 1630.
  Jane, 1630.
  John, 1634.
  Margaret, 1635.
Robins,
  Caroline, 1783.
Robinson,
  ———, 1601.
  Thomasine, 1613.
  Edward, 1618.
Rousall,
  George, 1804.
Rugley,
  Simon, 1567.
  Richard, 1578.

Rugley (*cont.*)
  John, 1580.
  James, 1580.
  Susan, † 1583.
  Mary, 1589.
  James, 1589.
  Margaret, 1595.
  Jone, 1595.
  Dorythie, 1601.
  Jeremie, 1603.
  Richard, 1605.
  Robert, 1624.
Rushe, ‡
  Susan, 1583.
Rycard,
  (*See* Ricard.)
Rye,
  Prudence, 1638.
  Mary, 1690.
  Tho., 1704.
  Amy, 1704.
  Elizabeth, 1721.
  Elizabeth, 1724.
  William, 1726.
  Mary, 1727.
  Stephen, 1728.
  John, 1742.
  Katharine, 1749.
  Mary, 1759.
  Benjamin, 1769.
Sabine,
  Mary, 1721.
  Mrs., 1725.
  Ann, 1761.
  Chibborue, 1763.
{ Sally,
{ Solly,
  William, 1624.
  Jeremie, 1627.
  Jonas, 1631.
  Richard, 1634.
{ Sauders,
{ Saunders,
  Mary, 1696.
  Mary, 1714.
Sawkins,
  Mich., 1718.
  Jno., 1718.
  Edward, 1726.
  Richard, 1728.
  Elizabeth, 1755.
Sawyer,
  Joane, 1680.
  Eve, 1680.
Sayer,
  Christofer, 1580.
  Elizabeth, 1580.
  Jane, 1582.
  John, 1585.
  Jone, 1597.
  James, 1614.
  James, 1674.
  Mildred, 1719.
Sharpe,
  Ann, 1702.

---

† See also foot-note, p. 156.   * See Baptisms, 1794, p. 77.
† Rushe (?) ‡ Rugley (?)

INDEX OF BURIALS, (*pp. 112—155.*)

Sharpe *(cont.)*
Martha, 1702.
Shepherd,
Robert, 1563.
Sheppey,
John, 1638.
John, 1641.
Sherman,
Davie, 1571.
(Wife of
Robert), 1606.
Robert, 1621.
Shipwell,
Dinah, 1718.
Shoveler,
John, 1623.
Shrubsole,
Elizabeth, 1678.
Elizabeth, 1681.
Rich., 1704.
Wid., 1740.
{ Silke,
{ Sylke,
Thomas, 1573.
Alexandra, 1682.
{ Simmous,
{ Simons,
John, 1594.
Jane, 1612.
Thomas, 1666.
Smith.
Mary, 1761.
Sarah, 1761.
Smithson,
Robert, 1606.
Thomas, 1677.
John, 1684.
John, 1793.
Smitten,
Ann, 1798.
Sole,
John, 1681.
Solly,
(*See* Sally.)
Spain,
Ann, 1790.
Stephen, 1790.
Austin, 1804.
Spillett,
———, 1799.
Sprat.
Ed., 1704.
Jane, 1747.
Robert, 1750.
Standard,
Ellis, 1573.
Robert, 1579.
Stark,
Mary, 1641.

Sterling,
Ursilla, 1630.
John, 1636.
Streeting,
Susanna, 1737.
Sturdy,
Annis, 1558.
Alice, 1566.
Robert, 1571.
Julyan, 1585.
Sturges,
Mary, 1665.
Sutton,
Elizabeth, 1766.
Stephen, 1781.
Edward, 1786.
Swift,
Abr., 1696.
Joane, 1696.
Tallis.
Richard, 1666.
Mary, 1675.
Tassell,
James, 1738.
Taverner,
Thomas, 1639
Taylor,
Silvester, 1611.
Terry,
Sarah, 1787.
Gibbon
Ladd, 1806.
Thomas, 1806.
Tofts,
Elizabeth, 1719.
Trapps,
Mary, 1634.
Elizabeth, 1638.
Trice,
Thomas, 1617
Tristram.
Edmund, 1593.
Turk,
John, 1759.
Turner,
Richard, 1664.
Susan, 1674
Richard, 1675.
Madam, 1698.
Tho., 1715.
Jane, 1715.
John, 1721.
Thomas, 1722.
John, 1747.
Hannah, 1765.
Uden,
——— 1611.

Underdonne,
Christian, 1569.
Upton,
John 1608.
Vier,
John, 1578.
Vitnell,
(*See* Whitnell.)
Waginer,
Mary, 1618.
Wales,
Mary, 1690.
Wardropp,
George, 1566.
Waters,
Elizabeth, 1773.
Webb,
Joseph, 1761.
John, 1766.
Mary, 1770.
Wells,
Egedius, 1558.
{ White,
{ Whyte,
John, 1634.
Sarah, 1674.
Richard, 1688.
Ann, 1691.
Richard, 1711.
Richard, 1712.
Sarah, 1767.
William, 1770.
Mary, 1773.
Mary, 1793.
Elizabeth, 1794.
Richard, 1796.
Richard, 1800.
Whitehead
Elizabeth, 1794.
{ Whitnell, or
{ Vitnell,
{ Whitnail,
Jno., 1711.
Ann, 1735.
Jane, 1741.
Wilcock,
Maryan, 1563.
{ Wilford,
{ Wilsford,
Lady, 1602
Sir Thomas, 1610.
Ann, 1622.
Elizabeth, 1634.
Mannering, 1638.
Williams,
Thomas, 1776.
John, 1795.

Williams *(cont.)*
William, 1806.
Ann, 1808.
James, 1809.
{ Winter,
{ Wynter,
Christofer, 1596.
Richard, 1639.
Elizabeth, 1676.
Elizabeth, 1726.
{ Wood,
{ Wode,
William, 1597.
Abraham, 1605.
Mary, 1608.
Anthony, 1608.
Katherine, 1633.
Richard, 1633.
Mary, 1662.
Judith, 1670.
Elizabeth, 1676.
Anne, 1679.
James, 1691.
(Wife of
Thos.), 1692.
Mary, 1778.
John, 1778.
John, 1778.
Christo-
pher, 1798.
George, 1804.
{ Wraight,
{ Wraite,
Richard, 1636.
Ann, 1636.
Nicolas, 1641.
{ Wraithe,
{ Wrathe,
——— 1600.
James, 1621.
Nicholas, 1629.
Elizabeth, 1728.
Young,
Grygorye, 1572.
Annis, 1583.
Thomas, 1585.
William, 1591.
Vincent, 1593.
Vincent, 1598.
Robert, 1656.
Thomas 1665.
Daniel, 1695.

FINIS.

www.ingramcontent.com/pod-product-compliance
Lightning Source LLC
Chambersburg PA
CBHW030832270326
41928CB00007B/1016